D1084677

MARX'S *CAPITAL* AND ONE FREE WORLD

Marx's *Capital* and One Free World

A Fundamental Reappraisal of his Political Economy

Tadao Horie
President and Professor of Economics
Ohtsuki College of Economics, Japan

Foreword by Murray Wolfson
Professor of Economics
California State University, Fullerton

St. Martin's Press   New York

First published in the United States of America in 1991

Printed in Hong Kong

ISBN 0–312–04800–9

Library of Congress Cataloging-in-Publication Data
Horie, Tadao, 1913–
Marx's *Capital* and one free world: a fundamental reappraisal of
his political economy/Tadao Horie; foreword by Murray Wolfson.
p. cm.
1. Marx, Karl, 1818–1883. *Kapital*. 2. Marxian economics.
3. Communism. 4. Marx, Karl, 1818–1883—Contributions in political
science. I. Title
HB501.M5H64   1991   90–8352
335.4′1—dc20   CIP

To Humanity

Contents

Contents ix

List of Figures

List of Tables

Foreword

The era spanned by Tadao Horie's work is one in which individuals concerned with social welfare struggled to come to grips with Marxism. These days, Marxism – certainly Marxism-Leninism – appears as the ossified doctrine of regimes that are not capable of meeting the most modest demands of their people. But not very long ago the doctrine seemed to have been vindicated by events: the insane European dash for empire in which America and Japan joined at the end; the hideous First World War, the vindictive peace at Versailles and the Second World War it helped to spawn. These made Lenin's account of imperialism all too plausible. The world wide economic collapse between the two great wars seemed to announce the collapse of capitalism that Marx had foretold.

Marxism offered an apparently scientific explanation of these events as well as a programme for salvation. In Japan it served as a model of economic growth that took root and dominated the postwar economics faculties of many of Japan's great universities. Somewhat anachronistically, it entered through this route into the thinking of some of the leaders of Japan's postwar industrial capitalism. But most important, Marxism in one or another form deeply influenced the ideology of the labour, environmental and anti-war movements.

Tadao Horie was one of those people who were at first entranced by Marxism but who early on came to see the dangers inherent in it. They came to believe it to be a snare which would entrap movements for social progress into dogma, ultimate isolation and atrophy. Theirs was a hard row to hoe since they were type-cast as enemies of progress rather than its true defenders. One can see from Horie's writing how much he had to endure and how tenaciously he had to fight to justify his convictions.

The world can see now that Tadao Horie was right all along. Hindsight helps.

Horie tells us how he visited the Soviet Union and saw the outcome of Marxism-Leninism for himself. This clear eyed journalist–professor concluded that Stalin was not just another Russian despot. Nor was he simply a mistake of history, the end product of a series of events set in motion by the nationalistic blunders of the last century. These influences were operative, to be sure, but Tadao Horie understood more deeply. Stalinism was not an aberration from Marxism but

xvi

followed logically from the rationalist strand Marx had derived from Hegel. Lenin elaborated and implemented those themes which Stalin drove to their ultimate conclusion. Certainty about the future given by the 'science of society' hardened into dogma and dictatorship as Marxism played itself out in economics, philosophy and politics.

In this collection of essays over thirty years Horie meets Marxism head on. Of course the rout of ideology has been driven by the practical failures of Marxist planned economies and the events that followed. But the intellectual groundwork for that disillusion was laid by the trenchant criticism by Tadao Horie in Japan and others elsewhere.

Wounded though it may be, Horie does not believe that Marxism is dead – safely forgotten. To be sure *perestroika* and humanist reinterpretations have tended to define Marxism out of practical existence. Yet one must wonder what would happen if Gorbachev and his reform were not to survive the transit to a more nearly market oriented economy? The present Soviet economy is admittedly out of control. What events would it take to for an ideologue to argue that Gorbachev is simply a revisionist who introduced all the instability of the capitalist market into the USSR?

The debacle in China preoccupies us all at this writing. It illustrates how the attempt to retreat from the command economy degenerated into what can best be described as special privilege and macroeconomic instability; it is closer to a corrupt mercantilism than to either planned communism or competitive capitalism. In the end the old dogma was invoked in Beijing to justify bloody repression.

It is impossible to say what the consequences would be of destabilisation in these two nations? Reversion to orthodoxy is one, but there certainly are others that are even more frightening.

Perhaps the most important reason to study Horie is that Marxism is a 'sigh of the oppressed' and revives periodically from within liberal and humane movements. However dangerous the consequences of its determinism, it is an intuitively plausible form of expression of the justified desire of the disadvantaged for progressive change. And so the lessons that Horie teaches may have to be learned over again. Where will Japan, England and America turn when the current conservative movement has played out its rope? Horie wants to tell us where not to go.

Through his work Tadao Horie reveals himself to his readers. This book shows us his intensity, conviction and concern. In so doing we gain the privilege of conversing with a citizen of Japan and the one peaceful world he seeks.

MURRAY WOLFSON

Preface

At this time in world history it seems already platitudinous to declare that the myth of the superiority of communism (socialism) over capitalism has lost ground. Is it not still surprising, however, that Marx's *Capital* is full of elementary errors and self-contradictions? Non-Marxists usually regard the book simply as outmoded and therefore useless. Canonical Marxists stick to a belief in its 'infallibility'. Marx-oriented liberals easily admit the existence of faults in it, but do not doubt in principle the validity of Marx's methodology and the world-view (*Weltanschauung*), dialectical materialism.

These three stances are all mistaken. *Capital* not only is outmoded but also contains inherent inconsistencies, mostly originating from the application of dialectics itself. This methodology causes throughout the book a series of fallacies of ambiguity mistaken for profundity. *Capital* is the alpha and omega of Marxism. If it includes fundamental defects, and I say that it does, the whole edifice of the Marxian ideological system must be re-examined from its foundations.

It is true that Marxism, since its birth, had been playing the role of gadfly, especially in the age of crude capitalism in the nineteenth century. With the appearance of the first communist state, USSR, Marxism-Leninism came to be deemed by communists during the inter-war period as the sole scientific guiding doctrine both for the abrogation of the capitalist system and for the construction of communist society. And the Soviet Union, behind its Iron Curtain, attaining a breakneck industrial growth in the first and second Five Year Plan periods, succeeded in impressing the illusion of 'the workers' paradise' on the outer world which had been in the agony of the Great Depression. Marx's insight into the fall of capitalism and the rise of communism seemed to be almost coming true. The horrors of agricultural collectivisation and the Great Purge were known only to specialists abroad.

After the Second World War, however, various unconcealed events occurred which discredited communism: the disclosure by Khrushchev in 1956 of the cruelty of Stalinism, the suppression of attempted democratic reforms in Hungary and Czechoslovakia in 1956 and 1968 by Warsaw Pact forces, the collapse of the halo behind Mao Zedong and his Great Cultural Revolution in the late 1970s, the military 'assistance to Afghan friends' by the Soviet Union in 1979 and withdrawal in 1988–9 in acknowledgement of its failure, the crushing of the Solidarity union in Poland by martial law in 1981 and its re-legalisation in 1989 under the pressure of the Polish people.

The advanced capitalist countries, which, according to Stalin, should have been in a long term contracting trend through cyclical ups and downs, realised an unprecedented economic growth through the 1960s and early '70s. It is true that since the 'oil shock' of 1973 the capitalist world suffered a lingering stagflation for several years, but is now again in the process of normal expansion. The communist countries, in contrast, have been troubled by their unsteady and inefficient economies. They are even borrowing colossal amounts of money from the 'moribund' capitalism to escape from their crises.

Thus by now it should be evident that the Marxian paradigm is of no avail in interpreting the present situation and dealing with difficulties arising therefrom.

In the early 1930s I was a university student believing in communism as the only way out from mass misery under capitalism. This conviction of mine collapsed when I travelled through the Soviet Union in 1936. First-hand observation let me know that the country was not necessarily a 'heaven on earth'. It was the same sort of experience as described by André Gide in his *Retour de L'URSS* which was severely denounced by the Soviet authorities. (Gide and I happened to be in Moscow on the same day.)

I was en route to Berlin, where the 11th Olympic Games took place, and which I attended as a member of the Japanese national football team. In Germany I found a society far more advanced than Russia. But these two countries had a curious characteristic in common, i.e. the excessive presence of Stalin's busts and Hitler's photographs displayed almost everywhere, an unmistakable symbol of one-party (= individual) rule and thought control.

After the Olympic Games we visited a few West European countries. In London, at the entrance of Hyde Park, I came across a soap-box orator, who professed himself to be a Trotskyite, appealing for donations in support of the People's Front government of Spain fighting against Franco forces in the Spanish civil war which had broken out about a month before. A communist youth was jeering at the speaker and a policeman standing nearby was listening to their dispute. It was a scene one could never expect to be met with in prewar Japan, an impressive example of freedom of speech and thought, real democracy.

In retrospect, I feel that the basis of my later work, the fundamental reappraisal of Marx's political economy, was formed, although still subconsciously, through this trip to Europe. I learned that Marxism was not necessarily an exclusive 'absolute truth' and realised the validity of an old Chinese saying: 'Explore the facts and seek the truth' (Shishi jiushi).

In 1949 a recession took place in the United States. According to Marxian economic-crisis theory, it was to develop inevitably into a grave world-wide depression. After the event, however, it turned out to be no more than a temporary panic. At that time I still believed, say 97%, in Marxism as far as its general theoretical framework was concerned. But reflection upon the outcome of this recession made me face the critical choice between Marxian 'truth' and reality. Of Hegel a plausible anecdote is told. Someone asked him: 'Your thoughts are great. But aren't they in some cases contrary to reality?' Hegel's answer was: 'So much the worse for the facts (Um so schlimmer für die Tatsachen).' Not being an idealist of his sort, I could not follow suit. I decided to carry out an exhaustive re-reading and re-thinking of the contents of *Capital*.

By the end of 1955 I already had confidence that the theoretical construction of *Capital* involved a coherent series of fundamental defects and contradictions, not 'dialectical' ones, but violations of the Aristotelian law of contradiction. But I could not find the opportunity to make public my arguments because the mental climate of Japanese intellectual society was peculiarly favourable to Marxism. It had been fostered before and during the war. In the dark 1930s the 'underground' activities of communists fighting against the relentless persecution by the ruling power bestowed upon them a mystical glory of martyrdom. During the war the indomitable and heroic resistance to it shown by some of them amplified the lustre of communism. Thus, after the end of the war during the early Occupation period, communist activists came to be regarded as 'warriors for liberty and peace' at least among the Marxist-oriented trade unionists and intellectuals. And liberals, lacking precise knowledge of Marxian ideology which is nebular and abstruse, were apt to develop the 'Marx-complex'.

The wind changed with the official criticism of Stalin by Mikoyan and Khrushchev at the XXth Congress of the Soviet Communist Party in February 1856. During the 'Thaw' period Stalin became the object of exposure and denunciation. In this atmosphere I managed to find a few magazine editors interested in publishing my essays on the fundamental criticism of Marxian economics. My argument aroused a furor in all schools (there are many in Japan) of Marxists; their volley of condemnation continued for about three years and I made counter-arguments one by one to virtually all of them. Then came the period of benign neglect. Although I went on developing my work through published papers and books, they kept silent as if I were non-existent. And yet my stand has been slowly but steadily gaining ground.

Internationally I wrote several articles in summarising my works in Japanese and sent them to friends in other countries in both 'East' and 'West'. Direct contacts were also made when I went abroad and when they visited Tokyo. My Western friends were usually quick in understanding my position and agreed with it. My Eastern friends showed keen interest in my criticism and were glad to have frank discussions with me on a private level.

Now political democratisation and economic restructuring are going on in the East countries in various forms and degrees, accompanied by ideological conflicts, economic difficulties, nationality problems, etc. In this turmoil the most fundamental and crucial problem is that of the 'infallibility' of Marxism-Leninism. Around this we can see three approaches. First, the ultra-leftists or conservatives still believe in it. Second, the moderate reformers avoid directly touching on it.[1] Third, the radicals clearly deny it. These patterns are also seen in the attitudes of the leftist reformers in the 'West' and the 'South'.

One thing to be noted here is the absence of a clear-cut cognisance of inherent faults in Marxian economics and philosophy even among the radicals squarely challenging the Marxian 'absolute truth', which is the origin of the wrong belief that Marxists know 'the future course of history' because they are guided by it and therefore qualified to lead the people.

Not that criticism of Marxism is in short supply. On Marx's philosophy, we have a long list of arguments, pro and con. On the economics of *Capital*, elaborate and minute studies, interpretations and controversies are piled up (especially in Japan). What is now needed is an integrated observation and rigorous reappraisal of the Marxian ideological system as a whole. Through this comprehensive inquiry, the immanent fallacy in Marxian determinism would be exhaustively elucidated. This purely intellectual work is an indispensable prerequisite for promoting democracy in varied societies and attaining mutually credible peace, One Free World, emancipated from dogmatism and assured by freedom of thought.

This book is devoted to the aim mentioned above. It is based on the eight essays written from 1959 through 1983. These have been amplified, corrected, backed with new data, etc. and edited to make them into a coherent whole. The arrangement of the essays is half chronological and half logical.

Chapter 1, 'Towards a Higher Stage of Marxian Economics' (*Waseda Economic Papers*, No. 4, 1959), is an inquiry into Marx's labour theory of value, disclosing a basic inconsistency involved in it. At this stage of research my arguments did not go beyond the realm of labour-value theory. I was aiming at a 'creative development' of Marxian economics through correction of defects inherent in *Capital*.

But gradually I became aware that my 'creative development' had been developing into a system of radical critique. Thus in Chapter 2, 'The Immanent Self-Contradictions in Marx's Labour Theory of Value' (*Waseda Economic Papers*, No. 18, 1979), his labour theory is not only put under a more rigorous reappraisal but also evaluated as 'true' solely in a purely abstract and simple model, having no use as an operational theory of relative prices. The author's evaluation of the celebrated 'transformation problem' is presented here in connection with the critique of the labour theory of value.

Then follows Chapter 3, 'An Error Common to the Transformation of Money into Capital and the Primitive Accumulation' (*Waseda Economic Papers*, No. 19, 1980). Chapters 1 and 2 are concerned with Chapters 1–3, Book I of *Capital*, where Marx explains the genesis of commodities and money on the basis of his labour-value theory. He proceeds to a theoretical exposition of 'the transformation of money into capital' in Chapters 4–7, its historical counterpart being 'the so-called primitive accumulation' in Chapters 26–31. My Chapter 3 covers these problems and brings to light a critical self-contradiction committed by Marx: He asserts in essence that pre-capitalist societies do and do not produce surplus value. Its concern with this problem has been a notable merit of Japanese Marxism, and I deal here also with that.

Chapter 4, 'The Fundamental Defects in the 'Laws' in *Capital*' (*Waseda Economic Papers*, No. 7, 1962. Original title: 'The Historical Limits of Marx's Cognizance'), deals with 'the general law of capitalist accumulation', Chapter 25, Book I and 'The law of the falling rate of profit', Chapter 13, Book III of *Capital*. Here is disclosed the most important self-contradiction in *Capital*. Marx begins with the assumption that technology progresses and so productivity rises. And yet, in the course of unfolding these laws, he unconsciously drops (forgets?) these assumptions and becomes trapped in a queer implication that productivity does not rise when it rises.

Chapter 5, 'Materialist Concept of History and the Structure of *Capital*', is composed of 'Dialectics and Economics in *Capital*' (*Waseda Economic Papers*, No. 10, 1967) and Section V 'Obligatory Correspondence of Production Relations to the Productive Forces' of 'Hegelian Fallacy in Marxian Economics' (*Waseda Economic Papers*, No. 12, 1972). Here we touch on Marx's methodology in *Capital*. First, the materialist concept of history, i.e. the law governing the replacements of social organisms, is reviewed. Then, its application, the explanation by means of 'dialectical triad', of the rise and fall of capitalism leading to the advent of communism, is followed and criticised.

Chapter 6, 'Hegelian Fallacy in Marxian Philosophy' (*Waseda Economic Papers*, No. 12, 1972. Original title: 'Hegelian Fallacy in Marxian Economics'), makes inquiry into the philosophical basis of *Capital*. Hegelian and Marxian dialectics as the negation of the Aristotelian law of contradiction is scrutinised. An unwarrantable interchange of the concept of contradiction with that of opposition and struggle is laid bare. The ambiguous character of the 'unity and struggle of opposites' is criticised. It is pointed out that the Hegelian fallacy inherited by Marx is the prime cause of the obscurity with the appearance of abstruseness that prevails in *Capital*.

Chapter 7, 'The law of the Falling Rate of Profit, Reproduction Scheme and the Imperialist Expansion' (*Waseda Economic Papers*, No. 20, 1981), sets out from the examination of Marx's self-contradictory argumentation embedded in the law of the falling rate of profit. It leads to the elucidation of the involvement of the same contradiction in Lenin's expanding reproduction scheme, which is nothing but a two-sector analogy of Marx's 'Hypothetical series' (one-sector model) illustrating the law. This contradiction, the neglect of the rise of the workers' real income which should be realised proportionate with the rise in productivity, is the origin of Marx's 'absolute impoverishment' theory and Lenin's explanation of imperialist expansion driven by people's 'half-starved' standard of living in the mother countries, both being contradictory to historical facts.

In the last chapter, 'Marxian Economics in the Contemporary World' (*Waseda Economic Papers*, No. 21, 1982), the author's experience is introduced of a lecture in China entitled 'The economic growth of world capitalism vs. the foresights of Marx and Keynes'. The discussions following the lecture revealed that the Chinese economists were emancipated in their mentality from the obstinate dogmatism in the period of the Great Cultural Revolution. But as far as their fundamental theoretical position was concerned they were still remaining faithful to Marx's political economy, although thereafter they began to loosen their interpretation of Marx's propositions here and there to their advantage in the analysis of contemporary capitalism and the building of Chinese-style socialism. The second section criticises the fallacy of the 'law common to all social systems', in substance, the law of the priority growth of Department I (means of production) as a requisite for economic development. The third section is newly added. This is a brief record of my discussion with some Soviet economists in a symposium held in Moscow in October 1983.

This book is not easy reading. But is does not contain inconsistencies as does *Capital*. If one reads *Capital* believing that it is without inherent faults, it becomes hopelessly confusing beyond comprehension. In pointing out clearly these defects and stating flatly what is wrong, this book should at least not be unintelligible and misleading in the manner of Marx's *magnum opus*.

Disclosure of truth might hurt and cause misgivings among some people concerned for a time. But, in the long run, it must be a positive way to trustworthy peace and the happiness of mankind. This is the belief underlying my work of more than thirty years. Marx himself, I believe, would be pleased with this book. He once wrote in the preface to the first German edition of *Capital*: 'Every opinion based on scientific criticism I welcome.'

TADAO HORIE

Acknowledgements

This book could not have been published in this form and content but for the aid of Professor Emeritus P. J. D. Wiles, London School of Economics, an old friend. He cordially took pains to elaborately examine my first, second and third manuscripts. He made numerous corrections and suggestions on facts, theoretical points, editorial arrangements, and English expressions and gave effective assistance for realising publication.

I tried hard to follow his advice in most cases. As for the difference of opinion on some theoretical matters, I am grateful that he gave me good impetus to make my thoughts stricter and, I hope as a result, more persuasive.

Professor Murray Wolfson, Oregon State University (now at California State University, Fullerton), and Professor Kurt Dopfer, Hochschule, St Gallen, Switzerland, also kindly helped me by presenting suggestions on the contents and strongly supporting me in the actualisation of this project. The pertinent Foreword written by Professor Wolfson, who is well versed in the subject, is heartily appreciated.

My long contact with Professor Martin Bronfenbrenner, Aoyama-gakuin University, Tokyo, has been helpful in fostering my idea of this work.

Thanks to Professor A.W. Peterson, my late-colleague at Waseda University, Tokyo, for checking my English. Professor Peterson has since passed away. May his soul rest in peace.

I am also indebted to Professor Paul Snowden, Waseda University, for his aid in preparing the index.

Mr T. M. Farmiloe, my publisher, has kept an encouraging eye on my work since he came to know it through Professor Wiles five years ago and his decision in favour of publication offers the English-speaking world a good opportunity to be acquainted with it. My deep appreciation is due for this.

Last but not least, I would like to express my gratitude to all my colleagues, friends and students who have been associated with me in relation to this work. It has been cherished and developed in the course of seminars, lectures and discussions with them

In spite of valuable suggestions and comments and the efforts of myself, it is be inevitable that my work will contain some defects and faults. It goes without saying that they are all of my responsibility.

1 Towards a Higher Stage of Marxian Economics: The Concept of 'Value' Fundamentally Re-examined and Developed

The theoretical backbone of Marxian economics has been fossilised. Not that the contemporary Marxists are idle in their analysis of the new phase of postwar capitalism. Nor that the socialist countries are not making rapid economic progress. The problem is that the economic theory which should serve as the guide in these and other fields is now turned into a fetter on further progress.

[*Note:* This chapter was written in 1959. When the socialist countries came to the turning point from extensive to intensive development in the mid-1960s, their economies slowed down in spite of their efforts of structural reform. The difficulties have continued until 1989.]

Marx, of course, is not responsible for the situation. *Capital*, as an economics text for the proletariat, has undoubtedly played a great historical role. But in the light of the latter half of the twentieth century, one cannot help feeling some Newtonian rigidity in Marx's way of thinking: for instance, in such expressions, employed by him in *Capital*, as 'the discovery of the natural laws', 'iron necessity', 'discovering it (the law of the falling rate of profit)', etc.[1]

It is particularly characteristic of vulgar economy [economics – T.H.] that it echoes what was new, original, profound and justified during a specific outgrown stage of development, in a period when it has turned platitudinous, stale, and false.[2]

This is Marx's own remark. I am not going to say that his accomplishments are 'platitudinous, stale, false'. However, mere repeating of the economic theory left by Marx is now of no value. What is wanted is its development. And development inevitably

1

includes some denial. The hypothesis of ether made a big contribution to physics in a certain stage of its development. Later, Einstein's relativity made the same hypothesis obsolete.

[*Note:* At the early stage represented by this chapter I attempted a 'creative development of Marxian economics'[3] as stated in the Preface. But, as later chapters show, it resulted in its fundamental and critical reappraisal.]

I   A NEWLY DEVELOPED INTERRELATION OF THREE CONCEPTS – LABOUR-TIME, VALUE AND PRICE

1   Why did Strachey abandon the labour theory of value?

When John Strachey published *Contemporary Capitalism* in 1956, many staunch Marxists severely criticised him for his 'degeneration to a servant of monopoly capitalism'. This is not the issue I am going to take up here, however. In that book, Strachey charged Marxian economics with a big theoretical debt which Marxians are obliged to pay off. He stated as follows:

if we take man-hours of socially necessary labour time as our unit of value, we shall have no way of expressing changes in the productivity of labour . . . the total product is a given figure.[4]

he [Marx] had no way of measuring the growth of the social product as a whole.[5]

A quotation of a passage from *Capital* will offer an explanation:

If the productivity of industry increases, the prices of the individual commodities fall . . . Suppose the same labour produces, say, triple its former product. Then, $2/3$ less labour yields individual products.[6]

In other words, if the productivity of labour increases three-fold, the amount of labour embodied in individual products is reduced to one-third: so their prices (values) fall to one-third. How about the total price (value)[7] of the three-fold total product? The amount of products is three-fold, and their respective prices are one-third. Then as a matter of course total price remains unchanged. If this is the law of the price movement based on the labour theory of value, we clearly have no way of measuring the growth of the total national product caused by an increase in productivity of labour. Strachey's criticism hits the mark. If Marxists want to blame him for abandoning the labour theory and shifting to Keynesianism, they should first try to develop the labour theory of value themselves.

2 Is equal labour-time always expressed by an equal price?

To answer this question, we need a rigourous examination of Marx's labour theory from the very beginning. He writes in Chapter 1, Book I of *Capital*:

> On the one hand all labour is, speaking physiologically, an expenditure of human labour-power, and in its character of identical abstract human labour. It creates and forms the value of commodities.[8]

He also writes '*However . . . productive power may vary*, the same labour exercised during equal periods of time, always yields equal amounts of value'[9] (emphasis – T.H.). Moreover, the amounts of value or labour embodied in the commodities can be grasped only though price. 'Price is the money-name of the labour realised in a commodity'[10] and it 'represents the expression of value in money'.[11] Furthermore, 'throughout this work [*Capital*]', Marx assumes, 'for the sake of simplicity, gold as the money-commodity',[12] and states that 'expression of the value [labour realised – T.H.] of a commodity in gold–x commodity $A = y$ money-commodity – is its money-form or price'.[13]

To sum up: however productive power may vary, equal labour-time always yields equal amounts of value and its one and only form of expression is price. Then the total price (as 'the expression of value') of commodities produced in equal labour-time must always remain constant, however much the physical amounts of the commodities increase as the result of productivity increase. Meanwhile, prices of individual commodities fall in inverse proportion to the rate of productivity increase. Table 1.1 is a hypothetical illustration of the above cases.

Case (1) of Table 1.1 is Marx's illustration in 'D. Money-form', Sec. 3, Chap. 1, Book 1 of *Capital* with my additional assumption that 1 ounce of gold embodies 1 hour of labour. Suppose that 20 yards of linen and 6 other commodities shown here are the total national product of a hypothetical society and that after some years the productivity of labour in that society increases three-fold. As is illustrated in Case (2), which is my own work, the total quantity of

Table 1.1   Productivity rises: total price of total commodities remains constant: prices of individual commodities fall

---

(1) Suppose that 1 ounce of gold embodies 1 hour of labour:

20 yards of linen = ⎫
1 coat   = ⎪
10 lbs of tea   = ⎪
40 lbs of coffee = ⎬ 2 ounces of gold = £2
1 qr of corn   = ⎪   (2 hours)
$\frac{1}{2}$ a ton of iron = ⎪
x commodity A = ⎭

Total £14 (14 hours) . . . . 14 hours = £14

(equal value = equal value)

(2) If 3-fold commodities are produced in the equal labour-time following productivity rise:

60 yards of linen = ⎫   ⎧ 20 yards of linen = £$\frac{2}{3}$
3 coats   = ⎪   ⎪   (price falls to $\frac{1}{3}$)
30 lbs of tea   = ⎪   ⎪
120 lbs of coffee = ⎬ 2 ounces of gold = £2.50 ⎨ etc.
3 qr of corn   = ⎪   (2 hours)   ⎪
$1\frac{1}{2}$ tons of iron = ⎪   ⎪
$3x$ commodity A = ⎭   ⎩ etc.

Total £14 (14 hours) . . . . 14 hours = £14

(equal value = equal value)

* Total quantity of the commodities increases 3-fold:
* Total price of the commodities remains constant:
* Prices of individual commodities fall to $\frac{1}{3}$.
(Attention!) Productivity of labour in gold industry remains constant.

Table 1.2   If productivity of labour in the gold industry also changes

---

(3) Suppose both the commodities and gold are produced 3-fold following productivity rise:

60 yards of linen = ⎫

etc.   = ⎬ 6 ounces of gold = £6   So (2 hours)

etc.   = ⎭

20 yards of linen = £2
($^2/_3$ hours)

(price remains constant)

etc.

Total £42 (14 hours) . . . . 14 hours = £28

* Total price of the whole commodity increases 3-fold (in identical proportion with productivity rise).
* Prices of individual commodities remain constant.

(4) If the commodities are produced 3-fold and gold only 2-fold in equal labour time:

60 yards of linen = ⎫

etc.   = ⎬ 4 ounces of gold = £4   So (2 hours)

etc.   = ⎭

20 yards of linen = £1$^1/_3$
($^2/_3$ hours)

etc.

etc.

* Total price of the whole commodity increases 2-fold (in identical proportion with productivity rise in gold industry):
* Prices of individual commodities fall to $^2/_3$ (rate of productivity rise in gold ÷ rate of productivity rise in other commodities).

(5) If the commodities are produced 3-fold and gold alone 4-fold in equal labour time:

60 yards of linen = ⎫

etc.   ⎬ 8 ounces of gold = £8   So (2 hours)

etc.   = ⎭

20 yards of linen = £2$^2/_3$

($^2/_3$ hours)

etc.

Total £56 (14 hours) . . . . 14 hours = £56

* Total price of the whole commodity increases 4-fold:
* Prices of individual commodities rise 1$^1/_3$-fold.

---

commodities produced in the equal labour-time increases three-fold and yet its total price remains unchanged, the prices of respective commodities falling to one-third.

With this value-price structure it is evidently impossible to measure the growth of the total national product or the rate of increase of labour-productivity in this society. To make the matter worse, this price system is an *unrealistic* abstraction in the literal sense of the word. A prerequisite to rendering a price movement of this kind possible is the assumption that the productivity of labour in the gold industry remains unchanged. However, in the ever-changing real world, it cannot do so. Marx himself pointed out that 'only in so far as it is itself a product of labour, and, therefore, potentially variable in value, can gold serve as a measure of value.'[14] So let us examine in Table 1.2 the case where the productivity of labour in the gold industry also changes.

As shown in case (3) if the productivity of labour rises three-fold both in the industries producing the commodities and in the gold industry, the total price of all the commodities also rises three-fold, but the prices of individual commodities remain unchanged. If the productivity rise in the gold industry alone is two-fold, as in case (4), then the rise in the total price of all the commodities would also be just two-fold. And the prices of individual commodities would fall to two-thirds. In case (5), however, the productivity rise in the gold industry alone is assumed to be four-fold and consequently the total price of all the commodities also rises four-fold and the prices of individual commodities $1^1/_3$-fold. The generalised formulation of the above examples is given in Table 1.3.

This formula shows that: When gold is used as money – this is the assumption given by Marx himself – the thesis of Marx that 'however productive power may vary, the same labour exercised during equal periods of time, always yields equal amounts of value' (emphasis – T.H.) becomes invalid when price is the only form of the expression of value. The price ('the expression of the value in money') of the product of an equal amount of labour (value) is subject to change in either direction.

Moreover, Marx's usage of the concept 'value' is equivocal. By it he sometimes means 'labour(-time) embodied in commodities' and at other times 'price' which is the 'expression of value in money'. (For more detailed explanation on this, see Section II of Chapter 2 in the present volume.) And the 'value' in the above-cited passage, ('yields equal amounts of value') is just one case of the latter usage, i.e., value = price.

Table 1.3   Relation between prices and productivity changes in commodity-producing and gold industries.

amount of labour	$t_0 \dots \dots \to t_1$
('dead' and living labour)	$a \dots \dots \to a$
	$\left(\begin{array}{l} k_1 = \text{rate of change in productivity} \\ \quad \text{of commodities} \end{array} \right)$
total social product	
(total quantity of use-value)	$b \dots \dots \to (1+k_1)b$
total price of b	$\left(\begin{array}{l} k_2 = \text{rate of change in productivity} \\ \quad \text{of gold} \end{array} \right)$
$\left(\begin{array}{l} \text{gross national product} \\ \text{in terms of money} \end{array} \right)$	$c \dots \dots \to (1+k_2)c$
prices of commodities	$p \dots \dots \to \dfrac{1+k_2 p}{1+k_1}$

Note: 1. Only when $k_1 = k_2$ do prices of the commodities remain constant, and the rate of increase in the amount of the national product expresses the rate of rise in the production of labour (e.g. case (3) of Table 1.2).

  2. When $k_2 = 0$ c remains constant and p falls to $1\frac{1}{1+k_1} p$ (e.g.).

Thus, my statement above, 'The price . . . of the product of an equal amount of labour . . . ', can be rewritten as follows: The value of the product of the equal amount of value is subject to change in either direction. Let me illustrate this contradictory proposition utilising the examples of foregoing Tables 1.1 and 1.2.

Table 1.1   14 hours = £14 (14 hours)
An equal value (14 hours) is always expressed in an equal value (£14).

Table 1.2   14 hours = 14 hours
£14 < £42, 28, 56
Equal values (14 hours, £14) are expressed in different values (£42, 28, 56).

The relation between the amount of labour, 'substance' (see citations, notes 47, 49 and 51 of Ch. 2 in the present volume) of value, and prices, the expression of value in money, is not an unchanging one such as 2 hours = £2, 14 hours = £14, etc. Or more generally, it is wrong to think that the value of a labour-time is always expressed in terms of c price. The total price of the product of labour of an hour, when the rate of change of productivity in the gold industry is denoted by k_2 is a variable, $(1+k_2)c$. Prices of the individual commodities p, when the rate of change of productivity in the commodity-producing industries is denoted by k_1 are $\frac{1+k_2}{1+k_1}p$. The proposition of Marx that the 'value [= price, expression of value in money — T.H.] of commodities is in inverse ratio to the productiveness of labour'[15] is valid only in the particular case of $k_2 = 0$. The commodity price (= value) is the dependent variable of two independent variables, k_1 and k_2. Marx's fault was in disregarding one of the independent variables, k_2.

Some readers may insist that Marx was clearly conscious of this variable, citing the following sentences in Sec.1, Chap. 3, Book I of *Capital*:

> With those [commodities] . . . whose value rises, simultaneously with, and proportionally to, that of money, there is no alteration in price. And if their value rise is either slower or faster than that of money, the fall or rise in their prices will be determined by the difference between the change in their value and that of money.[16]

The rise of value of commodities and money means the fall of their labour-productivity. Applied to the foregoing Table 1.3 it is when k_1 and k_2 have negative numerical values. This is rather an unintelligible situation. In its stead let us think of the case of productivity-rise and paraphrase his statements as follows: With those commodities whose productivity rises, simultaneously with, and proportionally to, that of money, there is no alteration in price. And if their productivity-rise is slower or faster than that of money, the fall or rise in their prices will be determined between the change in their productivity and that of money. In my algebraic expression:

If $k_1 = k_2$, then $P_t = P_0$
If $k_1 < k_2$, then $P_t > P_0$
If $k_1 > k_2$, then $P_t < P_0$

Thus, it is clear that in the particular passage cited above Marx is aware of the variable relation between value (amount of labour) and price (the expression of value in money) of the commodities. (In my foregoing Table 1.2, 14 hours are expressed in £42, £28, £56, etc.) And yet on the other hand, he maintains that an equal amount of labour, however productivity may vary, yields an equal amount of value. (In my Table 1.1, 14 hours are always expressed in £14.) And in this case, 'if the productivity of industry increases, the prices of the individual commodities fall', as already cited. This latter price-mechanism was that which troubled John Strachey, because, then, we have 'no way of measuring the growth of the social product as a whole'. It is this confusion of Marx (for detailed explanation, see Section II (Subsection 2) Chapter 2 of the present book) that must be confirmed and put in order.

3 How to fill the gap between 'constant price' and Marx's price?

Strachey gave up the labour theory of value and chose 'contemporary methods for measuring the economy' that 'employ money, pounds or dollars or what you will, as their unit of value, correcting, of course, by means of index numbers for changes in the value of money'.[17] It is, in a word, the method of employing the statistician's 'constant prices' of the base year or the given year.

Here let us look back to case (3) in Table 1.2 and to the case of $k_1 = k_2$ in Table 1.3. When the rate of change in productivity of labour in the industries producing ordinary commodities and that of the gold industry are identical, commodity prices remain unchanged. Of course, in reality these two rates do not stay equal over a period of time. But the prices of, say, the base year can be collected and a hypothetical 'constant price', estimate of output change, arrived at by index number procedures.

Needless to say, Marxists are able to make use of the constant prices obtained by statistical methods without performing such a fundamental re-examination of the labour theory of value. In dealing with the real gross national product, industrial production index, quantum index of external trade and so on, Marxian economists are already enjoying the benefits of the constant price. In socialist countries it is utilised in the calculations for national economic planning. The tool is already being employed. The difficulty lies in the inflexibility of Marx's value-price system which prevents direct theoretical contact with this efficient tool. However, the groundwork to fill this gap is already laid. All we need do is to pick up one of the two independent variables affecting the change in commodity prices, the one subconsciously dropped by Marx!

[*Note:* Later the author's reappraisal reached the conclusion that the labour-time calculation of Marx is possible only in a simple, abstract model-world and, therefore, the two variables, k_1 and k_2 are operationally impractical. This, however, does not prevent Marxists from understanding the concept of 'constant price' and utilising already existing statistical constant prices.]

II DOESN'T TERTIARY INDUSTRY CREATE VALUE?

1 Questioning the 'law' of the falling tendency of the proportion of tertiary industry

Another aspect of Marx's labour theory of value which needs a radical reappraisal is its peculiar interpretation of the labour expended in tertiary industries.

According to the popular view of present-day Marxists, commerce, banking, education, medical treatment, entertainment, passenger transport, etc., belong to unproductive industries creating no value. Therefore, they explain, the constant capital, variable capital and profit of these industries are transferred from surplus value created in the material branches of production through the process of re-distribution of the national income. (*Note*: On the basis of this reasoning, Marxists denounce the inclusion of income accruing from tertiary industry in the amount of national income in the capitalist countries as a sort of 'watered' or 'double' calculation. They see in the high proportion of tertiary industry income an index of deep-rooted decay of monopoly capitalism.)

[*Note:* For example, Joseph M. Gillman denotes unproductive expenditures by the symbol u which stands for 'the salaries and wages of the unproductive workers and for all the sales, advertising and all other administrative expenditures as well as for taxes'. Moreover he thinks all these expenditures are to be deducted from surplus value.[18]]

It is true that we are surrounded and almost choked with a flood of wasteful and even harmful 'service' industries, extravagant advertising, and television murder-films and the like. Set aside the continued growth of medicine, education and passenger transport, etc., in order to make the Marxists' attack on these corruptions logically consistent, a fatal flaw in their theoretical construction must be removed. Unfortunately, Marxian argument as summarised above contains within it a perfect self-contradiction.

The story is simple and clear-cut. It is an 'orthodox' Marxian view that 'the law of the falling tendency of the rate of profit' persists in the long run in spite of various counteracting causes. The rate of profit in this case means the proportion in fractional terms of the total amount of surplus value produced in the branches of material production to the amount of total capital in these industries. Now, if constant capital, variable capital and profit of the tertiary industry are all to be derived from the surplus value of the material branches of production, and a profit (p) for these latter is still to be left over, the total capital expenses ($c + v$) in tertiary industry must naturally be smaller than national surplus value. Then the proportion in fractional terms of the total capital in tertiary industry to that in the industries engaged in material production must also be smaller than the rate of profit. Therefore, if the falling tendency of the rate of profit is a 'natural law' of the capitalist society, 'the law of the falling tendency of the proportion of tertiary industry' must also exist as a logical sequence, the latter figure always being smaller than the rate of profit.

But in the real capitalist world, wasteful and useful tertiary industries alike are continuing their rapid growth and Marxists are rightly attacking the former. It is nothing but an obvious self-contradiction to defend the law of the falling rate of profit, on the other hand, and simultaneously call the tertiary industry an unproductive parasite that grows by feeding on surplus value. For the sake of clarity 'the law of the falling rate of the tertiary industry' is given symbolical illustration in Table 1.4.

Table 1.4 The law of the falling rate of tertiary industry

$$s = p_1 + c_2 + v_2 + p_2$$

$$\therefore\ s_1 > c_2 + v_2$$

$$\frac{s_1}{c_1 + v_1} = p'$$

$$\therefore\ p' > \frac{c_2 + v_2}{c_1 + v_1}$$

1: industries of material production
2: tertiary industry

Therefore, when p' becomes smaller, $\frac{c_2 + v_2}{c_1 + v_1}$ also becomes smaller, the numerical value of the latter always being smaller.

2 Can commercial business operate without capital? Origin of the confusion

Two operations are necessary to release us from this deadlock. One is the re-examination of the law of the falling tendency of the rate of profit. I concluded in 1956 that the law as such embraces serious confusion in logic.[19] The second operation is the exposure of the illusive

nature of the thesis that tertiary industry does not create value and is
maintained by surplus value produced only in the material branches.

Marx himself did not think that all of the tertiary industries fail to
create value. He clearly acknowledges the conception of the
'production of *immaterial things*'[20] (emphasis – T.H.) in *Theories of
Surplus Value*. In Sec, 4, Chap. 1, Book 2 of *Capital* he points out that
'there are certain independent branches of industry in which the
product of the productive process is not a new material product, is not
a commodity. Among these only the communications industry . . .
transportation proper . . . or transmission of communications, letters,
telegrams . . . is important.'[21] And taking up the transportation
industry as representative of them, Marx clarifies his view that the
transportation process of both goods and passengers creates value and
surplus value.

> what the transportation industry sells is change of location . . . the
> exchange-value of this useful effect is determined, like that of any other
> commodity, by the value of the elements of production (labour-power and
> means of production) consumed in it plus the surlus value created by the
> surplus labour of the labourers employed in transportation. This useful effect
> also entertains the very same relations to consumption that other
> commodities do. It is consumed individually its value disappears during its
> consumption; if it is consumed productively so as to constitute by itself a
> stage in the production of the commodities being transported, its value is
> transferred as an additional value to the commodity itself. The formula for
> the transport industry would therefore be $M - C \left\{ {L \atop MP} \right. \ldots P - M'$, since it is
> the process of production itself that is paid for and consumed, not a product
> separate and distinct from it.[22]

Thus, as far as the 'branches of industry in which the product of the
productive process is not a new material product' are concerned,
Marx's view and that of contemporary Marxists, who should be his
faithful followers, are partly different. The latter regards only *freight*
transportation and *productive* transmission of communications as
value-creating.[23]

Concerning another field of tertiary industry, the circulation
branches such as commerce and banking, both Marx and contemporary Marxists maintain that value is not created in these industries.[24]
This assertion, however, plunged Marx into intractable confusion of
logic which is reflected in the national income theory of contemporary
Marxists.

Table 1.5 shows in a properly arranged form the figures given by
Marx for the explanation of commercial capital's rôle in the formation
of the average rate of profit.

Table 1.5   Participation of commercial capital in the formation of the average rate of profit

---

(1)   Commercial capital abstracted:
annual total product of industrial capital
$720c + 180c + 180s = 1080$: $p' = 20\%$

(2) $100C$ of commercial capital joins in:
product of industrial capital is sold
to commercial capital at the price of 1062
and the latter sells it at 1080:
Industrial capital $900C$ gains $162s$: $p' = 18\%$
Commercial capital $100C$ gains $18s$: $p' = 18\%$

The merchant in this illustration annually buys 1062 (read Yen, dollars or pounds, etc. as you will) of goods and sells them at 1080, gaining the difference of 18 which constitutes his profit. He is supposed to feel no need of subtracting maintenance cost of office building or employees' wages or any other item.

This exceedingly lucrative business can be found only in the dream world of abstraction. Marx believed he had succeeded with these figures in explaining the participation of commercial capital in the formation of the average rate of profit, because of his unrealistic assumption that 'the merchant has no overhead expenses . . . aside from the money-capital'[25] the diminution of which was out of consideration.

Based on such an assumption, it is no wonder that the merchant can count as profit all the differences between buying and selling. But this is no real explanation.

Of the origin of 'overhead expenses' and profit of commercial capital, Marx stipulates that they are all deducted from the surplus value produced in the material branches of production,[26] of course, leaving some profit for them. Using the formula of Table 1.4:

$$s = p_1 + c_2 + v_2 + p_2$$

In the numbers of Table 1.5

$$s = 162p_1 + 0c_2 + 0v_2 + 18p_2$$

Thus, the unrealistic nature of Marx's illustration comes to be clearly visible.

In the Soviet *Political Economy–Textbook*, a similar sort of wrong abstraction is applied in explaining the participation of commercial capital in the formation of the average rate of profit, as shown in Table 1.6 in a form arranged by the author.[27]

Table 1.6   Participation of commercial capital as seen by *Political Economy*

Commercial capital abstracted from:
$800c_1 + 100s = 900$ $\hspace{4cm}$ $p' = 12.5\%$
Commercial capital, $200C_2$, added:
   Commercial capital buys the whole commodities of 900 value-units sells them at 900 and gains profit 20.

   Industrial capital $800C_1 \rightarrow 80p_2$ $\hspace{2cm}$ $p' = 10\%$
   Commercial capital $200C_2 \rightarrow 20p_2$ $\hspace{2cm}$ $p' = 10\%$
(Remaining question) $100s = 80p_1 + 0C_2 + 20p_2$
   Replacement of $200C_2$ is impossible.

As shown, in this model economy, the industrial (material sector) capital $800C_2$, produces 900 total social product, of which 100 is surplus value. The profit-rate is 12.5%. But for the accomplishment of the reproduction process some amount of commercial capital, say $200C_2$, is needed. If the commercial capital buys 900 value-units of products at the price of 880 and sells them at 900, then, $100s$ is divided into $80p_1$ and $20p_2$, giving rise to the average rate of profit of 10% between the industrial and commercial sectors.

This illustration from *Political Economy* involves a mistake similar to that of Marx in the above case. In Table 1.5, commercial capital consists only of 100 *money*-capital, without any constant and variable capitals. In Table 1.6, $200C_2$ of physical capital is appropriated, which is supposed to be divided into constant and variable capitals. However, $200c_2$ gains in a given period, e.g., one year, only $20p_1$. In the case of the industrial capital, it obtains the gross sales of 880, which should be 800 for the replacement of consumed capital and $80p_1$. But the commercial sector cannot find any fund at all for the replacement of $200C_3$.

This pattern of incorrect reasoning occupies the central position in the national income theory of contemporary Marxists. Figure 1.1 is the illustration of national income distribution found in *Political Economy*.

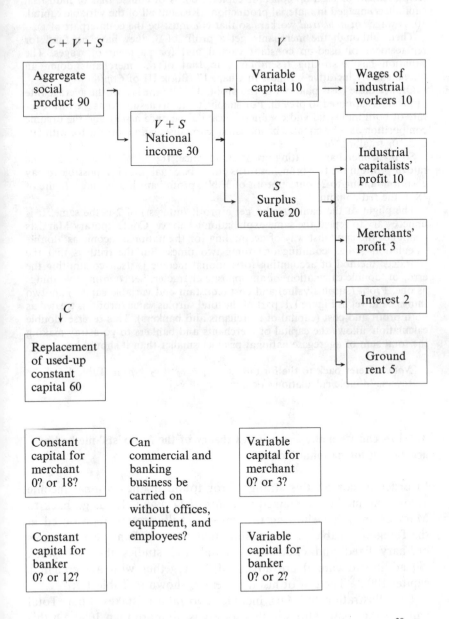

Figure 1.1 National income distribution as seen by *Political Economy*[28]
(with comments by T.H.)

'Replacement of used-up constant capital', 60, is of course that of industrial capitalists engaged in material production. (Reason: all of the variable capital, 10, is wages of *industrial* workers so that $60c$ must be the counterpart of v).

Then, although the merchants get a profit of 3, they have no fund for replacement of used-up constant capital and for payment of wages. The situation has a striking resemblance to that of the merchants doing an unrealistically lucrative business in Chap. 17, Book III of *Capital*.

Or, are these costs paid out of the profit, 3? Here the law of the average rate of profit is supposed to prevail. For simplicity, let us assume that the turn-over rate of both industrial and commercial capital be once a year and the organic composition also be equal. The industrial capitalists gain a profit, 10, with $60c$ and $10v$ totalling $70c$.

So if the merchants getting profit, 3, advance, $18c$ and $3v$ totalling $21c$, the rate of profit in the two branches turns out to be equal. But, is it possible to pay costs amounting to 21 out of profit of 3? No, profit vanishes leaving a figure of 18 in the red column.

The plight of the bankers who get a profit (interest) of 2 is the same. It is unnecessary to repeat the same explanation as above. Contemporary Marxists denounce the capitalist way of accounting for the national income as 'double calculation' – i.e., counting one thing two times. But the truth is that the Marxists' method of accounting for national income is itself committing the error of 'double calculation' of an opposite character, i.e. counting two things as one. Profit (surplus value) and cost (constant and variable capital) are two things. And yet in Figure 1.1, part of the total surplus value (profit) is treated as both profit and cost (capital of merchants and bankers). This reverse 'double calculation' allows the capital of merchants and bankers to go astray making the total sum of aggregate national product smaller than it should be.

[*Note:*   Refer back to the formula $s = p_1 + c_2 + v_2 + p_2$ in Table 1.4. Reverse 'double calculation' occurs of $c_2 + v_2$.]

3   How can we make a consistent theory of the Marxists' method of accounting for national income?

In order to correct this strange error found in the national income accounting method contained in *Political Economy*, let us go back to Marx again. After showing the unrealistic illustration reproduced in the foregoing Table 1.5, he admits that the merchant also advances ordinary fixed and circulating capital and studies the case when '50 additional capital are advanced . . . together with a merchant's capital 100'.[29] The gist of his argument is shown in Table 1.7.

This illustration by Marx includes two fatal mistakes. First: Total value of the commodities in this society is no more than 1080. Of this the capitalists and workers of the industrial branch buy $1054^2/_7$. The

Table 1.7   When 50_c is added to 100_c of money-capital of merchant

---

Total product of industrial capital:
$$720c + 180v + 180s = 1080$$
Industrial capitalist sells it at
$$1054^2/_7 = 900c + 154^2/_7 \quad \text{to the merchant}$$
$$\text{Industrial capitalist's } p' = 17^1/_7\%$$
Merchant sells it at $1130\,(1080 + 50$ for replacement$)$
$$1130 - (1054^2/_7 + 50) = 25^5/_7 \ldots \text{merchant's profit}$$
$$\text{Merchant's } p' = \frac{25^5/_7}{150} = 17^1/_7\%$$

---

merchant buys the remaining commodities valued at $25^5/_7$ with his profit. The commodities are sold out. The merchant still has money of 50 value with which he must buy goods for replenishment. Of course he cannot get them.

Second: The product valued at 1080 in the beginning is valued at 1130 after undergoing operations undertaken by merchant's capital. Commercial business has produced value! *Capital* tells us in Sec. 2, Chap 6., Book 2 that 'costs of circulation . . . do not enter into the value of commodities'.[30] But here the cost of circulation 50 entered into the value of commodities.

This was an 'error' pointing in the right direction. Now the merchant secured at least *money* for replacement. What should he do then to obtain necessary *goods*?

Consider the following: The industrial capital alone cannot realise the value produced, so that a certain amount of commercial and banking capital is needed to complete the process of re-production. Meanwhile, use-values are produced only in the industrial branches. Now suppose that the re-production process of a hypothetical society goes on with $70C$ of industrial capital, $21C$ of commercial capital and $14C$ of banking capital and the annual product of the industrial capital is $80G$ of goods (use-values). These goods are distributed among industrial, commercial and banking branches in proportion to their respective capital invested. In this way we can avoid the perplexing situation that the merchant has money for replacement but cannot find goods on the market. Let us illustrate the story in the form of Table 1.8.

Table 1.8   New interpretation of national income distribution

(A)   Society with smaller proportion of circulating departments

Industry	$60c + 10v + 10s = 80$	... produces $80G$
		obtains $80 \times \frac{70}{105}G$
Commerce	$18c + 3v + 3s = 24$	obtains $80 \times \frac{21}{105}G$
Banking	$12c + 2c + 2s = 16$	obtains $80 \times \frac{14}{105}G$

(B)   Society with larger proportion of circulating departments

Industry	$48c + 8v + 8s = 64$	... produces $64G$
		obtains $64 \times \frac{56}{105}G$
Commerce	$24c + 4v + 4s = 32$	obtains $64 \times \frac{28}{105}G$
Banking	$18c + 3v + 3s = 24$	obtains $64 \times \frac{21}{105}G$

Case (A) of this table serves as an answer to the error in the illustration of national income in *Political Economy*. Here, merchants and bankers hold not only profit, but also capital, which is lacking in the illustration of that textbook.

This table also helps us escape from the rule of 'the law of the falling proportion of tertiary industry'. Suppose the society of case (A), on account of irrational activity spurred by profit-incentive, now advances more of the total capital, 105, to commercial and banking business than before, as in the case (B). Here the goods produced diminish while the expended amount of value (quantity of 'dead' and 'living' human labour) remains unchanged. This society becomes poorer in terms of useful goods.

[*Note:* If we think of case (B) as a model of the present-day capitalist society accompanied by much waste, and (A) as the case when more useful goods are produced as a result of rational and planned economic activity, the difference, 16, of output of goods falls roughly under the third item of Paul A. Baran's 'potential economic surplus' i.e. 'output lost because of the irrational and wasteful organization of the existing productive apparatus.']^{31}

How about the fields which Marx calls the branches of 'immaterial production' in connection with Table 1.8? These are the industries which do not produce use-values, but offer 'services' with 'useful effects' analogous to consumption or production goods: e.g. medicine and education. The process of producing services, viewed from the standpoint of expending abstract human labour, is nothing but creation of value and surplus value. Therefore the item 'Industry' in (A) and (B) of Table 1.8 should be regarded as representing both goods-producing and service-producing industries and figures 80 and 64 as the abstract expression of output of goods and services.

There may be criticism of this kind: 'You have spoiled the Marxian theory of national income and pushed it down to the level of bourgeois national income accounting. This amounts to voluntary surrender of a valuable weapon of criticism in the theoretical struggle against contemporary decaying capitalism'.

My answer is: 'Just the opposite!' Generally speaking, it is true that material products are the basis of the maintenance and expansion of social reproduction. But they do not suffice. For that purpose, maintenance and enlargement of the 'service' industry of training technical experts plays an essential rôle. Branches offering 'useful effects' analogous to consumption and production goods are needed. Some commercial function is also indispensable. On the other hand, the arms and munitions industry belongs to the department of material production which 'creates value'. And yet it is nothing but a heavy and troublesome burden to society. When we examine the loss in production and circulation of a capitalist country or study more efficient ways of organising man-power and resources in a socialist country, the 'orthodox' Marxist method of excluding unproductive industries from the national income account may give rise to an invisible but real obstacle. This barrier will remain as long as there is theoretical confusion about 'double calculation' and the 'law' of the falling proportion of tertiary industry. Parting from belief in these fatal errors means only gain, not loss. The way will be opened to grasp the concepts of national income, total social product and its process of re-production with rigorous theoretical consistency on the basis of the labour theory of value. The development of the fundamental Marxian economic theory in this direction will offer a more effective weapon for the correct analysis of capitalist societies and for efficient construction in socialist countries.

4 Fundamental re-examination and development of the concept of 'value'

Lastly, it is necessary to throw light upon the difference between the concept of 'value' of Marx and his 'faithful' followers and that which I have developed from it. From the correct recognition of the fact that commercial and banking business does not produce *use-values*, Marx established an incorrect thesis that 'costs of circulation do not enter into the value of commodities', and the labour of workers in circulation departments does not produce value.[32] But office buildings, account books, necessaries of life consumed by commercial employees, etc., from the view-point of abstract human labour realised in them, are evidently *value*, and these employees also work longer than their necessary labour time. Their surplus labour time also produces surplus value. Marx ignored this 'dead' and 'living' labour just because it does not produce use-values. This was the origin of the whole confusion which I have explained here. My job was just to point out what had been twisted beyond recognition.

[*Note:* According to Ronald L. Meek, it is not only that 'the labour theory was good science in Marx's time but also that it is good science today'. But it must be recognised that Marx's labour theory originally involved in itself inconsistent arguments.[33]]

5 Supplementary notes added in 1984

(1) Table 1.8 can be expressed in the form of an input–output table (Figure 1.2). For simplicity, let us add two departments, commerce and banking, together. Then, we obtain $30c + 5v + 5s = 40$, a single circulation department.

O〱I	G	S	f.d.		t.o.
			L	C	
G	40	20			80
S	20	10	5	5	40
f.s.	W 10	W 5			
	P 10	P 5			
t.i.	80	40			120

Figure 1.2   National income distribution in the form of an input–output table

[*Note:*   G = goods, S = services, f.d. = final demand, C = capital, W = wages, P = profit, f.s. = final supply, t.i. = total input.

If we regard the figures for the circulation department as those representing the whole tertiary (service) industry, then this table would be of use for illustrating the input–output relation between goods-producing industry and service-producing industry.

(2) In connection with Table 1.8, I asserted, 'The way will be opened to grasp the concept of national income, total social product and the process of re-production . . . *on the basis of the labour theory of value.*' But now I feel the necessity of an important qualification: Table 1.8 and Figure 1.2 are meaningful on the basis of the labour theory of value only so long as they remain in the abstract world of hypothetical figures. If we want to develop them to a multi-sector operational input–output table based on statistical data, we must rely upon actual prevailing prices having nothing to do with labour value.

(3) In 1959 it was appropriate to say: 'According to the popular view of present-day Marxists, commerce, banking, education, medical treatment, entertainment, passenger transport, etc. belong to unproductive industries creating no value. Since the late 1960s, however, in Soviet Russia and Japan, Marxists' interpretation of unproductive labour has been remarkably changed. These unproductive industries have gradually been transferred into the grouping of productive industries, even commerce which Marx categorically classified as unproductive. Now some Japanese and Soviet economists include commerce in the category of productive industry. For instance, Y.A. Pevzner does so contending that 'value is created, not only in production, but also in every link of re-production . . . until a commodity (or service) reaches the consumer, or until the moment consumption begins'.[34] So do all Soviet official statistics.

These are the revisions in the right direction in an age in which workers engaged in tertiary industries occupy about half or more of the whole labour force in the advanced capitalist countries.

If these workers do not create value, the labour-value theory of Marx comes to be inapplicable to the majority of the working population! And yet, Nobuo Iimori, a Japanese economist, who himself extends the scope of productive labour to all the service industries except commerce criticises Pevzner as follows: 'Commercial labour does not create value . . . This is a fundamental proposition of labour-value theory by Marx. If commercial labour creates value, the total amount of value in a society is to be increased indefinitely through expansion of the pure circulation department.'[35]

This criticism shows a fatal misunderstanding of the labour-value theory by its defender himself. In Figure 1.2 above, the total amount

Table 1.9   The ratio of the workers engaged in tertiary industries in
major countries (%, 1975)

	Japan	US	UK	FRG	France
All industries	100	100	100	100	100
1. & 2. industries	48.5	33.0	43.6	53.3	49.9
tertiary industries	51.5	67.0	56.4	46.7	50.0

[Note: Primary industries: Agriculture, forestry, marine product industry. Secondary industry: Mining, manufacturing, building, electricity, gas, waterworks. Tertiary industries: Transportation and communication, finance and insurance, whole sale and retail business, services, non-classifiables.]

Source: OECD, Labour Force Statistics, 1964–75.

of value of this hypothetical society is 120 units. Expansion of the circulation industry is possible only through contraction of goods-producing industry. Thus, for the circulation industry 120 units of value is an unattainable limit of its expansion. Indefinite increase of total social value though expansion of circulation industry becomes possible *only when labour force increases indefinitely*. This should be the logical corollary of the labour theory of value.

[Note: See Ch. 8, Sec. III, subsection 2, in the present book for further particulars of this problem.]

2 The Immanent Self-Contradictions in Marx's Labour Theory of Value: In Connection with the Transformation Problem

I IS THE LABOUR-VALUE THEORY REALLY VALID IN *CAPITAL*?

1 Necessity of distinguishing between profundity and ambiguity

It must be surprising and almost unbelievable to nearly all the readers of *Capital*, if I say that the book is full of primitive errors in logic, not to speak of numerous problematical points in economics proper. But it is true, I have been endeavouring for more than twenty years (written in 1979) to offer an understandable picture of the economic system of *Capital*. Without persuasive demonstration of these basic defects, it is impossible to describe precisely what is meant by *Capital*, in which ambiguity very often takes the appearance of profundity.

Lenin's remark in his *Plan of Hegel's Dialectics (Logic)* is famous:

> If Marx did not leave behind him 'Logic' (with a capital letter), he did leave the logic of *Capital*, . . . In *Capital*, Marx applies to a single science logic, dialectics and theory of knowledge of materialism (three words are not needed: it is one and the same thing) which has taken every thing valuable and developed it further.[1]

For those who have unconditional faith in the truthfulness of Marxism-Leninism the above statement of Lenin might be sufficient to convince them of the absolute perfection of *Capital*, composed as it is in terms of dialectical logic, which is thought to be superior to formal logic. However, the dialectics itself is the origin of most of the systematic defects in logic inherent in *Capital*. The core of my argument is that the so-called 'logic of contradiction' (dialectics) is nothing more than fallacy of amphiboly.

[*Note:* 'Dialectical logic' is usually called 'logic of contradiction *(Widerspruch)*' as it is thought, by Hegel, Marx and their followers, to be a system of logic which supersedes the Aristotelian law of contradiction in describing motion, change, opposition, struggle, etc. (For more detailed explanation, see Section I, Chapter 6.) 'Fallacy of amphiboly' in this context is used as a general term for various kinds of fallacies mistakenly believed in as the 'logic of contradiction', for instance, fallacies of equivocation, insufficient disjunction, improper anthropomorphism, begging the question, etc. These are examined and disproved all through this book.]

Let us now look, from this methodological point of view, at some concrete examples, in the sphere of labour-value theory, of inconsistent and self-contradictory reasoning found in *Capital.*

2 The Labour-time calculation as the basis of the labour-value theory

(1) The two-fold meaning of the labour theory of value

According to Marx, the labour of the working class is the only element which produces value in the capitalist society. Of the whole produced value, the labourers receive the equivalent of their necessary labour (the wages for maintaining their life, or '*v*', the value of labour-power), and that of their surplus value is exploited by capitalists. There is no other way than a communist revolution to abolish this unfair and unjust society. Thus the labour theory of value and the theory of surplus value developed on it constitute the kernel of Marxian revolutionary theory. This is the reason why Marxists stick to the labour-value theory at all costs.

This theory, interpreted in the broad sense that labour is the basic element which sustains the social life of mankind, is an 'eternal truth.' Marx himself wrote in his letter of 11 July 1868 to Kugelmann as follows:

Even a child knows that any nation cannot live on if they stop working just two or three weeks, not to speak of one year.[2]

This is with regard to 'living labour.' In terms of present day economics it means that labour is the elementary and indispensable factor for the maintenance of national income as flow.

Labour is also needed for the accumulation of national wealth as stock consisting of capital goods and consumer goods which are durable. These are the embodiments of 'past (dead) labour'. In Chapter 49, Book III of *Capital* we read:

> If we think back to the beginnings of society, we find no produced means of production, hence no constant capital . . . But Nature there directly provides the means of subsistence . . . also gives . . . the time . . . to transform . . . other products of Nature into means of production: bows, stone knives, boats, etc. This process among savages, considered merely from the substantive side, corresponds to the reconversion of surplus labour into new capital [making of the initial means of production – T.H.]. In the process of accumulation, the conversion of such products of excess labour into capital [formation of additional constant capital over and above the replacement of existing capital – T.H.] obtains continually.[3]

It is an unmistakable fact that from ancient times mankind has been increasing its wealth through labour in this way. Marx's labour theory of value, however, not only means that labour has been the mainstay of income and wealth of mankind, but also asserts that, therefore, labour alone decides the value of commodities and is the one and only factor which accounts for the relative price system. Is the latter contention valid?

(2) The labour-value theory of the early British economists

The great thinker, John Locke, who lived in seventeenth-century England, where agriculture and simple manual trades were prevalent, had this to say:

> I think it will be but a very modest computation to say, that of the produces of the earth useful to the life of man, nine-tenths are the effects of labour . . . For whatever bread is more worth than acorns, wine than water, and cloth or silk than leaves, skins or moss, that is wholly owing to labour and industry. Nay, if we will rightly estimate things as they come to our use, and cast up the several expenses about them – what in them is purely owing to Nature and what to labour – we shall find that in most of them ninety-nine hundredths are wholly to be put on the account of labour.[4]

Unlike in the contemporary world, where a gigantic oil-tanker in the ocean is operated by a crew of around twenty and an unmanned water-power station in the mountain is run by remote control, in a pre-industrial society sustained by manual trades the labour-value theory had a solid empirical basis.

But, is the computation of the labour embodied in products as easy as the old British economists thought it to be?

As for the beginning of 'the beginnings of society' Marx referred to, where even stone knives do not exist yet, one need think only of homogeneous 'living labour'. Another classic example is the state of primitive society described by Adam Smith:

> In that early and rude state of society which precedes both the accumulation of stock and the appropriation of land, the proportion between the quantities of labour necessary for acquiring different objects seem to be the only circumstance which can afford any rule for exchanging them for one another. If among a nation of hunters, for example, it usually costs twice the labour to kill a beaver which it does to kill a deer, one beaver should naturally exchange for or be worth two deer. It is natural that what is usually the produce of two days' or two hours' labour, should be worth double of what is usually the produce of one day's or one hour's labour.[5]

> 2 days (or hours) = 2 days (or hours) one beaver is worth two deer (of same value)

Let us interpret Smith's implicit assumption as follows: (1) labour is homogeneous; (2) it is the one and only factor of production. Then, labour-value theory, as a labour-*time* theory of value, is perfectly consistent. The unit of measurement is time (week, day, hour, minute . . .).

But Ricardo's interpretation of Smith's primitive society is different. He thinks:

> Even in that early state to which Adam Smith refers, some capital . . . would be necessary to enable him to kill his game. Without some weapon, neither the beaver nor the deer could be destroyed, and therefore the value of these animals would be regulated, not solely by the time and labour necessary to their destruction, but also by the time and labour necessary for providing the hunter's capital, the weapon . . . Suppose the weapon necessary to kill the beaver was constructed with much more labour than that necessary to kill the deer . . . one beaver would naturally be of more value than two deer.[6]

Bigger dead labour		smaller dead labour
2 days		+ 2 days
One beaver	has more value than	two deer

In this simple model a labour-time calculation is still possible, because weapons are supposed to perish in one-time use and the dead (past) labour embodied in them to be measured in a time-unit, the day.

Then Ricardo proceeds to a more precise and complicated inquiry into relative values of commodities. And he writes:

> If we suppose . . . the same quantity of labour to be always required to obtain the same quantity of gold . . . I shall suppose . . . all alterations in price to be occasioned by some alteration in the value of the commodity of which I may be speaking.[7]

If a certain quantity of gold can be obtained with two days' living labour using a simple tool, embodying three days' labour, which perishes in one-time use, then, the quantity of labour required for the production of gold is *knowable* in terms of direct labour-time unit. It is five days. But in the real world the production process of gold beginning from mining gold ore and ending in the shape of gold bullion or coin requires innumerable kinds of past labour whose degrees of 'pastness' are innumerably different. And living labour in the last process of production, say, in the mint, is not homogeneous. Skilled or high-quality labour must be weighted. For instance, one real hour must be counted as three hours. The same thing also applies to all the kinds and degrees of past labour because they are not homogeneous. Thus, in practice, a direct labour-time computation of the 'quantity of labour materialised' in a certain quantity of gold is impossible, and if done, it has to be fictitious. (Detailed explanation raising some more reasons for the impossibility of the direct labour-time calculation is given in the following Sec. (4).)

John Gray, one of the Ricardian Socialists, came up with the idea that a planned and reasonable society could be brought forth by reforming the 'system of exchange' on the basis of the labour theory of value. He declared:

> Labour is the source of wealth, or 'original purchase money that is paid for everything'.[8]

> Money should be merely a *receipt*, an evidence that the holder of it has either contributed a certain value to the national stock of wealth, or that he has acquired a right to the said value from someone who has contributed it.[9]

> An estimated value being previously put upon produce, let it be lodged in a bank, and drawn out again whenever it is required; merely stipulating, by common consent, that he who lodges any kind of property in the proposed National Bank, may take out of it an equal value of whatever it may contain, instead of being obliged to draw out the self same thing that he put in.[10]

> Shall we retain our *fictitious* standard of value, gold, and thus keep the productive resources of the country in bondage? Or, shall we resort to the

natural standard of value, *labour*, and thereby set out productive resources *free*?[11]

But in his scheme Gray did not advocate a direct labour-time calculation, as the following quotations show:

> All goods . . . should be transmitted from their respective factories to the national warehouses, and here, to the price of material and labour already expended . . . direct cost, should be added the per centage, or profit, fixed by the Chamber of Commerce, to pay the various expenses of rent, interest of capital, management, salaries, depreciation of stock, incidents, and all national charges; and this being done, would form the retail price of goods.[12]

> The average price of labour being once determined . . . we should have attained, for the first time . . . an *immutable standard of value* . . . if it were determined that a pound, for example, should be the payment for the labour of one man for a week, consisting of six days, or seventy-two hours . . . a pound note from that time forth would be just another name for a *week* of reasonable exertion.[13]

> Somewhere on our future race-course, we must have a *starting point*, consisting of a *minimum* rate of weekly wages . . . from which minimum price of labour all other things would . . . take their *proportionate* money price, through the operation of the principle of individual competition.[14]

From the above statements of Gray it is clear that he did not intend a labour-*time* calculation of value. His plan of an ideal social system controlled by the National Bank is developed in money units, pounds, shillings and pence. If he wished to make a direct(?) labour-time calculation, he could do it by equating one pound with seventy-two hours, £1 = 72 hours, and, with the help of this conversion-coefficient, working out the 'labour-hours' congealed in all the goods concerned. But, is GNP, thus computed of, say, 7,200,000,000,000 'hours' thought to be real labour-hours, a 'quantity of labour' in any substantial meaning? Is it not just another name for £100,000,000,000?

Robert Owen presented his version of labour theory of value in his *Report to the County of Lanark*, of a plan to improve the social conditions there.

> The natural standard of value is, in principle, human labour, or the combined manual and mental powers of men called into action . . . To make labour the standard of value it is necessary to ascertain the amount of it in all articles to be bought and sold. This is, in fact, already accomplished, and is denoted by what in commerce is technically termed '*the prime cost*' [emphasis – T.H.] or the net value of the whole labour contained in any article of

value, . . . the material contained in or consumed by the manufacture of the article forming a part of the whole value . . .

The profit of production will arise . . . from the value of the labour contained in the article produced . . . Its exact amount will depend upon what . . . shall be proved to be the present real value of a day's labour . . .

It would require an accurate . . . consideration . . . to determine the exact value of the unit or day's labour . . . a standard of value . . . a more slight and general view . . . that this unit need not represent a less value than the wealth contained in the necessaries and comforts of life which may now be purchased with five shillings.[15]

Here we should note the following: 'day's labour', say ten hours, is countable and known. But how about its 'value', five pieces of one-shilling coin or the wage-goods which can be purchased with these coins? Is it countable and knowable that they are produced by ten hours of labour? It should be impossible as I explained in the cases of Ricardo and Gray. If 'labour hours' embodied in them were made 'known', it must be nothing other than a fiction, the result of a calculation in the direction from shillings to 'hours', ten *real* hours of skilled labour being counted as thirty hours, just because one day's skilled labour is paid fifteen shillings.

Later in 1832 Owen opened the National Equitable Labour Exchange in London. The 'labour-time calculation' adopted in that institution is given an exact description by G. D. H. Cole:

Owen's 'Labour Notes' have been often misunderstood. He did not propose to value, and he did not actually value, all goods solely in accordance with the numbers of hours spent in producing them. Apart from the value of the material, which was calculated in money at current market prices, he recognised different kinds of labour as differing in value, accepting as the basis of differentiation the actual money rates of wages payable to various types of workers. The price of an article was calculated by adding together the money value of the material, the current time-wages for the hours spent on the work, and a penny in the shilling for the expenses of the Exchange. The total in pence was then divided by 6, 6*d*. being taken as the average price of an hour's labour. The result of this sum was the numbers of hours of 'labour-time' incorporated in the article. Thus materials 6*s*., six hours' skilled labour at 1*s*. per hour = 6*s*., commission 1*d* per 1*s*. = 1 *s*.; total 13*s*., which at 6*d*. per hour = 26 hours of labour-time.

Nothing would have been lost or gained by this translation or re-translation of pounds, shillings and pence into labour-time, if the goods had really been worth the sums asked for them. But some were worth more and some less, and there appears to have been no adequate arrangement for valuation on the basis of what Marx subsequently called 'socially necessary labour-time'. One might take twelve hours to make what another would make in six; and, while for some articles it was fairly easy to fix a standard time allowance, for others there was nothing for it but to accept the estimate of the maker. Thus some articles were priced too high and some too low; and when the Exchange opened, naturally people bought what was cheap, and left what was dear on the hands of the promoters. And, as the Exchange did not stand to make a profit in any case, it could not afford to make a loss.[16]

Here again we see a calculation in the reverse order, from price-units to hours, the computed figures being no more than prices in disguise of 'hours'.

(3)   Marx's criticism of Gray and support for Owen are both out of focus

Marx's stand is that the labour-time calculation is impossible in the commodity producing societies where social production proceeds privately and, therefore, anarchically. Thus he is strongly critical of John Gray who, according to Marx's interpretation, intended to carry into effect a direct labour-time calculation system in the British commercial society at that time. Marx refers to Gray in *A Contribution to the Critique of Political Economy*:

> John Gray was the first to set forth the theory that labour-time is the direct measure of money in a systematic way. He proposes that a national central bank should ascertain through its branches the labour-time expended in the production of various commodities. In exchange for the commodity the producer would receive an official certificate of its value, i.e. a receipt for as much labour-time as his commodity contains, and this bank-note of one labour week, one labour day, one labour hour, etc., would serve at the same time as an order to the bank to hand over an equivalent in any of the commodities in its warehouses.[17]

Marx, who regards Gray's 'bank-note of one week . . . one labour hour, etc.' as impracticable, criticises him as follows:

> Since labour-time is the intrinsic measure of value, why use another extraneous standard as well? Why is exchange-value transformed into price? Why is the value of all commodities computed in terms of an exclusive commodity, which thus becomes the adequate expression of exchange-value, i.e. money? This was the problem which Gray had to solve. But instead of solving it, he assumed that commodities could be directly compared with one another as products of social labour. But they are only comparable as the things they are. Commodities are the direct products of isolated independent individual kinds of labour, and through their alienation in the course of individual exchange they must prove that they are general social labour.[18]

Marx reconfirms this viewpoint later in *Capital* referring to his argument in *A Contribution to the Critique of Political Economy*:

The question . . . why does not money directly represent labour-time, so that a piece of paper may represent, for instance, *x* hours' labour, is at bottom the same as the question on why, given the production of commodities, must products take the form of commodities? This is evident, since their taking the form of commodities implies their differentiation into commodities and money. Or, why cannot private labour . . . be treated as its opposite, immediate social labour? I have elsewhere examined thoroughly the Utopian idea of 'labour-money' in a society founded on the production of commodities. (*A Contribution* . . . , p. 83,ff.) [19]

The crux of Marx's argument above is: Value of commodities cannot be directly measured by labour-time. It is measured indirectly only in money (price) units. Gray should have understood this. But in its stead he imagined that commodities, products of individual private labour, could be produced and distributed as if they were the products of socially planned labour. On that account Gray invented a Utopian idea of a bank-note in terms of labour-time units, which could be feasible only in an economic system of 'immediate social labour' (a centrally planned economy with socialised means of production, in modern terminology).

Marx is wrong on two points. First, he describes it as if Gray actually proposed a bank-note of one labour *week*, one labour *day*, one labour *hour*, etc., on the grounds of several citations from Gray's writings *The Social System*, *A Treatise on the Principle of Exchange* and *Lectures on the Nature and Use of Money*.[20] This is Marx's misreading. Nowhere in the two books quoted by Marx does Gray suggest a direct labour-time calculation. His scheme is that: 'The average price of labour being once determined . . . an immutable standard of value' . . . should have been attained and 'a pound note . . . would be just another name for a week' (72 labour-hours). But as I already explained above, a week (72 hours) computed by dint of money-units is a fiction, just another name for a pound, not vice versa.

The second point is Marx's erroneous belief in the feasibility of a literal direct labour-time calculation in a society of 'immediate social labour', which presumably led him to the misinterpretation that Gray suggested bank-notes in terms of labour-time units.

On the basis of this wrong conviction (a detailed explanation is given in the following section) Marx offers a misplaced praise to Robert Owen:

Owen's 'labour-money' (*Arbeitsgeld*) is no more 'money' than a ticket for the theatre. Owen pre-supposes directly associated labour, a form of production that is entirely inconsistent with the production of commodities. The certificate of labour is merely evidence of the part taken by the individual in the common labour, and of his right to a certain portion of the common product destined for consumption.[21]

If this 'labour-money' means a 'convenient medium',[22] proposed in Owen's *Report to Lanark*, which permits the exchange of 'all articles with each other at their prime cost', this is just a medium of monetary calculation, although Owen himself thinks that by this device 'the amount of labour in each' article can be represented. If it means the 'labour-note' issued by the National Equitable Labour Exchange, the labour 'hours' filled in these notes were no more than prices fictitiously called 'hours' as already explained. Here let me quote again Cole's remark: 'He did not actually value all goods solely in accordance with the number of hours spent in producing them.'

Thus Owen is praised for pricing proposals almost indistinguishable from Gray's, simply because he proposes altered social institutions.

(4)   The so-called 'labour-time calculation' of Marx, Engels and the Soviet economists

Marx thought that the labour-time calculation in the literal sense of the word could only come into operation in the society with the socialised ownership of the means of production. It is clearly shown in the following passage in Chapter 1, Book I of *Capital*:

> Let us now picture to ourselves . . . a community of free individuals, carrying on their work with means of production in common, in which the labour-power of all the different individuals is consciously applied as the combined labour-power of the community . . . The total product of our community is a social product. One portion serves as fresh means of production and remains social. But another portion is consumed by the members as means of subsistence . . . We will assume . . . that the share of each individual producer in the means of subsistence is determined by his labour-time. Labour-time would, in that case, play a double part. Its apportionment in accordance with a definite social plan maintains the proper proportion between the different kinds of work to be done and the various wants of the community. On the other hand, it also serves as a measure of the portion of the common labour borne by each individual, and of his share in the part of the total product destined for individual consumption. The social relations of the individual producers, with regard to their labour and to its products, are in this case perfectly simple and intelligible, and that with regard to not only to production but also to distribution.[23]

Engels presented a remarkably optimistic view of this matter in *Anti-Dühring*:

> From the moment when society enters into possession of the means of production, the labour of each individual . . . becomes at start and directly social labour. The quantity of social labour contained in a product need not then be established in a roundabout way; daily experience shows in a direct way how much of labour is contained in a steam-engine, a bushel of wheat of last harvest, or a hundred square yards of cloth of a certain quality. It could therefore never occur to it still to express the quantities of labour put into the products, quantities which it will then know directly and in their absolute amounts, in a third product, in a measure which, besides, is only relative, fluctuating, inadequate, though formerly unavoidable for lack of a better, rather than express them in their natural, adequate and absolute measure, *time* . . . . It will not express the simple fact that the hundred square yards of cloth have required for their production, say, a thousand hours of labour in the oblique and meaningless way, stating that they have the *value* of a thousand hours of labour.[24]

A society referred to by Marx and Engels here corresponds to 'the first stage of communist society . . . just emerged from capitalist society', by the definition of Marx in *Critique of the Gotha Programme*, where 'the individual producer receives back from society – after the deductions have been made – exactly what gives it . . . his individual quantum of labour.'[25]

But can a direct labour-time calculation be 'perfectly simple and intelligible' in such a society? No: just as in the British commercial society at the time of Gray and Owen, a skilled worker's one hour must be counted as, say, 'five hours', if he obtains five-fold wage. And quantities of labour contained in all the means of production and consumption cannot be measured in direct labour-time units. 'That the hundred yards of cloth have required for their production a thousand hours of labour' is not an ascertainable 'simple fact', as we showed in connection with a citation from Ricardo (see note 7). If any 'labour-time' computation were tried, it should inevitably result in a fictitious one as practised in the National Equitable Labour Exchange.

Marx and Engels belonged to a generation who died without seeing realised socialist countries. But now it is about two-thirds of a century since the birth of Soviet Russia. We have a group of countries where the means of production are fundamentally owned in common. Yet in these societies we cannot meet such things as a labour-certificate with a par value of, say, 'one hour' or a pair of shoes with a price (hour?)-tag of 'ten hours and thirty minutes' and so on.

The impossibility of labour-time calculation in the contemporary socialist societies is explained away by the revision of the original theory of Marx and Engels. They thought the labour-time calculation could be introduced already in the lower phase of communist society, as shown in the above-cited statements. But in Soviet Russia the period of transition from money-calculation to labour-time calculation was postponed until the advent of the 'higher phase of communist society' where distribution is to be made 'to each according to his needs.'[26] The Programme of the Communist Party of the Soviet Union, adopted by the 22nd Congress of the CPSU on 31 October 1961, decided that:

> The material and technical basis of communism will be built up by the end of the second decade (1971–80), ensuring the abundance of material and cultural values for the whole population; Soviet society will come close to a stage where it can introduce the principle of distribution according to needs . . . Thus, a communist society will in the main be built in the USSR . . .
> It is necessary in communist construction to make full use of commodity-money relations . . . such instruments of economic development as cost accounting, money, price, production cost, profit, trade, credit and finance play a big part. With the transition to the single communist form of people's property and the communist system of distribution, commodity-money relations will become economically outdated and will wither away.[27]

According to the *Political Economy–Textbook* of the USSR:

> With the advent of communism, the attainment of a high level of productive forces which guarantees the abundance of products, the establishment of complete rule of single communist ownership, the change of labour into life's prime need, the commodity production and circulation existing under socialism will come to be superfluous. Money will become unnecessary. The direct distribution of products without using money according to needs among the members of society will be organised. The society will gradually make calculation of labour directly with labour-hours, without relying upon value and its form.[28]

[*Note:* In Soviet Russia and among Marxists in general the first or lower phase of communism is called *socialism* and its higher phase simply *communism*. Lenin had already made the following remark in 1917: 'generally called socialism, but termed by Marx the first phase of communism'.[29]]

Can you imagine that from 1 January 1981 onward money, price, profit, credit etc. 'will become outdated and wither away' being substituted by 'simple and intelligible' labour-time calculation and labour-hour notes? This is rather a matter of common sense. (This sentence was written in 1979. In October 1983 I had a chance to visit Moscow and Leningrad and could confirm that Russians were still using rubles and kopeks as the units of business calculation, but not *chasy* (hours) and *minuty* (minutes). On 25 April 1984 Soviet President Konstantin Chernenko told Communist Party officials that it was wiser to 'leave behind the superficial concept of the ways and time frame of transition to the supreme phase of communism that was current during a certain period'. This statement involves as its logical corollary an unlimited postponement of the expected transition from monetary calculation to labour-hour calculation.[30]

But for certainty let me offer a detailed illustration. The labour-time calculation is impossible even in the higher stage of communist society because:

First, human labour is not homogeneous: in, say, an automobile factory, its chief engineer should be of higher ability than its gatekeeper. If this were a communist society of lower phase or a capitalist society, the difference in ability is explicitly displayed as the difference in wage level. For instance, the former obtains five times higher wages than the latter does. Then, one hour's labour in physical terms of the chief engineer should be counted as 'five hours' in an economic calculation. This is not a real length of time, but an economic quantity bearing the name of a time-unit. Apparently Marx had a view that this unreasonableness could be avoided by a 'reduction' of skilled labour into simple labour:

> Skilled labour counts only as simple labour intensified, or rather, as multiplied simple labour, a given quantity of skilled being considered equal to a greater quantity of simple labour. Experience shows that this reduction is constantly being made.[31]

Well, 'experience shows' that when one hour of a skilled labourer produces five times as much value as that of a simple labourer, the former receives five times as much wages as that of the latter. This should be Marx's illustration. But it is no more than a value-calculation in the fictitious name of 'hours'. The unreasonableness of counting one real hour as 'five hours' still remains.

Now, suppose this automobile factory were in a society where 'the productive forces have increased with the all-round development of the individual, and all the springs of co-operative wealth flow more abundantly' and the dominating rule is: 'From each according to his ability, to each according to his needs.'[32] Here the levels of consumption of the chief engineer and the gatekeeper would not reflect the difference in their abilities; they might be about the same. And yet the difference in abilities will continue to exist. And the costs of education and those of goods and services necessary for the execution of their respective tasks should be higher for the former than for the latter. Thus, one hour's labour of the former is more valuable than that of the latter. So that one labour hour of the chief engineer must be counted as, say, 'three' labour hours.

Second, the difficulty in the calculation of 'past labour': the total amount of labour 'materialised' in the finished products, automobiles, consists of the 'living labour' expended by the automobile workers plus the 'past (dead) labour' embodied in materials, power, in depreciation cost of machinery and factory building, etc. One of the materials, for example, steel sheets, is the product of living labour of steel workers and the various kinds of past labour which, in their turn, absorbed unskilled and skilled living labour (which must be counted as x-fold hours of unskilled labour) in various time-points of the past. Thus, the total labour 'hours' embodied in an automobile, if added up somehow, are something purely nominal having no substantial connection with real physical hours.

Third; the trouble concerning fertility and conditions of location. For instance, the amount of labour 'hours' embodied in the same quantity and quality of iron ores, material for steel sheets, extracted from mines of various richness are bound to be different. But, at the same time the values of the same commodities must be expressed in the same price or same labour 'hours': the 'hours' which are different and one and the same!

Fourth; the problem of supply and demand. Marx asserts in *German Ideology* that: 'with the abolition of the basis of private property, with the communistic regulation of production . . . *the power of the relation of supply and demand is dissolved into nothing*'[33] (emphasis – T.H.). This line of thought is developed, in *Capital*, into a 'perfectly simple and intelligible' direct labour-time calculation as cited above. Then, how about in a communist society of higher phase? There it is assumed that 'all the springs of cooperative wealth flow more abundantly'. And yet it should be clear that it can not mean *unlimited supply fulfilling unlimited demand* of all the members of the society. We are now living on our 'small planet' and acutely know the obstinate existence and pressure of scarcity. Irrespective of living in an advanced capitalist society or in a communist society of higher phase, what is needed for a reasonable management of production and exchange is not an illusory direct labour-time calculation system, but an elastic price-mechanism, the relation of supply and demand.

Lastly, let us further suppose a communist society of higher phase consisting of 'all-round individuals' who can be engaged in any kind of work. For instance, the chief engineer and the gatekeeper can change their posts and they can even take the office of the general secretary of the communist party; a fully egalitarian (but very unrealistic) society, where labour power might be homogeneous. But all the same, the values of goods and services allotted to consumption and production cannot be computed by the 'direct labour-time calculation' due to the other grounds enumerated above. And if it were done somehow, it would be no more than a fiction.

Now let us examine the so-called 'simultaneous equations for the calculation of total labour expended' proposed by a Russian economist, V. K. Dmitriev, in 1904 (see Table 2.1). According to Minoru Oka who expounds the idea in his *Introduction to Economic Planning*:

X_1, X_2, ... X_n represent the total labour expended for the production of each unit of various products, t_1, t_2, ... t_n living labour expended for the production of each unit, a_{11}, a_{12}, ... a_{1n} input-coefficient of various products P_1, P_2, ... P_n, for producing one unit of a product P_1. If input-coefficients (a_{ij}) and the quantities of living labour expended are known, numbers of the equations and those of the unknowns come to be the same, so that the whole set of these equations can be solved in any numerical value of n.[34]

Table 2.1   Dmitriev's simultaneous equations for the calculation of labour expended

$$X_1 = a_{11} X_2 + a_{12} X_1 \ldots . a_{1n} X_2 + t_1$$
$$X_2 = a_{21} X_2 + a_{22} X_2 \ldots . a_{2n} X_2 + t_2$$
$$\cdots\cdots\cdots\cdots\cdots\cdots\cdots\cdots\cdots\cdots$$
$$\cdots\cdots\cdots\cdots\cdots\cdots\cdots\cdots\cdots\cdots$$
$$X_n = a_{1n} X_n + a_{2n} X_n \ldots . a_{nn} X_n + t_n$$

[Note by T.H.]   In Marxian terminology:
$X_i = c_i + v_i + s_i$; $a_{i1} X_1 + a_{i2} X_2 + a_{in} X_n = c_i$;
$t_i = v_i + s_i$

On first reading one may accept the feasibility of direct aggregation of the total labour expended. But, Oka goes on to a difficulty:

> The biggest theoretical difficulty in this direct labour calculation lies in the heterogeneity of labour . . . living labour expended (t_1, t_2 . . . t_n) must be reduced to standardised simple labour. However, the coefficients for the direct reduction of heterogeneous labour are nearly unobtainable. As indices of heterogeneous living labour expended, we may adopt wages expended W_i in place of living labour expended (t_i).

$$X_i = a_{i1} X_1 + a_{i1} X_2 \ldots . a_{in} X_n + W_i$$

In this case X represents, not the total quantity of labour expended, but 'cost' designated in money-units.[35]

In other words this X is not $c + v + s$, but only $c + v$ because W is v. In order to fill this gap Oka relies on Strumilin's idea that the principle of distribution under socialism is: 'To each according to his labour.' The application of this principle means that the ratio of each labourer's wages, v, in the whole value he created, $v + s$, should be one and the same for all the labourers. Thus Oka proposes to replace W in the above equation by $W(1 + s')$, s' being average or aggregate s/v. The equation acquired in this way is, Oka explains, substantially Strumilin's labour-value calculation, which makes possible the measurement of the total labour expended, taking into account of the heterogeneity labour.[36]

Now, what we obtain by $W(1 + s')$ is the total sum of wages and profit, not in labour hours, but in monetary units, for instance, 500 rubles. If we could assume a conversion-coefficient of, say, 1 ruble = 2 hours, then 500 rubles would be counted as 1,000 'hours'. But, as already explained, these are *not real* hours.

Moreover, in the explanation of the equations, the input-coefficients, (a_{ij}), are assumed to be known. But, how do they come to be known? For instance, if 200 rubles (not 200 hours) of steel sheets are needed to produce an automobile (P_1) of 1,000 rubles (not 1,000 hours), then the input-coefficient, e.g., a_{21}, should be 0.2. Now the total 'hours' of labour expended in the production of an automobile can be obtained from the input-coefficients thus computed in money-units or living labour 'hours' which are just wages and profit in disguise. The total amount of labour calculated in this way of, say, 2,000 'hours' is nothing but another name for 1,000 rubles.

In May 1921 when socialist economic construction was started in Soviet Russia which had just emerged from the chaos of civil war and intervention, the People's Commisariat of Finance made a proposal to establish a 'labour unit' called 'Trud' (labour) which should take the place of the ruble. This new unit was to be linked with the prewar price system in gold rubles by a certain conversion coefficient. This scheme was not realised. But if it had been, 'Trud' notes must have been just another paper-money having nothing to do with 'direct labour-time calculation.'[37]

To sum up: The 'direct labour-time calculation' fancied by Marx and Engels and their followers is merely formalistic and without substance because of: first; the fictitious character of the 'reduction' of complex labour into simple labour; second; the meaninglessness of the measurement by time-unit of 'past labour'; third; the irrationality of counting the different quantities of labour accruing from the difference in fertility and conditions of location of land, as one and the same quantity; fourth; the impossibility of dissolving the relation of supply and demand into nothing. These faults apply to any society – irrespective of socialist, capitalist or simple commodity producers' – where differences in quality of labour exist, and division of labour, exchange and roundabout production are in operation.

(5) The labour-time calculation of value of commodities in 'Capital'

Marx fell into the error of assuming that 'perfectly simple and intelligible' direct labour-time calculation could be practised in a socialist society. As for the commodity-producers' society based on the private ownership of means of production, however, Marx contends that direct labour-time calculation is impossible because the character of production is anarchical and products take the form of commodities which express their value (quantities of labour embodied in them) indirectly through the medium of other commodities as equivalents, their accomplished form being money. 1 quarter corn = x cwt iron in Chapter 1, Book I, and 20 yards linen = £2 in Chapter 3, Book I of *Capital*, mean x hours = x hours, i.e. two commodities or a commodity and money on the left and right side of the equations embody the same amount of labour but the amount itself is unknown.[38] Marx writes:

> Money as a measure of value is the phenomenal form that must of necessity be assumed by that measure of value which is immanent in commodities, labour-time.[39]

But a valid conversion coefficient between money and labour-time is unobtainable for the reasons already given, and if obtained, as in the case of Robert Owen, it would inevitably be an unreal one, conversion being executed from money term to labour-time.

And yet, Marx argues as if it were possible to make direct labour-time calculation of the quantities of labour embodied in commodities and its conversion into money terms. In Chapter 6, 'Buying and Selling of Labour-Power', Book I, he writes:

> Suppose that in this mass of commodities [wage-goods – T.H.] requisite for the average day there are embodied 6 hours of social labour . . . This quantity of labour forms the value of a day's labour-power . . . If half a day's average social labour is incorporated in three shillings, then three shillings is the price corresponding to the value of a day's labour-power.[40]

If the relations – value of wage-goods for 1 day = 6 hours of average social labour = 3 shillings – is *known*, then 3 shillings represents 'the value of a day's labour-power'; in other words, we obtain a valid and real conversion coefficient of 6 pence = 1 hour.

Remember here Marx's starting proposition was that in the commodity production the direct application of measurement by the labour-time embodied in the products is impossible. The logical corollary should be that the above relations mean, from the viewpoint of labour-time calculation, x hours = x hours = x hours, x being *unknown*. In the same social framework, commodity production, unknown at the beginning of argument is later treated as known. This is nothing but a self-contradiction.

Nevertheless, Marx continues to assume x hours are *known* in the following illustrations in *Capital*. In Chapter 12, Book I we read: 'If one hour of labour is embodied in six pence [It is not knowable that a six pence coin is a product of one labour-hour – T.H.] a value of six shillings will be produced in a working-day of 12 hours.'[41] In Chapter 17: 'If the value created by a working-day of 12 hours be, say, six shillings.'[42] Thus, 6 pence = 1 hour, is assumed. And in Chapter 13, Book III: 'Suppose £100 are the wages of 100 labourers for, say, one week.'[43] That is, reduced to the wage of one labourer for one day, about 3 shillings representing 6 'hours' of necessary labour in 12 hours of a working-day. This division of a working-day into the necessary and surplus labour by halves is Marx's fundamental assumption all through the three Books of *Capital*.

3   *Capital* fails to prove the validity of the labour theory of value

Marx develops his argument in *Capital* on the assumption that the conversion coefficient, 6 pence = £1 hour, were really obtainable. This gives the reader the impression that, say, a commodity of 1 were the product of 40 'hours' of labour and the gross national product of Great Britain totalling £5 billion were 200 billion 'hours' if 'directly measured' by labour-time. As shown in the historical instances of 'labour notes' by Robert Owen or 'Trud bills' proposed by the People's Commisariat of Finance in the early days of the USSR, what is feasible is the computation only in the opposite direction, from the existing price system to the 'labour hour' system, which is in substance the same price system with a different name. Also, as in an imaginary automobile factory and in Dmitriev's simultaneous equations, the attempt to make direct labour-time calculation inevitably ends in a price calculation which is just called an 'hour' calculation.

It is not successfully demonstrated in *Capital* that the existing price system has behind itself a corresponding 'labour-hour' (= value) system, or in Marx's words: 'Money as a measure of value is the phenomenal form that must of necessity be assumed by that measure of value which is immanent in commodities, labour-time',[44] in the capitalist society, the object of analysis by Marx in *Capital*.

The world in which the labour(-time) theory of value applies is that such as Adam Smith's 'early and rude state of society which precedes both the accumulation of stock and the appropriation of land' (with homogeneous labour as the sole factor of production), or an abstract model assumed by Michio Morishima 'for the construction of the prototype of the labour theory of value',[45] etc. In the society at the time of John Locke where manual labour was predominant, the labour theory of value might have had a certain substantial meaning as an approximation. Or the Ricardian theory interpreted as the '93% Labour Theory of Value', in the sense that 'labour input in an average product be taken as proportional to all factor costs', might have been also a useful approximation.[46]

The labour(-time) theory in *Capital* is not 93%, but 100%. 'Labour is not only the measurement unit but also the value-creating *substance*'[47] [Emphasis – T.H.]. And it is substantially applied to the capitalist society in which the measurement of value of products by labour-time unit is excluded by the very nature of that society, anarchical production. This is an evident self-contradiction in Marx's reasoning. We should say that an effective labour(-time) theory of value cannot exist in a *Capital* purged of this error and made consistent.

II THE CONFUSION INVOLVED IN THE LABOUR-TIME = VALUE = PRICE SYSTEM

Now we proceed to the re-examination of the relationship between quantity of labour (expressed in 'hour' units), value and price in Part 1 'Commodities and Money', Book I. Here Marx develops his labour theory of value as the principle underlying the existing system of relative prices and thus establishes the fundamental premises for his system of economic science. This basic theoretical operation already contains impermissible inconsistencies as illustrated below.

1   The value = price system throughout *Capital* is $xL = xV = x\sigma V = x\sigma P$

(1)   The case of $xL = xV$

First, let us re-confirm Marx's fundamental propositions on the three notions of quantity of labour (measured in hour-unit), value and price. In Chapter 1, Book I we read:

> All labour is, speaking physiologically, an expenditure of human labour-power, and in its character of identical abstract human labour, it creates and forms the value of commodities.[48]

> Human labour-power in motion, or human labour, creates value, but is not itself value. It becomes value only in its congealed state, when embodied in the form of some object.[49]

The same thing is expressed in reverse order also in Chapter 1:

> A use-value, or useful article . . . has value only because human labour in the abstract has been embodied or materialised in it.[50]

Marx then refers to the quantitative measurement of that value:

> How . . . is the magnitude of this value to be measured? Plainly, by the quantity of the value-creating substance, the labour, contained in the article. The quantity of labour, however, is measured by its duration, and labour-time in its turn finds its standard in weeks, days, and hours.[51]

Expressed in a plainer way, these four sentences mean: Human labour, being expended at the *present* time is a value-creating substance, but not value itself. The same labour, grasped at some time point in the *past*, as already expended and embodied in the product, is value. How is the magnitude of this value measured? Of course, by the length of labour-time. This length must be the same in the same product, whether it is observed at present or after it has turned past. Let me formulate it as follows:

$$xL \text{ (quantity of labour)} = xV \text{ (quantity of labour)}$$
$$x \text{ hours} = x \text{ hours}$$

(length of labour being expended)	(length of labour already expended)

(2) The case of $L = V = P$

In the context of the above-quoted statements, the substance of the value-concept is x hours, identical with the amount of labour expended. And x is (as if) *known* in this case.

But at the same time Marx asserts the impossibility of the value of commodities being measured by labour-time units. (I have already mentioned this self-contradiction.) From a series of relations, 1 quarter corn $= x$ cwt iron $= 20$ yards linen $= £2$ (gold coin) . . . , we should assume that, x hours $= x$ hours $= x$ hours $= . . . = x$ hours, x being *unknown*. The length of labour-time, i.e. the magnitude of value, of a commodity has no other way of being expressed than by the equation with a certain quantity of some other commodity or, in general, by a certain amount of money, in other words, price.

Marx writes: 'Price is the money-name of the labour realised in a commodity. (Ch. 3, Book I).[52] 'Price represents the expression of value in money' (Ch. 21, Book III).[53]

Let us formulate the idea as follows:

$$xL = xV = xP$$

(quantity of labour)	(magnitude of value)	(money-name of value)
(labour being expended)	(past labour expended)	(past labour expended)
x hours	x hours	x hours

xL, xV and xP should be all equal in their magnitudes because their common essence is x hours.

But, x being unknown, the relation really knowable is only:

xV : $x\sigma P$ (σ = constant)
(value of x hours corresponds with xσ price)

If the price of 1 quarter corn is £2, we can assume its value to be $x^1/_\sigma$ hours. But x remains unknown. If x is known, for instance:

1 quarter corn = £2
(80 hours)   (80 hours)

then, we can obtain a conversion coefficient between 'hours' and price:

40 hours = £1   or   2 hours = 1 shilling
$\therefore \sigma = \frac{1}{40}$ or $\therefore \sigma = \frac{1}{2}$

But x should remain unknown in the commodity-producer's society where production is anarchical so the goods produced have to take the form of commodities which bear price-tags, but not labour-hour-tags. Thus what is knowable in practice is price alone. The concept of value in this context ($x\sigma P$, money-name of value) clearly can have no common measure with that defined as x (*known*) hours of labour expended in the past.

(3) Value as a system of price and $P_t = \frac{1}{1+k_1} P_0$

Now we turn our attention to Marx's usage of the term 'value' as a synonym of price (as the expression or money-name of value) throughout *Capital*. He writes in Chapter 1, Book I:

> However . . . productive power may vary, the same labour exercised during equal periods of time, always yields equal amount of value. But it will yield . . . different quantities of value in use.[54]

If the term 'value' in this case is interpreted as x hours expended in the past, the first sentence of the above quotation turns out to be self-explanatory and meaningless. The same labour exercised in a certain length of time is equal whether measured at present or after it becomes past. What Marx means here should be: The same length of labour-time, x hours, when its productivity varies produces different quantities of goods, but their total value is always the same and is expressed by the same total price.

Let me cite two more instances of the term 'price' used by Marx as the expression or synonym of value:

> The value of commodities is in inverse ratio to the productiveness of labour. And so, too, is the value of labour-power, because it depends on the values of commodities . . . The value of money being assumed to be constant, an average social working-day of 12 hours always produces the same new value, six shillings . . . If, in consequence of increased productiveness, the value of the necessaries of life fall, and the value of a day's labour-power be thereby reduced from five shillings to three, the surplus value increased from one shilling to three. (Ch. 10, Book I)[55]

Here the *value* of the necessaries of life, the *value* of a day's labour-power and the surplus *value* (therefore, the values of various commodities) are all expressed in shillings, by *price* amounts. The values can have no other expression than prices.

In the following case, Marx directly uses the term *price* instead of value:

> If the productivity of industry increases, the *price* [emphasis – T.H.] of individual commodities falls. There is less labour in them . . . Suppose, the same labour produces, say, triple its former product. Then $2/3$ less labour yields the individual product. (Ch. 13, Book III)[56]

First, let me add one sentence: Accordingly the *price* of the commodities falls to $1/3$. 'The productivity of industry' is the same thing as the 'productiveness of labour'. So, in short, the above quotation means: 'The *price* of commodities is in inverse ratio to the productiveness of labour.' Thus it is now evident that Marx uses value and price as synonyms.

Let us re-confirm here that the same word, value, in Marx's terminology expresses two things quite different in quality. First:

$$\begin{array}{ccc} \text{value-creating substance} & & \text{value} \\ xL & = & xV \\ \text{(living labour, } x \text{ hours)} & & \text{(past labour, } x \text{ hours)} \end{array}$$

Value means 'past labour, x hours', x being assumed to be known because 'living labour, x hours', should be known. Second:

$$\begin{array}{ccc} \text{Value} & & \text{price (expression of value)} \\ xV & : & x\sigma P \\ (x \text{ hours}) & & (\yen, \pounds, \$, \text{ etc.}) \end{array}$$

This price as an expression of value is called by Marx sometimes value and sometimes price. In this case, value is not x hours, but $x\sigma P$ (¥, £, $, etc.) Thus Marx falls into the confusion of treating two different things as identical, $xV = x\sigma P$. In detail:

value	=	value	=	Price
xV	=	$x\sigma P$	=	$x\sigma P$
x hours		¥, £, $, etc.		¥, £, $, etc.

Now let us designate $x\sigma P$ called value by $x\sigma V$ in order to distinguish it from $x\sigma p$ called price. Then we get the equation:

xV	=	value	=	$x\sigma P$

According to Marx's line of reasoning xV and $x\sigma V$ are essentially the same thing because they are values, i.e. 'congealed' labour measurable in labour-time unit. But as already shown[57], a valid conversion coefficient between labour-time and money is unobtainable. Therefore, the above 'equation' does not make sense.

Of the two meanings of value-concept, the first one, x hours, is no more than a tautology: The same hours of labour being expended and already expended are of the same quantity. This value-concept is of no use in the value-price system of Marx's economics. The value concept applied throughout *Capital* is the second one, value = price, $x\sigma V = x\sigma P$ (except in the cases where the different turnover times and compositions of capitals are analysed in some parts of Books II and III).

Now come back to Marx's fundamental proposition governing the value-price system in *Capital*: 'The value (price) of commodities is in inverse ratio to the productiveness (productivity) of labour.'[58] This can be reduced to the following formula:

$$P_t = \frac{1}{1+k_1} P_0 \tag{2.1}$$

[*Note:* P_0: Price of commodities at the beginning
  P_t: Price of commodities after labour productivity changed
  K_1: The rate of change of productivity in the production of commodities

If we apply this formula to Marx's statement (of the previous page, restated by T.H.) 'If the productivity of industry triples, the price of the commodities falls to $1/3$.': If productivity rises 3 times: $k_1 = 2$.

$$P_t = \frac{1}{1+2} P_0 = \frac{1}{3} P_0$$

Now let us apply it to the above-quoted (see note 54) proposition in Chapter 1, Book I (paraphrased by T.H. for clarity). 'The same quantity, the same hours, of labour produces, when its productivity varies, different quantities of commodities. But the total value [= price, because value is expressed only in price form – T.H.] remains the same'.

Suppose x hours remain constant and its productivity changes by k_1:

$$G_t = (1 + k_1) G_0 \tag{2.2}$$

As the value-price of commodities is in inverse ratio to the productivity of labour as shown in the above formula (2.1), the total value-price of the commodities produced remains the same as illustrated below:

$$G_t P_t = (1 + k_1) G_0 \frac{1}{1+k_1} P_0 = G_0 P_0 \tag{2.3}$$

In Marx's example of concrete numerical values (see note 56), if the productivity triples, i.e. $1 + k_3 = 3$, and 3-fold commodities are produced, the value-price of an individual commodity falls to $1/3$, so that the total value-price of the commodities remains unchanged:

$$G_t P_t = (1 + 2) G_0 \frac{1}{1+2} P_0 = G_0 P_0$$

Such is the relationship between labour productivity and value-price in *Capital*. In this context, value is always identical with price (expression of value). So the relationship between the quantity of labour, value and price in *Capital* can be expressed by the following self-contradictory formula:

Value-creating	Value created	Value	Price
xL	= xV	= $x\sigma V$	= $x\sigma P$
x hours	x hours	¥, £, \$, etc.	¥, £, \$, etc.

Here let us reconfirm Marx's confusion in his value-price system. Value, xV, is 'labour in its congealed state',[59] x hours. Value, $x\sigma V$, is 'the phenomenal form of labour-time', [60] x hours. They are (thought to be) the same thing. And yet $x\sigma V$ is expressed only in price, x hours being unknown in the commodity producers' society. Thus xV and $x\sigma V$ do not have a commensurable unit which proves their identity.

2   In the beginning part of *Capital*, $xL = xV = x\sigma V$: $(1 + k_2)\,x\sigma P$

This labour = value = price system, $xL = xV = xsV = x\sigma P$ and $P_t = \frac{1}{1+k_1} P_0$, contains in it that which contradicts Marx's labour-value theory itself. Note that the proposition, 'The value of commodities is in inverse ratio to the productiveness of labour', is valid only when 'the value of money is assumed to be constant' as cited above.[61] And, throughout *Capital*, Marx assumes, 'for the sake of simplicity, gold as the money-commodity'.[62] That the value of gold-coin is constant means the quantity of labour embodied in it is constant, hence the productivity of producing it is unchanged.

The aforesaid assumption, $P_1 = \frac{1}{1+k_1} P_0$ is presented in Chapter 12, 'Concept of Relative Surplus-Value', Book I. When the productivity of producing a basket of wage-goods is generally rising ($k_1 > 0$), in the fairly long term, it is an unrealistic abstraction to assume that the productivity of producing gold coin alone remains unchanged, its rate of change being denoted by k_2, where $k_2 = 0$. Abstraction is the process of disengaging the essential concept, factor, relation, function, etc. from intricate phenomena. The propositions, hypotheses, formulae, laws, etc., properly abstracted, however unrealistic they may seem, are realistic in the sense that they represent essential features in the chaos of realities. But the assumption of $k_2 = 0$ in a long-term analysis in which k_1 changes in general is literally unrealistic as it misses an essential variable, $k_2 \gtrless 0$

But in the beginning part of *Capital* Marx himself admits that k_2 must be a variable in the long-term macro analysis.

(1) $P_t = \frac{1}{1+k_1} P_0$ in Chapters 1 and 3, Book I of 'Capital'

This confusion in Marx's argument is already disclosed in Section I (Subsection 2), Chapter 1 in the present book. So here let us reconfirm the crux of the matter in brief in order to reach and examine a problematical concept of *relative value*.

In Chapter 3, Book I of *Capital*, we read:

> Only so far as it is itself a product of labour, and, therefore, potentially variable in value, can gold serve as a measure of value.[63]

> The values of commodities remaining constant, their prices vary with the value of gold (the material of money), rising in proportion as it falls, and falling in proportion as it rises.[64]

As the value is in inverse ratio to the labour-productivity, the statement above can be paraphrased as follows: The labour-productivity of commodities remaining constant, $k_1 = 0$, their prices vary with the productivity of producing gold coin, $k_2 \gtrless 0$, rising in proportion as it rises, and falling in proportion as it falls.

$$P_t = (1 + k_2) P_0 \qquad (k_2 \gtrless 0) \qquad\qquad (2.4)$$

Up to this part of *Capital*, the determining factors of the values or prices ($x\sigma V$ or $x\sigma P$) are two variables, k_1 and k_2. We can express this relation by putting formulae (2.1) and (2.4) together as follows:

$$P_1 = \frac{1+k_2}{1+k_1} P_0 \qquad\qquad (2.5)$$

Let us note that Marx lays hold of essentially the same thing already in Chapter 1 as a relation between relative form and equivalent form of values:

> The equation, 20 yards of linen = 1 coat, becomes 20 yards of linen = 2 coats, either because the value of the linen has doubled [the productivity in producing the linen has fallen by one-half – T.H.], or because the value of the coat has fallen by one-half [the productivity in producing the coat has doubled – T.H.]; and it becomes 20 yards of linen = 1/2 coat, either, because the value of the linen has fallen by one-half [the productivity has doubled – T.H.], or because the value of the coat has doubled [the productivity has fallen by one-half – T.H.].[65]

For clarity, the relations above can be expressed as follows by applying formula (2.5).

$$P_t = (1 + k_2) P_0$$

k_1: the rate of change of productivity in producing linen
k_2: the rate of change of productivity in producing the coat
P: quantity of the coat (indirect expression of the value of the linen)

(1a)   If $k_1 = -0.5$, $k_2 = 0$, then $P_t = \frac{1+0}{1-0.5} 1$ coat $= 2$ coats
∴ 20 yards of linen $= 2$ coats

(1b)   If $k_1 = 0$, $k_2 = 1$, then $P_t = \frac{1+1}{1+0} 1$ coat $= 2$ coats
∴ 20 yards of linen $= 2$ coats

(2a)   If $k_1 = 1$, $k_2 = 0$, then $P_t = \frac{1+0}{1+1} 1$ coat $= 1/2$ coat
∴ 20 yards of linen $= 1/2$ coat

(2b)   If $k_1 = 0$, $k_2 = -0.5$, then $P_t = \frac{1-0.5}{1+0} 1$ coat $= 1/2$ coat
∴ 20 yards of linen $= 1/2$ coat

In accordance with these illustrations Marx concludes:

> The labour-time [xL, x hours] . . . respectively necessary for the production of the linen and the coat, and therefore the value of these commodities [xV, x hours and $x\sigma V$ expressed in the quantity of the commodity in equivalent form, or more in the general, $x\sigma P$ in ￥, £, \$, etc. – T.H.] may simultaneously vary in the same direction, but at unequal rates, or in opposite direction, or in other ways. The effect of all these possible different variations, on the *relative value* [$x\sigma V$ in kind or, more in general, $x\sigma P$ in ￥, £, \$, etc. – T.H.] of a commodity, may be deduced from the results of (1a), (1b), (2a) and (2b).
>
> Thus real changes in the magnitude of value [xV, x hours], are neither unequivocally nor exhaustively related in their expression, that is, in the equation expressing the magnitude of *relative value* [$x\sigma V$ in kind or, more in general, $x\sigma P$ in money unit]. The *relative value* of a commodity may vary, although its *value* remains constant. Its *relative value* may remain constant, although its *value* varies; and finally, simultaneous variations in the magnitude of *value* and in that of its *relative expression* [= relative value – T.H.] by no means necessarily correspond in amount.[66] (emphasis – T.H.)

The relation between value and the so-called *relative value* or *relative expression* of value in the above sentences can also be expressed by applying my foregoing formulae to the case of $x\sigma V$ in kind (equivalent form of value).[67]

$$P_t = \tfrac{1}{1+k_1} P_0 \tag{2.6}$$

$$P_t = \tfrac{1+k_2}{1+k_1} P_0 \tag{2.7}$$

k_1 : the rate of change of productivity in producing linen or any commodity in the 'relative form of value'[68]

k_2 : the rate of change of productivity in producing coat or any commodity in the 'equivalent form of value'

P in (2.6) : the quantity of coat (equivalent form) or the magnitude of *value*

P in (2.7) : the quantity of coat (equivalent form) or the magnitude or *relative value*

Value, P in (2.6), changes subject to the change of k_1 alone, but *relative value*, P in (2.7), changes subject to the changes of k_1 and k_2. Hence, it follows that 'simultaneous variations in the magnitude of value and its relative expression [relative value] by no means necessarily correspond in amount'.

(2)   If $P_t = \tfrac{1}{1+k_1} P_0$, then $xL = xV = x\sigma V = x\sigma P$. If $P_t = \tfrac{1+k_2}{1+k_1} P_0$ then $xL = xV$: $(1+k_2) x\sigma V = (1+k_2) x\sigma P$

Here let us confirm the difference between the value-price system applied throughout *Capital* and that in its beginning part. The former case is in my representation:

Living labour	Value	Value	Value
xL	$= \quad xV$	$= \quad x\sigma V$	$= \quad x\sigma P$
x hours	x hours	¥, £, \$, etc.	¥, £, \$, etc.

Since x-hours (of past labour) of the value $= xV$ of a certain commodity is unknowable, there is no other means of expressing itself than the 'phenomenal form',[69] i.e. money-form, value $= x\sigma V$, which is identical with price $= x\sigma P$. In short an unknown but specific amount of the value $= xV$ (x hours) should always be expressed in a specific amount of price $= x\sigma P$ (¥, £, \$, etc.). However the productivity of the commodity concerned may vary, this relation of correspondence between labour-amount and price sum, $xV{:}x\sigma P$, remains the same by dint of the assumption, $P_t = \frac{1}{1+k_1}P_0$, or $P_t = \frac{1+k_2}{1+k_1}P_0$ when $k_2 = 0$, because the productivity-rise in the production of a certain commodity is, in other words, the fall in the amount of labour embodied in it (xV) in inverse ratio, and this, in turn, means the fall of its price $x\sigma P$ in the same ratio.[70]

But, the fixed correspondence between value and price, $xV{:}x\sigma P$, is manifestly denied in Chapters 1 and 3, Book I, as shown in my following representation:

Living labour	Value	Related value	Price
xL	$= \quad xV$	$: \quad (1+k_2)x\sigma V$	$= \quad (1+k_2)x\sigma P$
x hours	x hours	quantity of	¥, £, \$, etc.
		used-value or	
		¥, £, \$, etc.	

Here it is impossible for x hours (xV) to find a specific corresponding amount of commodity or money in the equivalent form because they are variables independent of x hours, i.e. $xV{:}(1+k_2)\,x\sigma V$ or $x\sigma P$.

It is worthy of note that of these two relations, xV and $x\sigma P$, the former is wrongly applied in the long-term analyses throughout *Capital*.

3 The way to put the two contradictory value = price systems in order

The value = price system, $xV{:}(1+k_2)x\sigma P$ based on the assumption, $P_t = \frac{1+k_2}{1+k_1}P_0$, $k_1 \gtrless 0$, $k_2 \gtrless 0$, can be consistently applied in the long-term macro analysis. But in the middle of Chapter 3 Marx declares:

> Henceforth we shall consider the value of gold to be given, as in fact, it is momentarily whenever we estimate the value of a commodity.[71]

Henceforth $k_2 = 0$. And Marx proceeds to the analyses of Chapter 12 'The concept of relative surplus value', Book I, Chapter 25 'The general law of capitalist accumulation', Book I, Part 3 'The law of the tendency of the rate of profit to fall', Book III, etc., where the long-term macroscopic situations in which the productivity-rise in producing commodities in general, $k_1 > 0$, is the prerequisite of his reasoning so that the value of gold, $P_t = \frac{1}{1+k_2}$, should also be considered variable. The assumption, $k_1 > 0$, $k_2 = 0$, in a long-term analysis is an evident antinomy. What should Marx have done in order to escape from this confusion? He should have abandoned the self-contradictory assumption, $P_t = \frac{1+k_2}{1+k_1} P_0$, $k_2 = 0$, and applied $P_t = \frac{1+k_2}{1+k_1} P_0$, $k_1 \gtrless 0$, $k_2 \gtrless 0$, in general, and, when necessary, adopted the assumption, $k_1 = k_2$, i.e. the rate of change of the productivity in producing the commodities in general, and that of the gold coin are equal. Then, irrespective of the degree of changes in k_1 and k_2, the price level remains always the same, $P_t = P_0$. This might be called a theoretical constant price system based on the labour-value theory, an abstract Marxian counterpart of the statistical constant prices computed from the current prices with the help of GNP deflator when contemporary economists think in 'real' terms.

In Marxist-Leninist schemes, such as the hypothetical series representing the law of the falling rate of profit,[72] simple and expanding reproduction schemes, etc., expressed only in terms of value, we have no means of indicating the changes in the quantity of produced use-values.[73] This is the fatal reason why the exact quantitative approach is excluded in Marxian economics. If we make use of the constant price system based on the labour theory of value, $P_t = \frac{1+k_2}{1+k_1} P_0$, $k_1 = k_2$ the expression of the quantitative changes in use-values comes, it might seem, to be feasible.

4   In practice the operations applying the formulae, $P_t = \frac{1+k_2}{1+k_1} P_0$, are impossible

Here we deal with the fundamental problem left over which is concerned with the viability of Marx's labour theory of value. Are the formulae, $P_t = \frac{1+k_2}{1+k_1} P_0$, $P_t = \frac{1+k_2}{1+k_1} P_0$, operational in practice? Can we obtain the numerical values of k_1 and k_2? $1 + k_1$ and $1 + k_2$ indicate the changes in the quantities, respectively, of commodities in general and money produced with a certain amount (hours) of labour. In their inverse form, $\frac{1}{1+k_2}$, $\frac{1}{1+k_2}$ they indicate the quantities (hours) of labour embodied in a certain commodity. So if we could somehow know the numerical values of k_1 and k_2, it would be possible to measure the labour-productivity in the literal sense of the term. However, this possibility is excluded because the labour expended or embodied in the commodities, x hours, are not knowable, as already explained above.

This 'unknowableness' is Marx's contention itself as far as the commodity-producers' societies are concerned. And yet, at the same time Marx pushes through his argument on the assumption that (or, as if) direct labour-time calculation is possible. Let me quote once again his definite statement on this point:

> How . . . is the magnitude of . . . value to be measured? Plainly, by the quantity of . . . labour, contained in the article. The quantity of labour . . . is measured by its duration, and labour-time in its turn finds its standard in weeks, days and hours.[74]

Here at least he definitely claims that the value of a commodity is to be measured directly by labour-time units. And it looks really feasible in his illustration following the quotation above:

> The introduction of power-looms into England probably reduced by one-half the labour required to weave a given quantity of yarn into cloth. The hand-loom weavers . . . continued to require the same time as before; but for all that, the product of one hour of their labour represented after the change only half an hour's social labour, and consequently fell to one-half its former value.[75]

This is the place where Marx explains that the labour which forms the substance of value is not individual labour, but the socially necessary labour of the average technical level. So he is supposed to explain that, when power-looms come to be prevalent, the labour-time, say, 1 hour, of hand-loom weavers spent in making a certain quantity of cloth, is evaluated as only half an hour of the socially necessary labour-time.

For the correct description of the above case he should have stated that 'one hour of their [hand-loom weavers' individual] labour represented after the change only half an hour's social labour.' But his statement here is that 'the *product* [emphasis – T.H.] of one hour of their labour represented . . . only half an hour's social labour.' This is Marx's fatal misapprehension. The cloth woven by one hour's living labour of a hand-loom weaver or half an hour's living labour of a power-loom weaver should *contain*, in addition, some *past labour* spent in yarn, depreciation of tool or machine, shop or factory, etc. Let us designate this past labour, respectively, by c hours and c^1 hours for the product of a hand-loom weaver and that of a power-loom weaver, then the individual value of labour embodied in the cloth of the hand-loom weaver is $c^1 + 1$ hours which is evaluated only as $c^1 + 1/2$ hours of socially necessary labour, c and c^1 of course remain unknown. What is knowable is only their prices.

Why did, or rather could, Marx not make this calculation? The reason seems to be significant and interesting. As c and c^1 are unknown, the individual value of the cloth and the social value of it, $c + 1$ hours and $c^1 + 1/2$ hours, can not be grasped as fixed numerical values in terms of hours. But if the cloth could be produced by living labour alone, i.e., by weaving motion alone without making use of yarn, tool or machine, workshop, etc., then, c and c^1 being zero, the individual and social values of the cloth would be counted as fixed amounts, 1 hour and $1/2$ hour respectively. The reciprocals of these figures, $\frac{1}{1 \text{ hour}}$ and $\frac{1}{1/2 \text{ hour}}$, indicate the difference between the productivity of the hand-loom weaver and that of the power-loom weaver, the productivity of the latter being twice as high as that of the former.

In this way Marx makes possible what is impossible. He succeeds in the conversion of the living labour expended in the process of weaving the cloth, the value-creating substance, $v + s$, into the value embodied in it, $c + v + s$, past labour, by taking no account of c, $c = 0$. This disregard of c, $c = 0$, or rather confusion of $c > 0$ and $c = 0$, constitutes an essential feature of Marx's labour-value theory. Another illustration from the same Chapter 1 follows:

When Marx studies the various cases of shifts in the exchange rate between the two commodities, 20 yards of linen = 1 coat, as shown in the statements quoted above (see notes 65 and 66), specific numerical values, 2 coats, $1/2$ coat, etc., are to be obtained only if the direct measurement of the labour 'hours' embodied in coat and in linen is possible. For that purpose c (past labour) must be disregarded, $c = 0$, as Marx does in the citation below:

> By making the coat the equivalent of the linen, we equate the labour embodied in the former to that in the latter $[c_1 + v_1 + s_1 = c_2 + v_2 + s_2 -$ T.H.]. Now it is true that the tailoring, which makes the coat, is concrete labour of a different sort from the weaving which makes the linen. But the act of equating it to the weaving $[v_1 + s_1 = v_2 + s_2 -$ T.H.] reduces the tailoring to that which is really equal in the two kinds of labour, their common character of human labour.[76]

The equation, $c_1 + v_1 + s_1 = c_2 + v_2 + s_2$, should be impossible because c_1, c_2 hours are unknown. Only by confusing $c + v + s$ with $v + s$

(countable living labour), or by disregarding c, $c = 0$, could Marx here 'equate the labour embodied in the former (coat) to that in the latter (linen)'. Strictly speaking, equating labour hours for tailoring and weaving $v_1 + s_1 = v_2 + s_2$, would be possible only if they were simple and homogeneous ones. In this unrealistic case these living labour hours might be assumed to be directly countable. But in practice these two different kinds of labour with probably different degrees of skills could be 'reduced' to fictitious 'labour hours' only from wage rates.

Let us examine another case. In Chapter 3, Book I Marx writes: 'Suppose that in this mass of commodities [wage-goods – T.H.] requisite for the average day there are embodied 6 hours of social labour . . .'[77] But the concrete numerical value, 6, would be obtainable only by making an unreal assumption that living labour alone is sufficient in the production of wage-goods; in other words $c = 0$.

Marx further assumes that 'If half a day's [6 hours'] average social labour is incorporated in three shillings, then three shillings is the price corresponding to the value of a day's labour-power.'[78] In order to find out the quantitative ratio, 6 hours (of social labour) = 3 shillings (6 hours embodied in shilling coins), again we need the unreal assumption that simple and homogeneous living labour alone is sufficient in making coins.

Thus Marx's labour = value = price system seems to be operational, as if it can convert living labour into value (past labour) = price (phenomenal form) only through his ambiguous argument which assumes implicitly that commodities and coins can be produced by living labour alone.

It is crystal clear that goods cannot be made by living labour alone except in the unreal world where simple and homogeneous living labour is the sole factor of production that counts. It was Marx's fundamental error and the origin of his confusion that he applied his direct labour-time calculation to the capitalist society, the object of his analysis in *Capital*, where it is manifestly unapplicable.

III   THE SIGNIFICANCE OR RATHER INSIGNIFICANCE OF THE SO-CALLED TRANSFORMATION PROBLEM

Lastly, let me refer to the relation of my argument here with the well-known 'Transformation Problem' which, says Sweezy, 'has occupied a central position in most discussions of Marxian economics since Engels published Volume (Book) III of *Capital* in 1894'.[79] 'The problem is undoubtedly important, in so far as its solution is vital to the logical consistency of the Marxist vision', says Laibman.[80] The essence of the problem is 'the apparent contradiction between the value accounting of Volume (Book) I of *Capital* and the price-of-production accounting of Volume (Book) III', as Morishima and Catephores point out.[81]

It is true that this problem has occupied a central position in the discussions for and against Marx's labour-theory and that its solution has been thought to be vital for Marxists as the proof of logical consistency in *Capital*. However, I would like to clarify why it is at least improper that it has been given such an eminent status. In the whole edifice of the three Books of *Capital*, the problem is of no more than subsidiary importance. There exists another problem of pivotal significance to Marx's economics and Marxian ideology in general.

1 On labour, value, price and price of production

One of the difficulties in understanding the transformation problem is the equivocal usage of the words 'value' and 'price' by Marx himself and by those who are concerned with the problem. My arrangement of the concepts 'labour', 'value' and 'price', in Sec. II above, shown in the following summarised form, would help to put the confusion involved in order:

value-creating substance	value	value	price
xL	$= \quad xV$	$= \quad x\sigma V$	$= \quad x\sigma P$
x hours	x hours	¥, £, $, etc.	¥, £, $, etc.
(labour being expended)	(labour expended)	(value in money name)	(money name of value)

By 'value' Marx means in some places 'labour expended', xV, and in other places 'value in money name', $x\sigma V$, which are two things of different dimensions. But Marx thinks that they are one and the same in essence because 'labour expended', x hours, gives commodities 'value', of, say, $1/2$ x shillings (1 hour $= 1/2$ shilling).[82] For him, 'value' (labour expended, xV) is 'substance', and 'value' (value in money name, $x\sigma V$) or 'price' (money name of value, $x\sigma P$) – they are synonyms for Marx – is its 'phenomenal form.'[83] xV and $x\sigma V$ or $x\sigma P$ have a common measuring unit, labour-time, according to Marx. A distinct recognition of this confusing terminology, which is unrecognised in the transformation discussions, is needed for strict interpretation of Marx's labour(-time)-value theory.

In this connection let us note the fact that for Marx labour-time calculation was a sort of actuality. Modern economists, Marxist and non-Marxists alike, know that labour-time calculation is meaningful only under strongly restrictive assumptions, only in an unrealistic abstract world. But Marx was confident that in 'a community of free individuals . . . with means of production in common' (an *actual* social system in the future),[84] the regulation of production and distribution comes to be 'perfectly simple and intelligible' by putting *literal* labour-time calculation into practice. This illusion of a planned economy without money was one of the fundamental causes of retarded economic progress in the communist countries[85] and the tragic massacre in Kampuchea. These influences of Marx's wrong reasoning upon historical events, derived from his confusion of the world of hypothesis with reality, are also out of the reach of the transformation discussions. But they surely deserve due attention.

Now, the crux of the matter is that x hours in my formula above are unknowable in the real capitalist (or communist) world as I already explained in detail. A conversion-coefficient, σ, of $x\sigma P$ can not be fixed, so that only price (not $x\sigma P$, but one having no link with direct labour-time calculation) is available. Marx's labour value theory, $xL = xV = x\sigma V = x\sigma P$, does not hold good.

My conclusion is endorsed by Wiles who says: 'Marx's value is an Aristotelian substance and price an Aristotelian accident; therefore we can only know anything empirically about price . . . value is unknowable.'[86] Dickinson asserts bluntly: 'Values and prices are quantities of different dimensions, measured in different units. Values are measured in quantities of labour-time. Prices are measured in terms of money . . . The idea of equating the sum of the prices (or of any prices) to the sum of the values (or of any values) is nonsense.'[87]

2   The transformation of values into prices

It is generally acknowledged that Marx was incorrect in his transformation calculation because he left constant and variable capitals in value ($x\sigma V$) terms.[88] These should have been first transformed into prices (not $x\sigma P$, but prices of production).[89] Wolfson declares: 'Marx's own solution was a jumble of value units and price units, whereas a consistent system ought to be stated in one or the other. Not both at once.'[90]

As a prerequisite for the transformation of $x\sigma V$ into price of production, there must be made a conversion of xV (x hours) into $x\sigma V$

(value in money name). σ of $x\sigma V$ is unknowable in the real world. An unrealistic assumption of homogeneity of labour is indispensable to make it knowable. Thus existing calculations by many theorists in various ways which aim at correcting this defect of Marx's method are all developed on the basis of homogeneity of labour combined with other extremely restrictive conditions.

Sweezy simply assumes that one unit of gold ($^1/_{35}$ ounce) is produced by one hour of labour, 1 hour = \$1,[91] just like Marx's assumption of 1 hour = $^1/_2$ shilling (in both cases homogeneity of labour is implied) and then proceeds to the transformation calculation of $x\sigma V$ into price of production in the form of a simple reproduction scheme with three departments.

Seton starts his analysis with 'the n-fold subdivision of the economy . . . closely allied to the familiar Leontief matrix' in which products are 'reckoned in terms of labour value' and then 'this system of "*value*" flows' is 'translated into *price* terms.'[92]

Samuelson begins with 'Adam Smith's 'early and rude state', where . . . it takes one hour to hunt a deer and two hours of equally simple labour to hunt a beaver'. He arranges the two animals in a Leontief-like model.[93] And he formulates 'the singular case of equal internal compositions of (constant) capital',[94] on the basis of which 'Marx has been preserved from all pitfalls'.

Morishima reduces 'all sorts of labour to the homogeneous *human labour in the abstract*', and constructs an n-sector input-output model based on that assumption.[95] Then he inquires into an 'additional condition required for the validity of Marx's algorithm' (conversion of values into production prices), an assumption of 'linearly dependent industries' which is 'weaker than the traditional condition of equal value-compositions of capital and the condition of "equal internal compositions of capital" . . . by Samuelson . . . (but) still very restrictive'.[96]

Laibman adopts 'a geometric approach' in which the unit of account is 'labour-time, unskilled, homogeneous and socially-necessary'. His 'main result . . . is that prices of production are uniquely determined as to scale as well as proportions'.[97]

The transformation calculations cited above and many others existing but not mentioned here are all of highly abstract character. It is noteworthy that Marxists see in them justification of labour – and surplus value theory, while Marx critics find in them ground for negating its validity.

Sweezy knows that 'the real world is one of price calculation', and yet he does 'not deal in price terms from the outset'. The reason is that: 'As long as we retain value calculation, there can be no obscuring of the origin and nature of profits as a deduction from the product of total social labour . . . value calculation makes it possible to look beneath the surface phenomena of money and commodities to the underlying relations between people and classes.'[98]

Seton declares that 'the internal consistency and determinacy of Marx's conception of the transformation process . . . have been fully vindicated' by his analysis. But he is strongly critical of 'the body of the underlying doctrine, without which the whole problem loses much of its . . . raison d'être. The assumption of equal 'rates of exploitation' . . . has never been justified . . . Above all, the denial of productive factor contributions other than those of labour, on which the whole doctrine of the surplus value rests, is an act of *fiat*.'[99]

Samuelson writes of his 'case of equal internal composition', that 'its disparities from realism help to elucidate the objections to Marx's procedures more cogently than do many of the sometimes sterile commentaries on him.' His fundamental statements on the 'so-called transformation problem' are: 'Contemplate two alternative and discordant systems, write down one. Now transform by taking an eraser and rubbing it out. Then fill in the other one. *Voila*! You have completed your transformation algorithm.' 'Stripped of logical complication and confusion, anybody's method of solving the famous transformation problem is seen to involve returning from the unnecessary detour taken in Volume (Book) I's analysis of value.'[100]

Laibman criticises 'the erase and replace exercise' of Samuelson by emphasising the priority of 'the concept of transformation from values to prices (not the other way around), even though the mathematics of the transformation procedure between the proportions of the two systems is reversible . . . in verifying the transformation concept, main emphasis must be placed on the prior nature of the values as moments of the production relations of the society, which determine exchange relations, and not vice versa.'[101]

Now I should submit my evaluation of these two contrary assertions. First, the priority of the value system claimed by Marxists is unwarranted. It is valid only in the abstract world. We, including Marxists, know that in the real world only prices are knowable, so that values are out of the question. Marx started with the premise that the labour-time calculation is impossible, the x in x hours is unknowable.

Nevertheless, in the process of his analysis Marx treats x as a known quantity. This is an evident self-contradiction. This mistake is repeated in Marxists' contention that the value system is the root and the price system is its derivative in the *real* capitalist society.

Thus, I agree with Marx critics in denying the validity of the value system. However, I feel that we already have enough correct solutions if their final aim were to demonstrate the invalidity of value system. Wiles has this to say: 'The transformation is a gigantic boondoggle for mathematically inclined intellectuals.'[102]

Some more variant solutions expected in the future would further elaborate the transformation arguments. They might be of fascinating interest from the viewpoint of strict logic and mathematical procedure. However, they would have no relevance to the main theme of *Capital*, the inevitable transition from capitalism to communism, which should be placed under a strict reappraisal in the context of the contemporary world. (More explanation on this point is given later in connection with the law of the falling rate of profit.)

Speaking of variants, here I present an exceptional one, already existing, based on the denial of 'the dogma of homogeneous labour'.[103] Krause starts with two kinds of concrete and heterogeneous labour expended in producing coal and iron. 'The money relation induces a particular relation for the concrete labours themselves, called *abstract labour*.'[104] For the quantitative determination of abstract labour he applies the 'reduction-coefficients.' Homogeneous labour, which he excludes, is the case where reduction-coefficients are all equal to 1. In its stead he introduces a theoretical framework called 'standard reduction', by dint of which 'the transformation problem, ineluctable under the assumption of homogeneous labour, vanishes'.[105] However, the standard reduction is 'the mere logical possibility . . . regardless of whether it corresponds to reality'. The elegance of his mathematical procedures combined with the originality of his idea seems quite attractive in itself. But it has nothing to do with the literal reading and rigorous reappraisal based on it of *Capital*, intended for changing the real world.

3   On the rate of surplus value and the rate of profit

For Marx 'profit is . . . a converted form of surplus value, a form in which its origin and the secret of its existence are obscured and extinguished . . . profit is the form in which surplus value presents itself to the view, and must initially be stripped by analysis to disclose the latter.'[106] 'The rate of surplus value is . . . an exact expression for the degree of exploitation of labour-power by capital.'[107] 'In the relation of capital to profit' (the rate of profit), the real nature of profit-making, i.e. exploitation of surplus value, 'is cloaked in mystery and appears to originate from hidden qualities inherent in capital itself.'[108]

Thus the existence of surplus value and a unique (or everywhere equal) rate of surplus value is an unquestionable postulate of Marx's inquiry into the law of the motion of the capitalist society.

Therefore Marxists concerned with the transformation problem attach primary importance to the equal rate of surplus value as an attestation of the exploitation by capitalists of labourers.

However, can the equal rate of surplus value be retained in the process of transformation of values into price? When the organic compositions,[109] c/v, are different among industries or enterprises, it is evident that the rates of surplus value, c/s, and the rates of profit, $s/c+v$, cannot be equal. If s/v are equal $s/c+v$ must be different, and *vice versa*. For instance, in Sweezy's Table IV 'Value Calculation' s/v are equal and $s/c+v$ are different, and in Table IVa 'Price Calculation' s/v or, to be exact, $p(\text{profit})/w(\text{wages})$ are different and $s/c+v$ or $p/c+w$ are equal.[110]

However, in the real world s/v (surplus value/variable capital, or surplus labour hours/necessary labour hours) is unknowable. What we can obtain are various p/w (profit/wage) on the microscopic level or a unique p/w as a macroscopic aggregation. The latter p/w is the only available substitute for a uniform s/v. Should this p/w be called 'the rate of exploitation'? Rather, the concept of 'exploitation' itself should be re-examined, although here I would not go further into this subject.

At this point I would like to draw attention to one thing which also lies outside the interests of the transformation discussants: Marx's self-contradiction involved in his argument on surplus value. In Marx's simple reproduction scheme (Ch. 23, Book I and Ch. 20, Book II) the prerequisite is the existence of a certain amount of the means of production or constant capital. Therefore, he needs 'the so-called primitive accumulation' (accumulation by usurpation, Part VIII, Book I) to explain the beginning of the capitalist reproduction, because he thinks that the pre-capitalist societies have no capital, hence obtain no surplus value. On the other hand, he refers elsewhere to the existence of surplus labour, product or value in these societies and its conversion into capital (accumulation of capital) even in the

Table 2.2   Sweezy's Table IV and Table IVa

Value Calculation[a]

Department	Constant capital	Variable capital	Surplus value	Value
I	225	90	60	375
II	100	120	80	300
III	50	90	60	200
Totals	375	300	200	875

[a] The rate of surplus value is here assumed to be $66^2/_3$ per cent.

Price Calculation

Department	Constant capital	Variable capital	Profit	Price
I	288	96	96	480
II	128	128	64	320
III	64	96	40	200
Totals	480	320	200	1000

'beginnings of society' (the stone age)[111]. Surplus and capital exist, and at the same time do not exist, in pre-capitalist society! The next chapter is an attempt to examine this confusion of Marx and put it in order.

In the three department simple reproduction schemes of the Bortkiewicz–Sweezy solution constant capitals are *given* just as in Marx's scheme. So Marx's confusion on the origin of constant capital does not appear. In the input–output type solutions of Seton and Samuelson capital goods and consumer goods have substitutability from the beginning. Thus the inquiry into the primitive acquisition of capital goods is needless. Therefore Marx's confusion on this point is also out of their scope.

4 The incompatibility and continuity between Book I and Book III

It is an acknowledged understanding that the argument of Book I is developed in terms of value ($x\sigma V$) and that of Book III is in terms of *price*. Marx himself states in Book III: 'In Books I and II we dealt with the value of commodities. On the one hand, the *cost-price* has now been singled out as a part of this value, and, on the other, the *price of production* of commodities has been developed as its converted form.'[112]

I take sides with the advocates of incompatibility of value system and price system on the ground stated above, i.e., the σ in $x\sigma P$ is unknowable.

But this incompatibility is the problem between Book I and Parts 1 and 2 of Book III. Here I feel it necessary to confirm the usually neglected continuity between Chapter 25 of Book I and Part 3 of Book III. The value $x\sigma V$ in Part 1 of Book I is that of commodities in an abstract simple commodity-producers' society. However, the value in Chapter 25, 'The general law of capitalist accumulation', is that of commodities in a logically simplified capitalist society. Here Marx deals with the total social capital as an aggregation of all the individual capitals.[113] In this case c/v is, of course, unique, just as in the case of the same organic composition shared by every individual capital and price is $x\sigma P$, not price of production. Thus discrepancy between value and price (of production) does not arise, and nor does the difficulty in connection with the uniform s/v, the different c/v and the average $p/c+v$.

In Parts 1 and 2 of Book III the premise is the existence of inter-industrial differences of organic composition, hence the transformation problem. In the succeeding Part 3, however, Marx comes back again to the analysis of the total social capital. (£100c + £100v, etc., shown at the outset of Chapter 13 of *Capital* (see Table 2.3 below) should not be interpreted as individual capitals, but as models of total social capital.) In Chapter 25 of Book I he pursues the relation between c and v, c/v, and in Part 3 of Book III that of c, v and s ($=p$ in this case), $s/c+v$. In this way his pursuit of 'the economic law of motion of modern society'[114] which is undertaken in Chapter 25 of Book I is succeeded and completed in Part 3 of Book III. And in both parts the term 'value' means $x\sigma V$ and 'price' $x\sigma P$ which are thought to be the same thing. Borrowing Wiles's language, the Aristotelian philosopher in Book I became an Englishmen in Parts 1 and 2 of Book III, and returned to be an Aristotelian in Part 3 of it.

5   A self-contradiction occupying the central position in the economics of *Capital*

'The law of the tendency of the rate of profit to fall' in Part 3, Book III is the cornerstone of *Capital* and Marxian ideology in general. It is an 'infallible' law, not invented, but 'discovered'[115] by Marx, working with 'iron necessity toward inevitable results',[116] a 'scientific' demonstration of the unavoidable fall of capitalism and the rise of communism predicted in the *Communist Manifesto*. This 'infallible' law is unwarranted, however, as we show in the following.

Three main points of Marx's argument vindicating the inevitable collapse of capitalism are:

(1)   The ever-widening gap between supply[117] and demand[118] causing ever-intensifying economic crises.
(2)   The absolute impoverishment of the labouring class as a result of the subsistence wages of the employed labourers and the rise of the unemployment rate.
(3)   The fall of the rate of profit leading to the chronic stagnation of capitalist economy.

Beyond doubt, the fundamental premise of the law of the falling rate of profit is *productivity-rise*.[119] This is reflected in the heightening of the organic composition of capital in Marx's two sets of series illustrating the law of the falling rate of profit (see Table 2.3).

Table 2.3   Marx's two sets of series illustrating the law of the falling rate of profit[120]

$$50c + 100v + 100s$$
Pd_1 $\quad 100c + 100v + 100s = 300 \ (300G)$
$$200c + 100v + 100s$$
$$300c + 100v + 100s$$
Pd_2 $\quad 400c + 100v + 100s = 600 \ (30{,}000G)$

(in millions)
$$4c + 2v + 2s$$
$$15c + 3v + 3s$$

Note: Concrete figures of *G* (goods) are added by T.H. for quantitative clarity of explanation. *Pd* = Period.

Let us take up two of the above 'series' designated as Pd_1 and Pd_2 for simplicity of explanation. The organic composition of capital rises 4-fold from $100c/100v$ in Pd_1 to $400c/100v$ in Pd_2 reflecting the far more rapid rise of labour-productivity, which must let fall the value (= price, $x\sigma V = x\sigma P$) of commodities in inverse ratio. In Marx's own words: 'The value of commodities is in inverse ratio to the productiveness of labour. And so too, is the value of labour power.'[121] In the model capitalist society shown above the labour-productivity is assumed to rise 50-fold from Period 1 to Period 2. While $300G$ are produced by 300 units of labour in Period 1, $300,000G$ are produced by 600 units of labour in Period 2. One labour unit is £1 in money terms. (σ in $x\sigma V = x\sigma P$ is 1. Therefore, $1G = £1$ in Period 1 and $1G = £^1/50$ in Period 2. The productivity rises 50-fold and the value (price) of G falls to $^1/50$.[122]

And yet, Marx assumes 'a given wage'[123] in his explanation of the table above. This is the fatal self-contradiction. The wages of 100 labourers are 'given', £100, in both Pd_1 and Pd_2. Note that these are *nominal* wages. Real wages must have risen 50-fold from Pd_1 to Pd_2. 100 labourers in Pd_1, could buy only $100G$ with their £100. But in Pd_2 they obtain $5,000G$ with the same £100. And total money flow of £600 should buy up $30,000G$. Marx is unaware of this divergence between nominal amount of money and its real purchasing power.

Thus he erroneously thinks that the law unmistakably shows an unavoidably widening gap between supply and demand, and the wages of the labourers are given, £100 = $100G$. Then, if these employed labourers were burdened with the increasing number of unemployed, a lowering of the standard of living, 'the absolute impoverishment', of the working class as a whole becomes an inevitability. The law, however, as corrected by his own value (= price) mechanism changing inversely to productivity, logically represents a society where the standard of living of the employed labourers rises in direct proportion to the productivity-rise.

As for the increasing rate of unemployment, history shows that it is not a proven 'necessity'. It fluctuates in both directions.

[*Note:* In Marx's own words: 'The relative over-population becomes so much more apparent . . . the more the capitalist mode of production is developed.'][124]

Marx's wrong prediction of the inevitable tendency toward stagnation of the capitalist production is derived from the falling rate of profit. And this law is based on the premise that, in the terminology of contemporary economists, technical progress in the capitalist society is always capital-coefficient-raising. This is evidently unwarranted. There is also neutral and capital-coefficient-lowering technical progress.

6   On the continuity of Book II and Book III

Chapters 23 and 24, Part 7, Book I of *Capital* can be regarded as the illustration in the form of a one-sector model of simple and expanding reproduction in terms of value $x\sigma V$. It is succeeded by Chapter 20, 'The simple reproduction', and Chapter 21, 'Accumulation and reproduction on an extended scale', Part 3, Book II. This expanding reproduction scheme without technical progress is developed by Lenin's expanding scheme succeeding Marx's with one condition added: technical progress is indirectly expressed by the heightening of organic composition of capital. Accordingly, Lenin's scheme and Marx's hypothetical series illustrating the law of the falling rate of profit share an essential homogeneity. Lenin's scheme is the falling rate of profit in the form of a two-sector model. Therefore, it inevitably involves the defects inherent in Marx's series.

These faults common to Marx's law and Lenin's reproduction scheme are unacknowledged by the transformation discussants. The rigorous analysis of them is presented in Chapter 4, 5 and 7 of the present book. Chapter 6 is an inquiry into the methodological and philosophical basis of these errors.

Of course I am not going to say with this disclosure of Marx's (and Lenin's) fatal mistakes that there cannot be over-production and economic crises and so forth in the capitalist countries. I just feel it ought to be brought to light that the law 'discovered' by Marx is disqualified as an attestation of the inevitability of the ever-widening gap between supply and demand leading to the fall of capitalism and the rise of communism. I have never thought it unnecessary to change the present state of our society. But reforms should not be misguided by a wrong belief that capitalism goes into its own ruin through the dialectical movement of self-contradiction involved in the system itself. A theoretical cornerstone indispensable for reforms should be the confirmation of the definite inconsistency in logic immanent in the 'infallible' law on motion of modern society.

One word on our relationship with the communist countries. For the attainment of a really amicable co-existence of the two social systems, which should finally lead to One Free World, the myth of Marx's law alleged to vindicate the collapse of capitalism and the overall victory of communism must be liquidated not only as a matter of fact but also in its theoretical foundation. I hope that the radical reappraisal of the law developed in this book might be helpful to this end.

7 Epilogue

From these broad viewpoints with pressing relevance to the realities of the contemporary world, the transformation problem appears to be an over-cultivated field of subsidiary importance. A rigorous and integrated scrutiny of the main theme of *Capital*, the field hitherto almost deserted, should occupy a central position at this time of history. It is overdue.

3 An Error Common to 'The Transformation of Money into Capital' and 'The Primitive Calculation': Pre-Capitalist Societies Do and Do Not Produce Surplus

I NO SURPLUS VALUE IN THE PRE-CAPITALIST SOCIETIES?

Part II, Book I of *Capital*, entitled 'The transformation of money into capital', consists of Chapters 4 to 6, ending in the presentation of a question on our title subject. Its answer is given by Marx himself in Chapter 7, 'The labour-process and the process of producing surplus value', Part III. This is improper. Chapter 7 should have been included in Part II.[1] Chapters 4 and 5 tell us that an indispensable prerequisite for the transformation of money into capital is the appearance of labour-power as a commodity and that the pre-capitalist simple commodity-producers' society does not produce surplus value. The historical explanation corresponding to this theoretical description, the transformation of money into capital, is given in Chapters 26 to 32, in Part VIII, 'The So-Called Primitive Accumulation'. In Chapter 26 Marx points out that the fundamental precondition for the transformation of money and commodities into capital is the 'so-called primitive accumulation' which is 'nothing else than the historical process of divorcing the producer from the means of production',[2] in other words the process of production of labour-power as a commodity.

68

Money and commodities being thought *not* to be *capital*, the pre-capitalist feudal society, historical equivalent of the theoretical, abstract simple commodity-producers' society, should *not* be able to *produce surplus value*. Thus, 'the different momenta of primitive accumulation'[3] are enumerated in Part VIII as follows: 'The process of forcible expropriation of people'; [4] 'of the agricultural revolution . . . the forcible means employed';[5] 'The discovery of gold and silver in America, the extirpation, enslavement and entombment in mines of the aboriginal population, the beginning of the conquest and looting of the East Indies, the turning of Africa into a warren for the commercial hunting of black skins'.[6] The expropriations pictured here are *not* of the *surplus* in a society, but of the necessary portion without which the life and existence of the members of the society is endangered or destroyed. If we use the symbols '*s*' and '*v*' in a broad sense, this is the expropriation, not of '*s*', but of '*v*'.

But *at the same time*, Marx himself states in Chapter 26 that primitive accumulation is the process of 'transformation of feudal exploitation into capitalist exploitation'.[7] This feudal exploitation, in principle, should be that of surplus products and surplus value, '*s*', and *cannot be* the expropriation of necessaries of life, '*v*'. This point is clarified by Marx himself in Chapter 47, 'Genesis of capitalist ground-rent', Book III, and elsewhere.

Moreover, we find in Chapter 10, Book III a passage which clearly admits the existence of surplus value in a theoretical simple-commodity-producers' society abstracting from the ruling class in the historical feudal society:

> Suppose, the labourers themselves are in possession of their respective means of production and exchange their commodities with one another . . . In such a case, two labourers would, first, both have replaced their outlays, the cost prices of the consumed means of production, in the commodities which make up the product of their day's work . . . Secondly, both of them would have created equal amounts of new value, namely the working-day added by them to the means of production. This would comprise their wages plus the *surplus value* [emphasis - T.H.], the latter representing surplus labour over and above their necessary wants, the product of which would however belong to them.[8]

The historical counterpart of this description is 'Genesis of the Capitalist Farmer', Chapter 29, Book I and 'Genesis of the Industrial Capitalist', Chapter 31. The farmers, small guild masters and independent small artisans 'exploit wage-labour'(9) and turn themselves gradually into full-blown capitalist farmers and industrial capitalists. In these cases they expropriate the surplus labour 's' of the wage-labourers, not their necessary labour 'v'. The independent farmers and small artisans or theoretical simple commodity-producers create surplus value which belongs to themselves. When they lose their means of production and become employed workers, the surplus value they create goes into the pockets of their employers. In a word, Marx acknowledges the existence of surplus value in the pre-capitalist society.

Now it is readily to be seen that Marx's argument contains self-contradiction within it. He asserts in Chapter 5 that simple commodity-producers do not create surplus value.[10] And in Chapters 27 to 31, as far as 'the forcible means employed'[11] in the process of primitive accumulation are concerned, Marx is supposed to be in a position to deny the existence of surplus value in the pre-capitalist society. But in Chapter 10, Book III he clearly states that the simple-commodity-producers create surplus-value. And in Chapters 29 and 31, Book I, when he discusses the exploitation of feudal lords and that of farmers and small masters who are capitalists in the making, he presupposes the creation of surplus value within the feudal society. In what way was this confusion brought about? How should we put it in order?

II 'CAPITAL' AND 'SURPLUS' IN NARROWER AND BROADER SENSES BY MARX

The origin of this antinomy concerning surplus value lies in the twofold character of Marx's notion of 'capital'. On the one hand, he maintains that in the pre-capitalist societies there is no such thing as capital which constantly produces surplus value apart from the cases of old merchants and usurers whose capital 'acquires, but not produces' surplus. So he makes a mockery of Colonel Torrens who 'discovers the origin of capital'[12] in the first stick a savage seizes to strike down the fruit which hangs above his reach. A logical corollary is that there is no surplus value (and therefore no surplus products, no surplus labour) in the pre-capitalist societies where capital which produces surplus value does not exist.

On the other hand, Marx admits, or rather positively asserts, that mankind, since it emerged from an animal level standard of living, has always been using constant capital (or the means of production corresponding to it), doing surplus labour and producing surplus products and surplus value (if they go into markets). In Chapter 49, Book III he writes:

> If we think back to the beginnings of society . . . Nature there directly provides the means of subsistence . . . also gives . . . the time . . . to transform . . . other products of Nature into means of production: bows, stone knives, boats, etc. This process among savages . . . corresponds to the reconversion of surplus labour into new capital. In the process of accumulation, the conversion of such products of excess labour into capital obtains continually.[13]

Here Marx refers to exactly the same thing as told by Colonel Torrens which he ridiculed in Chapter 5, Book I. The savages described here expend surplus labour through which they acquire initial capital and accumulate additional capital. Then, it goes without saying that they expend necessary labour. The statements of Marx to the effect that necessary labour and surplus labour exist through any and all forms of societies can be found in many places in *Capital*:

> Variable capital is . . . only a particular form of appearance of the fund for providing the necessaries of life, or the labour-fund which the labourer requires for the maintenance of himself and family, and which, whatever be the system of social production, he must himself produce and reproduce. (Chapter 23, Book I)[14]

> If man were not capable of producing on one working-day more means of subsistence, which signifies in the strictest sense more agricultural products than every labourer needs for his own reproduction, if the daily expenditure of his entire labour-power sufficed merely to produce the means of subsistence indispensable for his own requirements, then one could not speak at all either of surplus product or surplus value. An agricultural labour productivity exceeding the individual requirements of the labourer is the basis of all societies. (Chapter 47, Book III).[15]

> Surplus labour in general, as labour performed over and above the given requirements, must always remain. In the capitalist . . . system, it merely assumes an antagonistic form . . . A definite quantity of surplus labour is required as insurance against accidents, and by the necessary and progressive expansion of the process of reproduction in keeping with the development of the needs and growth of population, which is called accumulation from the viewpoint of the capitalist. (Chapter 48, Book III).[16]

> If the labourer wants all his time to produce the necessary means of subsistence for himself and his race, he has no time left in which to work gratis for other. Without a certain degree of productiveness in his labour, he has no such superfluous time at his disposal; without such superfluous time, no surplus labour, and therefore no capitalists, no slave owners, no feudal lords, in one word, no class of large proprietors. (Chapter 14, Book I).[17]

Capital has not invented surplus labour. Wherever a part of society possesses the monopoly of the means of production, the labourer, free or not free, must add to the working-time necessary for his own maintenance an extra working-time in order to produce the means of subsistence for the owners of the means of production. (Chapter 8, Book I).[18]

The above examples will suffice to confirm that Marx recognises the existence of necessary labour (corresponding to 'v', variable capital, in terms of value) and surplus labour (corresponding to 's', surplus value, in terms of value) and surplus labour (corresponding to 's', surplus value, in terms of value) in human societies of all different stages of development. To sum up: Reviewing all through *Capital* it becomes clear that Marx finds, in all stages of human societies, constant capital in the wider sense (means of production), variable capital in the wider sense (necessary labour or necessaries of life corresponding to variable capital) and surplus (labour, products or value).

III   THE THEORETICAL PROCESS IN WHICH MARX FELL INTO ERROR

1   Hic Rhodus, hic salta!

In what way has this reasonable view of Marx on surplus which seems in accord with historical facts gone astray in 'the transformation of money into capital'? The first false step was that he chose the commodity circulation as the starting point of explanation of the problem.

The first distinction we notice between money that is money only, and money that is capital, is nothing more than a difference in their form of circulation. The simplest form of the circulation of commodities is $C–M–C$, . . . or selling in order to buy. But alongside of this form we find another specifically different form: $M–C–M$, . . . buying in order to sell. Money that circulates in the latter manner is thereby transformed into, becomes capital.[19]

The cotton that was bought for £100 is perhaps resold for £100 + £10 or £110. The exact form of this process is therefore $M–C–M'$, where $M' = M + \Delta M =$ the original sum advanced, plus an increment. This increment . . . I call *surplus value*. The value originally advanced, therefore, not only remains intact while in circulation, but adds to itself a surplus value or expands itself. It is this movement that converts it into capital.[20]

A noteworthy point here is Marx's clear-cut statement that the value originally advanced adds to itself a surplus value or expands itself *in circulation*. In other words he admits that surplus value comes out of or is produced in the process of circulation. This is a statement contradictory to his main stream of argument that surplus value cannot be produced in circulation as seen in the passages following the above citation:

> There is in an exchange nothing (if we except the replacing of one use-value by another) but a metamorphosis, a mere change in the form of the commodity . . . The exchange of commodities, which in its normal state is an exchange of equivalents, consequently, no method for increasing value.[21]

> If commodities, or commodities and money, of equal exchange value, and consequently equivalents, are exchanged, it is plain that no one abstracts more value from, than he throws into, circulation. There is no creation of surplus value.[22]

> The creation of surplus value, and therefore the conversion of money into capital, can consequently be explained neither by the assumption that commodities are sold above their value, nor that they are bought below their value.[23]

> We have shown that surplus-value cannot be created by circulation, and, therefore, that in its formation, something must take place in the background, which is not apparent in the circulation itself. But can surplus value possibly originate anywhere else than in circulation?[24]

Thus, Marx, who states that surplus value comes out of circulation process, repeatedly insists that surplus value cannot be created in circulation. Then, 'can surplus value originate anywhere else than in circulation?'

> The commodity contains a quantity of his (commodity-owner's = commodity-producer's) own labour . . . This quantity is expressed by the value of the commodity, and since the value is reckoned in money of account, this quantity is also expressed by the price, which we will suppose to be 10. But his labour is not represented both by the value of the commodity, and by a surplus over that value, not by a price of 10 that is also a price of 11, not by a value that is greater than itself. The commodity-owner can, by his labour, create value, but not self-expanding value. He can increase the value of his commodity, by adding fresh labour, and therefore more value to the value in hand, by making, for instance, leather into boots. The same material has now more value, because it contains a greater quantity of labour. The boots have therefore more value than the leather, but the value of the leather remains what it was; it has not expanded itself, has not, during the making of the boots, annexed surplus value. It is therefore impossible that outside the

sphere of circulation, a producer of commodities can, without coming into contact with other commodity-owners, expand value, and consequently convert money or commodities into capital.[25]

The conclusion of this passage is that the labour of the commodity-- owner (simple commodity-producer) does not create surplus value. Confronting this proposition with his reasonable statement in Chapter 10, Book III, cited in Section I,[26] to the effect that the labour of simple commodity-producers create surplus value the self-contradiction contained in Marx's argument becomes crystal-clear.

Then, how did Marx arrive at this strange conclusion? We see two sets of 'demonstrations' in the quotation above. The first one: If the value of a commodity made by a commodity-producer is, for instance, £10, the value of £10 cannot be at the same time both £10 and £11. Therefore, the labour of the commodity-producer creates value, but not surplus value. Does this make any 'demonstration'? It is self-evident that £10 cannot be £11. The real question is this: Of the whole value of £10 materialised in the commodity, does £X which expresses the value added by the labour of the commodity-producer contain surplus value or not? Marx does not probe this point, but declares, just on the ground of the above truism, that the commodity-producer's labour does not create surplus value.

The gross sales for this accounting period of your corporation were 10 billion Yen.

The amount of 10 billion Yen cannot at the same time be 10 billion Yen and 11 billion Yen, a value that is greater than itself. Therefore, your corporation could not raise any profit during the last accounting period.

If anyone used this sort of an argument, he would be treated as crazy. But Marx's 'demonstration' is just of the same nature.

The second 'demonstration': A commodity-producer makes leather into boots. The value of boots is greater than that of leather because the labour of the commodity-producer is added to it. But the value of leather is just as it was. It did not expand itself to create surplus value. Therefore, the labour of the commodity-producer does not create surplus value. In short, the value of boots is greater than that of leather by the amount of labour added by the producer. But the value of leather remains the same.

From this story, how can you draw the conclusion that the labour of the producer does not create surplus value? It is self-evident that the value of leather remains what it was, because it is an aggregation of various *past* labour expended by cattlemen, transporters, leather-makers, etc. The past cannot be changed. The question hinges on whether the labour added by the shoemaker contains surplus value or not. This kernel of the problem is invisible to Marx.

Of the gross sales of 10 billion Yen for this accounting period of your corporation, 5 billion Yen is the cost of (non-personnel) supplies. This cost, 5 billion Yen, remains what it was. It did not expand itself. It did not produce profits. Therefore, the whole sum of remaining 5 billion Yen is personnel expenditures which as a matter of course does not contain profits. Your corporation failed in raising profits.

If anyone talked like this, he would be regarded as having lost his senses. But just this is the error of Marx's 'demonstration'.

Now, Marx writes in Chapter 4 of *Capital* that surplus value is created (original value expands itself) in circulation.[27] But he states repeatedly in Chapter 5 that surplus value is *not* created in circulation.[28] And in the last part of that chapter he even denies the creation of surplus value by the 'commodity-owner' in the production process.[29] But Marx must explain away somehow or other that the merchant's capital acquires surplus value in circulation and his money is transformed into capital:

> It is therefore impossible for capital to be produced by circulation, and it is equally impossible for it to originate apart from circulation. It must have its origin both in circulation and yet not in circulation . . . .
> Our friend, Moneybags, who as yet is only an embryo capitalist, must buy his commodities at their value, must sell them at their value, and yet at the end of the process must withdraw more value than he threw into it at starting. His development into a full-grown capitalist must take place, both within the sphere of circulation and without it. These are, the conditions of the problem. Hic Rhodus, hic salta![30]

This reads like a typical dialectical statement being both affirmation and negation at the same time. Marx himself must have had full confidence in this 'dialectical contradiction'. But in reality this is no more than a fallacy of self-contradiction as explained below. First, he sets up a theoretical premise that money is transformed into capital *in* the process of *circulation*. It necessarily means that surplus value is produced in circulation. But at the same time, according to his other premise that exchanges are those among equivalents, there should be no room for increasing the value of any commodity concerned. In other words, there should be no creation of surplus value in circulation. Therefore, in the following pages he repeatedly stresses that surplus value cannot be produced in the process of circulation. Moreover he makes a 'demonstration' that a commodity-owner *in the process of production* can create value, but *not surplus value*. This inconsistency involved in his argument, of which he is unaware, drives him into writing the self-contradictory (seemingly dialectical) proposition: 'It is impossible for capital to be produced by circulation, and it is equally impossible for it to originate apart from circulation.'

2   The trick has at last failed

The explanation of what Marx believes to be dialectical contradiction, that surplus value must be produced 'both within the sphere of circulation and without it', begins at the outset of Chapter 6, 'The buying and selling of labour-power'.

> The change of value that occurs in the case of money intended to be converted into capital, cannot take place in the money itself . . . Just as little can it originate in the second act of circulation, the re-sale of the commodity, which does no more than transform the article from its bodily form back again into its money-form. The change must, therefore, take place in the commodity bought by the first act, $M-C$, but not in its value, for equivalents are exchanged, and the commodity is paid for at its full value. We are, therefore, forced to the conclusion that the change originates in the use-value, as such, of the commodity, i.e. in its consumption. In order to be able to extract value from the consumption of a commodity, our friend, Moneybags, must be so lucky as to find, within the sphere of circulation, in the market, a commodity, whose use-value possesses the peculiar property of being a source of value, whose actual consumption, therefore, is itself an embodiment of labour, and, consequently, a creation of value. The possessor of money does find on the market such a special commodity in capacity for labour or labour-power.[31]

The gist of his reasoning is as follows: The two acts of exchange, $M-C-M$, are both the exchange of equivalents in which there is no possibility of value being increased. Therefore, in order to bring about surplus value in exchange, $M-C-M + \Delta M$, which should be exchange of equivalents as well, the commodity bought by the first act of exchange must be the one which, in its consumption, produces a new commodity (embodiment of labour) and, consequently, creates new value (including surplus value.) The name of this commodity is labour-power. The process can be shown in the formula: $M-C_1$ (labour-power)–*P* (consumption of labour-power = production) –C_2 (new commodity) = $M + \Delta M$.

Thus we find already here the answer in an implicit form which Marx describes explicitly in Section 2, Chapter 7, boasting that 'the trick has at last succeeded'.[32] But Marx should not have included in his answer the buying of labour-power, 'a commodity, whose use-value possesses the peculiar property of being a source of value, whose actual consumption is an embodiment of labour'. The leading dancer in the *Rhodus* island theatre is a *merchant* who is going to transform money into capital. When he buys cotton what he can and must do is not to increase its value, but to take care not to decrease its value by wear and tear. He, as a merchant, is not in a position to consume the cotton for his own use. He sells the cotton at its value and yet he earns surplus value. How is it possible? The question Marx raised and his own answer might be paraphrased as follows:

> 'How does a merchant raise profit by first buying cotton and then selling it?'
>
> 'Oh, that is because the yarn manufacturer, who buys cotton from the merchant, employs labourers and lets them create new value including surplus value through the act of spinning cotton into yarn.'

Does this answer make sense? Marx stepped out in a wrong direction when he suggested the buying of labour-power.

The explicit answer Marx gives in Section 2, Chapter 7, is this: A yarn-manufacturer, who has 27 shillings at first, buys cotton for 20 shillings, spindles for 4 shillings and labour-power for 3 shillings. This labour-power or labourer expends labour worth 6 shillings in the course of making yarn. Thus the whole value embodied in the yarn is 30 shillings.

> 27 shillings have been transformed into 30 shillings; a surplus value of 3 shillings has been created. The trick has at last succeeded; money has been converted into capital.
>
> Every condition of the problem is satisfied, while the laws that regulate the exchange of commodities, have been in no way violated. Equivalent has been exchanged for equivalent. For the capitalist as buyer paid for each commodity, for the cotton, the spindle and the labour-power, its full value. He then did what is done by every purchaser of commodities; he consumed their use-value. The consumption of the labour-power, which was also the process of producing commodities, resulted in 20 lbs. of yarn, having a value of 30 shillings . . . He withdraws 3 shillings more from circulation than he originally threw into it. This metamorphosis, this conversion of money into capital, takes place both within the sphere of circulation and also outside it; within the circulation, because conditioned by the purchase of the

labour-power in the market; outside the circulation, because what is done within it is only a stepping-stone to the production of surplus value, a process which is entirely confined to the sphere of production.[33]

What Marx tells us here can be illustrated as shown in Figure 3.1.

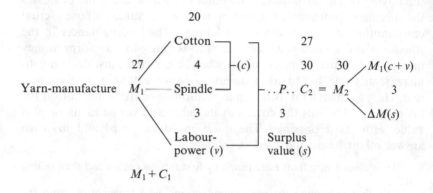

Figure 3.1   Marx's illustration of creation of surplus value

This elucidation of the creation of surplus value and the transformation of money into capital is in itself clear and consistent within the framework of labour-value theory. But this is the answer to the question presented in Chapter 5, 'How does a *merchant* raise his profit?' The answer above substantially means: 'The *yarn manufacturer* who buys cotton from the merchant obtains the profit = surplus value produced by the labourers.' Marx writes: 'He did what is done by every purchaser of commodities.' As a general rule it is only right for a purchaser of some commodity to consume it. So that the above statement seems quite strict and without any slip. But 'he' in this context must be a *merchant*, an embryo of the *commercial* capitalist. If a merchant consumes the commodity he bought, he will, far from gaining profit, suffer loss. Marx boasts that 'the trick has at last succeeded'. And the secret of this trick lies in the fact that he, himself unconsciously, substituted a yarn manufacturer for a merchant. So we must say that 'the trick has at last failed'.

Not that Marx has nothing to say on 'How does a merchant raise a profit by first buying cotton and then selling it?' He writes in Chapter 5:

If the transformation of merchants' money into capital is to be explained otherwise than by the producers being simply cheated, a long series of intermediate steps would be necessary, which at present, when the simple circulation of commodities forms our only assumption, are entirely wanting.[34]

This reads as if Marx intends to present 'a long series of intermediate steps' necessary to explain 'the transformation of merchants' money into capital' in Section II, Chapter 7. But there what we find is how a yarn manufacturer obtains surplus value. As a matter of fact the explanation of this 'long series of intermediate steps' is given in Chapters 16 to 18, Book III, in the description of commercial capital sharing in the formation of average rate of profit. The gist of it is as follows: Although commercial capital (labour of commercial workers) does not produce value, it gets transferred surplus value which industrial capital (labour of industrial workers) produces, by undertaking the commercial function of industrial capital as its own speciality and thereby sharing in the formation of the average rate of profit. This explanation is, again, a product of Marx's theoretical mistake, of which I already discussed in Section II. 'Doesn't Tertiary Industry Create Value?', Chapter 1.

IV   SUCCESSION OF CONFUSION FROM THE *TRANSFORMATION OF MONEY INTO CAPITAL* TO *PRIMITIVE ACCUMULATION*

1   Primitive accumulation in a society without surplus value

As disclosed in the foregoing Section III of this chapter, Marx arrived at the wrong conclusion that surplus value is not produced in pre-capitalist societies through his confusion in reasoning. This error is succeeded in Part III 'The Accumulation of Capital', Book I. 'Simple Reproduction', Chapter 23, is that in a capitalist society. It is an abstract model society where capitalists employ labourers by variable capital, let them work and produce surplus value, which is assumed to be consumed away by capitalists, so that the scale of reproduction is not expanded but remains simple.

> But that process must have had a beginning of some kind. From our present standpoint it therefore seems likely that the capitalist, once upon a time, became possessed of money, by some accumulation that took place independently of the unpaid labour of others, and that this was, therefore, how he was enabled to frequent the market as a buyer of labour-power.[35]

'Our present standpoint' here should probably be interpreted to be his view that there exists no surplus value in pre-capitalist societies. This assumption perfectly fits with his argument that the economic cycle which produces surplus value continuously must have had a beginning'.

Chapter 24, 'Conversion of Surplus Value into Capital', is the research on 'surplus value as capital, reconverting it into capital, . . . accumulation of capital'.[36] This means that the capitalist does not use up surplus value for consumption but appropriates it for additional investment and, therefore, expanded reproduction proceeds. We find the following passage in this chapter:

> The original conversion of money into capital is achieved in the most exact accordance with the economic laws of commodity production [the law of exchange of equivalents - T.H.] . . . Nevertheless, its result is:
>
> (1)   the product belongs to the capitalist and not to the worker;
> (2)   That the value of this product includes, besides the value of the capital advanced, a surplus value which costs the worker labour but the capitalist nothing, and which none the less becomes the legitimate property of the capitalist.[37]

This is an abridged repetition of the contents of Chapters 4 and 5. Money as such does not produce surplus value. But, with the appearance of labour-power, it is transformed into capital in strict accordance with the law of exchange of equivalents. The exploitation of surplus value starts. 'The trick has at last succeeded.'[38]

Now we read at the beginning of Chapter 26, 'Secret of Primitive Accumulation':

> We have seen how money is changed into capital [Chapters 4 to 7 – T.H.]; how through capital surplus value is made [Chapter 23 – T.H.], and from surplus value more capital [Chapter 24 – T.H.] But the accumulation of capital presupposes surplus value; surplus value presupposes capitalistic production; capitalistic production presupposes the preexistence of considerable masses of capital and of labour-power in the hands of producers of commodities. The whole movement, therefore, seems to turn in a vicious circle, out of which we can only get by supposing a primitive accumulation . . . preceding capitalist accumulation; an accumulation not the result of the capitalist mode of production, but its starting-point.[39]

The core of the problem is this: Capital cannot exist without surplus value and surplus value cannot be produced without capital. So Marx assumes, in order to cut off this vicious circle, a primitive accumulation of capital and labour-power. On the other hand, he retains the idea formed in Chapters 4 to 7 that money as such does not produce surplus value, nor does simple commodity-producer's labour do it either, and labour-power is the sole commodity capable of producing it. Thus in the process of the primitive accumulation the utmost emphasis is laid on the labouring class 'free from' means of production. Here comes his famous definition:

> The so-called primitive accumulation, therefore, is nothing else than the historical process of divorcing the producer from the means of production.[40]

Then, in the historical description of the following chapters, Marx puts stress on the use of force in the production of the labouring class and in the expropriation of wealth. This is not the expropriation of surplus value which normally exists in the pre-capitalist society (because surplus value is thought to be non-existent in the pre-capitalist society), but the usurpation of the necessities of life. Let me cite some typical passages. At the end of Chapter 27:

> The spoilation of the church's property, the fraudulent alienation of the State domains, the robbery of the common lands, the usurpation of feudal and clan property, and its transformation into modern private property under circumstances of reckless terrorism, were just so many idyllic methods of primitive accumulation. They conquered the field for capitalistic agriculture, made the soil part and parcel of capital, and created for the town industries the necessary supply of a 'free' and outlawed proletariat. [41]

In Chapter 31, 'Genesis of the Industrial Capitalist', we see the passage already quoted in Section 1 above:

> The discovery of gold and silver in America, the extirpation and entombment in mines of the aboriginal population . . .[42]

The paragraph text to the above citation is:

> The different momenta of primitive accumulation distribute themselves now, more or less in chronological order, particularly over Spain, Portugal, Holland, France, and England. In England at the end of the 17th century, they arrive at a systematical combination, embracing the colonies, the national debt, the modern mode of taxation, and the protectionist system. These methods . . . all employ the power of State, the concentrated and organised force of society, to hasten, hothouse fashion, the process of transformation of the feudal mode of production into the capitalist mode, and to shorten the transition. Force is the midwife of every old society pregnant with a new one.[43]

And the last sentence of this chapter is:

> Capital comes dripping from head to foot, from every pore, with blood and dirt.[44]

2 From feudal to capitalist mode of exploitation

On the other hand, all through *Capital*, as already pointed out in Sections I and II above, we find a chain of thought that labour in the human society in any and every stage of development is divided into necessary labour (v) and surplus labour (s), and mankind has continuously produced surplus products (surplus value, if commodity production is prevalent) making use of capital (or means of production). This line of thought inevitably intrudes into Marx's argument on primitive accumulation.

In Chapter 23, Book I, in the paragraph just before the statement 'some accumulation that took place independently of the unpaid labour of others',[45] he writes 'Variable capital is . . . only a particular form of appearance of . . . the labour-fund which the labourer requires . . . whatever be the system of social production'[46] (cited in Section II). Then he illustrates the case of a peasant doing compulsory service for his lord, who works 3 days a week on his own land and the other 3 days does forced work on the lord's domain. 'But from the moment that the forced labour is changed into wage-labour, from that moment the labour-fund which the peasant himself continues as before to produce and reproduce, takes the form of a capital advanced in the form of wages by the lord.'[47] This is an obvious contradiction to his argument on 'some accumulation independent of the unpaid-labour of others' in the next paragraph.[48] And yet Marx thus distinctly acknowledges the existence of surplus in the feudal society.

Let us proceed to Chapter 26. In its beginning Marx writes that 'surplus value pre-supposes capitalistic production'.[49] This inevitably means that surplus value does not exist in the pre-capitalist society. But, just a few pages later, he refers to 'the transformation of feudal exploitation into capitalist exploitation',[50] and in Chapter 29 even exploitation of 'wage-labour'[51] by a farmer in the feudal society. This exploitation should undoubtedly be interpreted as that of, not necessary labour 'v', but surplus labour 's' (product, or value).

We read at the beginning of Chapter 31, 'Genesis of the Industrial Capitalist':

Doubtless many small guild-masters, and yet more independent small artisans, or even wage-labourers, transformed themselves into capitalists, and (by gradually extending exploitation of wage-labour and corresponding accumulation) into full-blown capitalists.[52]

The labour of independent small artisans in this case should be understood to produce surplus value belonging to themselves, as Marx himself points out in the above-cited statement in Section I.[53] It goes without saying that wage-labourers here should produce surplus value which is appropriated by their employers who and whatever they may be.

In passing, if we take into consideration the appearance of such minute 'capitalists' as these, we are pressed to re-examine what Marx writes on 'the preexistence of considerable masses of capital'[54] at the beginning of Chapter 26. As to these 'considerable masses', in Chapter 9, Book I we find:

> The possessor of money or commodities actually turns into a capitalist . . . only where the minimum sum advanced for production greatly exceeds the maximum of the middle ages. Here, as in natural science, is shown the correctness of the law discovered by Hegel (in his 'Logic), that merely quantitative differences beyond a certain point pass into qualitative changes.[55]

This statement seems to exclude the possibility of the small capitalists coming into existence. Marx here perhaps thinks of 'the minimum sum' in the context of Chapters 13 and 14 where 'co-operation' and 'manufacture' are set as the starting points of capitalism. But the genesis of the capitalist can be theoretically explained with an independent small commodity-producer employing one labourer at the outset, and such cases must have existed in history as Marx himself writes in Chapter 31. We also find in Chapter 9, just before the above citation, the case of a 'small master' employing one or two labourers. Thus, we know that Marx's argument contains self-contradiction. Marx is not qualified to assert here the correctness of the law discovered by Hegel of the change from quantity to quality.

For understanding this self-contradiction the concept of 'the collective power of masses' would be a useful guidepost. Marx writes in Chapter 13, Book I:

> Capitalist production only then really begins . . . when each individual capital employs simultaneously the comparatively large number of labourers; when consequently the labour-process is carried on on an extensive scale and

yields, relatively, large quantities of products . . . both historically and logically, the starting-point of capitalist production . . . Not only have we here an increase in the productive power of the individual, by means of co-operation, but the creation of a new power, namely, the collective power of masses.[56]

'The collective power of masses' is in the German original *'Massenkraft'*,[57] and in the French version of *Capital* it is 'force collective'.[58] This is the concept first used by P. J. Proudhon in his famous book, *Qu'est-ce que la propriété?*[59] The gist of his assertion is that *property is theft* because it is unjust acquisition of the fruit of force collective. Proudhon's argument is thought to be a forerunner of Marx's theory of exploitation of surplus value. In Chapter 13 Proudhon's influence on Marx is evident. Here he contends that the starting-point is 'co-operation', which creates *Massenkraft* (force collective), yielding surplus value. In other words here he thinks that surplus value is not produced before technology reaches the stage of 'co-operation'.

Thus Marx falls into the inconsistency of explaining 'the genesis of capitalism' in the following two ways:

(1) with the appearance of small guild-masters, etc. employing just one or a few labourers, seizing surplus value from them, and growing up to full-fledged capitalists;
(2) with the taking root of 'co-operation', which first yields surplus value.

3 Correct theory of primitive accumulation in the light of stands taken by Uno and Ōtsuka

The point of my argument above is: The primitive accumulation interpreted by Marx is, on the one hand, a leap from the society without surplus value to the capitalist society which produces it, and on the other hand, 'the transformation of feudal exploitation [of surplus labour or product or value–T.H.] into capital exploitation [of surplus value–T.H.]'.[60] Now let us put this theoretical confusion in order. For this purpose it would be helpful to examine the value theory by Kōzō Uno and the historiology by Hisao Ōtsuka[61] in connection with the transformation of money into capital and with primitive accumulation.

As is well known, Uno is strongly critical of Marx's assumption of simple commodity-producers' society.[62] He asserts that the merchant-capital in the pre-capitalist society obtains its profits (surplus value) by 'exchange of non-equivalents',[63] i.e. by 'buying under value or selling over value, or buying under value and selling over value'. But, in my opinion, the assumption of a simple commodity-producers' society as a theoretical abstraction has suffcent validity and effectiveness to be a base for a fundamental explanation of the labour-value theory.[64] In this case, the labour of simple commodity-producers should be understood to produce surplus value belonging to themselves, as Marx himself admits in Chapter 10, Book III.[65] But the simple commodity-producers entering the stage in Chapter 5, Book I, do not create surplus-value, as already shown in Section III above. This is the contradiction to be criticised, of which Uno remains unaware. He thinks, following Marx, that the labour of the simple commodity-producer making leather into boots does not create surplus-value.[66] Thus, Uno inherits the wrong side of Marx's primitive-accumulation theory, i.e. a leap from the society without surplus value to the one producing it.

And yet he writes in another place, just as Marx: 'if one day's labour just sustains the power of the labourer to work one day and no more, then the historical development of mankind is utterly denied . . . No one can throw doubt on the fact that the productive-power of man has always been more than keeping up his own living.'[67] It is clear that Marx's confusion is inherited by Uno.

Standing out in marked contrast to 'Uno-Theory' is the so-called 'Ōtsuka Historiology'. Ōtsuka draws the following conclusion from his historical research:

> The genesis and social genealogy of modern capitalism (industrial capital) is not to be sought in the development of commerce in general and that of pre-capitalistic [commercial—T.H.] capital in particular, but in the independent and free development of the so-called middle-class-producers, especially in the independent development of industry and manufacture in the agricultural villages.[68]

> The historical formation of industrial capital is nothing but the process of self-dissolution of the middle-class-producers (farmers and small citizens as small commodity producers) into two poles, industrial bourgeoisie and proletariat. Therefore, this polarisation of middle-class-producers is indeed the fundamental moment of the development of modern capitalism.[69]

The middle-class-producer of Ōtsuka is the historical counterpart of the theoretical model, simple commodity-producer, of Marx. He is not the counterpart of the simple commodity-producer described in

Chapter 5, Book I, who does not create surplus value, but that of the simple commodity-producer in Chapter 10, Book III, who produces surplus value belonging to himself. (Or else, when the middle-class-producers dissolve themselves into two poles, the producers who fall down to wage-labourers must be thought to be expropriated, not of surplus value, but of a portion of necessities of life (necessary labour '*v*'), being given wages below subsistence level.) This historical process of polarisation depicted by Ōtsuka corresponds to 'the transformation of independent small artisans into small capitalists'[70] at the beginning of Chapter 31, Book I of *Capital* or the case of a 'small master'[71] in Chapter 9.

With our scrutiny so far of Marx's confusion in mind, we can now form a theoretical model of primitive accumulation which Marx should have written, or which is set right by corrections based on the good part of Marx's argument. After the illustration by Marx, 'the trick', in Chapter 7, Book I, the two formulae shown in Figures 3.2 and 3.3 are suggested.

One fundamental feature common to the formulae is that in both cases surplus value is created in the process of production. The fundamental differences are: (1) With a part of the initial capital (money) the simple commodity-producer buys means of consumption necessary for his life, but the capitalist buys labour-power (labourer). (2) The simple commodity-producer acquires surplus value created by himself, and the capitalist acquires surplus value created by labourer employed by him. These differences are caused by 'the historical process', which demarcate the two formulae, 'divorcing the producer from the means of production'.[72]

By way of precaution it should be made clear that by putting Marx's theoretical confusion in order with these formulae I never intend to disregard the historical facts, such as cheating (*nicht tauschen aber täuschen*) engaged in by merchants, the exchange of non-equivalents, the growth of a merchant into an industrial capitalist and various types of forcible usurpation in the process of primitive accumulation and so on. Needless to say that research into these historical facts should be advanced further. Only it must be pointed out that it is a fatal mistake to combine these historical facts with the wrong theoretical stand which denies the creation of surplus value by simple commodity-producers, independent small artisans, broadly speaking, by all categories of producers in any and every type of pre-capitalist society.

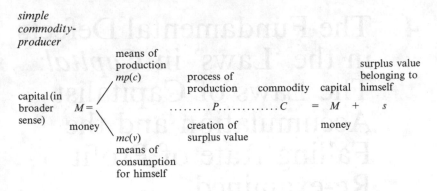

Figure 3.2   Simple commodity-producer's creation and possession of surplus value

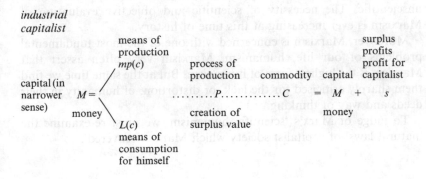

Figure 3.3   Capitalist's exploitation of surplus value created by labours

Lastly, my correct interpretation of primitive accumulation based on the right part of Marx's argument is still within the framework of Marxian labour-value theory. Of the labour-value theory, and the surplus value theory which sees the sole origin of surplus value in human labour, I am definitely critical, as this book shows.[73]

4 The Fundamental Defects in the 'Laws' in *Capital*: The Laws of Capitalist Accumulation and the Falling Rate of Profit Re-examined

For some people Marx is already a 'dead dog'.[1] For others he is still a symbol of infallibility. Both approaches, or rather non-approaches, are unscientific. The necessity of scientific and objective evaluation of Marxism is ever increasing at this time of history.

Moreover, Marxism is concerned with one of the most fundamental problems of our life, humanism. Marxism very often assert that Marxism is the highest form of humanism. But at the same time we find them sharply criticised for the lack, or distortion, of humanity in their deeds and way of thinking.

To judge of Marx's 'scientific humanism' we must re-examine the 'natural laws' of capitalist society which Marx 'discovered'.

I HEGEL'S VIEW ON 'CIVIL SOCIETY' AND MARX

Let us begin with an analysis of the philosophical aspect of Marxism. We have those famous passages written by Marx in the 'Afterword' to the second German edition to *Capital*:

> The mystification which dialectic suffers in Hegel's hands, by no means prevents him from being the first to present its general form of working in a comprehensive and conscious manner. With him it is standing on its head. It must be turned right side up again, if you would discover the rational kernel within the mystical shell.[2]

What Marx meant here can be summed up as follows: Hegel was wrong in viewing the development of the history of matter as that of

'Idea'. But his way of grasping the development of the world, the dialectic *per se*, is right and rational. So it can be used effectively if it is 'turned right side up again'.

This is the point on which much stress is generally laid in regard to the relation between Hegelian philosophy and Marx. (On this subject see my argument developed in Chapter 6.) But another point seems unduly neglected: the fact that Marx derived from Hegel not only his dialectics but also his view on the modern bourgeois society.

We find in Hegel's *Philosophy of Right* his foresight on the development of the modern bourgeois society which reminds us of some well-known sentences of *Communist Manifesto* and *Capital*. According to Hegel, the progress of modern bourgeois society, the increase of population and industrial power, brings on the accumulation of superfluous wealth on the one hand, and the poverty of the majority on the other as the result of simplified skills and lowered incomes caused by the development of large-scale production and division of labour. 'It hence becomes apparent that despite an excess of wealth civil society is not rich enough, i.e. its own resources are insufficient to check excessive poverty and the creation of a penurious rabble.'[3]

Now let us compare this with several quotations from Marx's writings chronologically arranged.

When society is in a state of progress, the ruin and impoverishment of the worker is the product of his labour and of the wealth produced by him. The misery results, therefore, from the *essence* of present-day labour itself. (1844)[4]

The modern labourer . . . instead of rising with the progress of industry, sinks deeper and deeper below the conditions of his own class. He becomes a pauper, and pauperism develops more rapidly than population and wealth. And here it becomes evident, that the bourgeoisie is unfit any longer to be the ruling class in society, and to impose its conditions of existence upon society as an over-riding law . . . Society can no longer live under this bourgeoisie, in other words, its existence is no longer compatible with society . . . What the bourgeoisie, therefore, produces, above all, is its own grave-diggers. Its fall and the victory of the proletariat are equally inevitable. (1848)[5]

Accumulation of wealth at one pole is . . . at the same time accumulation of misery, agony of toil, slavery, ignorance, brutality, mental degradation, at the opposite pole, on the side of the class that produces its own product in the form of capital.(1867)[6]

Along with the constantly diminishing number of the magnates of capital, who usurp and monopolise all advantages of this process of transformation, grows the mass of misery, oppression, slavery, degradation, exploitation; but with this too grows the revolt of the working-class, a class always increasing in numbers, and disciplined, united, organised by the very mechanism of the process of capitalist production itself . . . The knell of capitalist private property sounds. The expropriators are expropriated.(1867)[7]

The first quotation is from *Economic and Philosophic Manuscripts of 1844*, the second one from *Communist Manifesto* of 1848, the third and the fourth from *Capital*, Book I, the first German edition which appeared in 1867.

Hegel studied the economic conditions of England and its classical economics during his stay in Frankfurt (1797-1800) as a tutor in the home of a merchant.[8] The early 1820s, when Hegel was lecturing on *Naturrrecht und Staatswissenschaft*, was the latter period of the industrial revolution in England, where accumulation of wealth at one pole and that of misery and poverty at the other were developing in a horrible manner. Young Marx, who studied Hegel's philosophy of law in the early 1840s, was critical towards the idealism of Hegelian dialectics, but as far as the recognition of fundamental defects or contradictions of the modern bourgeois society are concerned, he apparently took quite the same view as Hegel, i.e. ever-increasing wealth of the minority and ever-increasing poverty of the majority. This view had not changed from *Economic and Philosophic Manuscript* of 1844 through Book I of *Capital* of 1867 and all through his life until his death in 1883.

[*Note:* The polarisation of British society to wealthy minority and poor majority was a general impression shared by the contemporaries in the second quarter of the nineteenth century. For instance, Gladstone, Chancellor of the Exchequer, made the following speech in the House of Commons on the 13th February 1843: 'It is one of the most melancholy features in the social state of this country that we see ... while there is at this moment a decrease in the consuming powers of the people, an increase of the pressure of privations and distress; there is at the same time a constant accumulation of wealth in the upper classes, an increase of the luxuriousness of their habits, and of their means of enjoyment.'[9]]

But in the second half of the nineteenth century the living conditions of the English working class tended to improvement, as Table 4.1 shows.

This table refers, of course, only to those employed. But even the Marxist economic historian, Professor E. J. Hobsbawm, University of London, had this to say: 'After 1848 the surplus population was absorbed, increasingly, into the capitalist market at home and abroad. Three industrial departments, mining, building and transportation, gave unskilled labourers ample chance of jobs.'[10] Thus Marx's

Table 4.1   Real wages in UK, 1841-80 (1850 = 100)[11]

1841	83	1851	102	1861	100	1871	121
1842	84	1852	102	1862	105	1872	122
1843	85	1853	105	1863	109	1873	128
1844	85	1854	96	1864	117	1874	133
1845	82	1855	85	1865	117	1875	135
1846	84	1856	96	1866	116	1876	137
1847	81	1857	96	1867	109	1877	133
1848	90	1858	102	1868	110	1878	132
1849	95	1859	104	1869	115	1879	137
1850	100	1860	103	1870	118	1880	134

conviction of an increasing mass poverty contradicts the historical realities in the latter half of the nineteenth century.

There was a marked difference between Hegel and Marx in seeking the solution to this contradiction in modern society. In looking for the reformed society, Hegel, with his 'closed' conception of the world, could not go beyond the Prussian state. Marx with his 'open' conception of the world and dialectics 'turned right side up', sought the eradication of the defects of modern society in the revolution, offsetting of bourgeois society, and the construction of the communist system by the proletariat who are the bearers of productive power of modern society.

This dialectics of development of capitalist society which leads to the negation of that society itself is the main theme of *Capital*. If the 'natural laws' described in *Capital*, the general law of capitalist accumulation, the law of the falling rate of profit, etc., had worked with 'iron necessity', the most advanced capitalist countries must have suffered the most violent contradiction of accumulation of wealth at one pole and that of poverty at the other and so the proletarian revolution would have broken out first in these countries.

Now it is clear that world history did not follow that course. The Russian revolution was the first one. Great Britain still preserves the capitalist system. And it is absurd to think that British society today has a wider gap between wealth and poverty than that of Marx's day and therefore is on the eve of the proletarian revolution. Nor is present-day Japan faced with a crisis of revolution fermented by ever-increasing accumulation of wealth on the one hand and poverty on the other.

This discrepancy between Marx's predictions and historical facts thereafter, shows us the necessity of re-examining the 'economic law of motion of modern society' developed in *Capital* which is the theoretical refinement of Marx's perspective on bourgeois society and revolutionary theory outlined in *Manifesto of the Communist Party*.

II   BASIC 'LAWS' DEVELOPED IN *CAPITAL*

1   Laws 'discovered' by Marx

It seems that Marx had a firm belief in his 'discovery' of laws of motion of society. Unlike Hegel's laws of development of society formulated 'upside down', in the sense that 'Idea' produced reality, Marx's laws, which were 'discovered'[12] – not 'invented' – by him, were inherent in society itself and so should have been infallible.

We know how Marx thought about the laws of society from the famous passage in the preface to the first German edition of *Capital*:

> Even when a society has got upon the right track for the discovery of the natural laws of its movement – and it is the ultimate aim of this work to lay bare the economic law of motion of modern society – it can neither clear by bold leaps, nor remove by legal enactments, the obstacles offered by the successive phases of its normal development. But it can shorten and lessen the birth-pangs.[13]

Man cannot arbitrarily change the laws of capitalist society because they objectively exist. However, by discovering and utilising them, we can 'lessen and shorten the birth-pangs' of transition to a higher and more rational society. This was his view of the laws of society and the aim of his economics. And it has been consistently followed by his followers. For instance, Dr Topekh, Soviet historian, who was in Tokyo in October 1959, told me something like this: 'The fundamental propositions of Marxian economics were not "invented", but "discovered" by Marx. So they are truth leaving no room for doubts, don't you agree?' My answer was, 'No'.

Here we must be aware of one thing: 'Laws' themselves should always be open to re-examination. 'Laws' (and working hypotheses) are formulated ('discovered' is rather misleading) by researchers through their observation of society. As a principle, they can include imperfection and errors. 'Laws' once regarded as perfect might be found unsatisfactory on second thought. 'Laws' once appropriate and

valid might become obsolete and useless following the development
and change of society itself. It is too easy-going to think that Marx's
laws are always true because they are not 'invented' but 'discovered' by
Marx. So let us now re-examine the two fundamental laws which are
closely interconnected and constitute the backbone of the economics of
Capital – the general law of capitalist accumulation and the law of the
falling rate of profit.

2 The general law of capitalist accumulation

The point of argument of the general law of accumulation in Chapter 25,
Book I of *Capital* is as follows: In capitalist society the rise of the so-
called 'organic composition of capital' – the ratio of constant capital to
variable capital – is slower than that of the 'technical composition of
capital' – the ratio of the mass of means of production to that of the
labour-power – which 'is an expression of the productiveness of
labour'.[14] As it is assumed that 'the increase or diminution of the
variable capital corresponds rigidly with the increase or diminution of
the number of the labourers employed',[15] the rise of the technical
composition of capital (or the labour-productivity) always surpasses
the increase in the number of the labourers employed. This means,
under Marx's assumption of 'a given wage' (see citation, note 19,
present chapter) that the ever-increasing supply of commodities with
the rise of labour-productivity always surpasses the purchasing power
of the working class and this gap becomes wider and wider as capitalist
society develops. Table 4.2 is an illustration by the author of Marx's
argument above, with additional concrete figures intended for precise
understanding.

Let us imagine a small model society with 100 workers. At first they
operate 300 units of means of production. Then, as a result of technical
progress, they come to be able to operate 30,000 units of means of
production, or if the workers were doubled, 60,000 units of means of
production. According to Marx's terminology, the technical composition of capital rose 100 times, or in a more usual expression, the labour
productivity rose 100 times.

[*Note:* For the purpose of showing the rise of labour-productivity,
number of products is a better and more accurate measure than number of
means of production. The latter means machinery, factory building, raw
materials, fuel and power, etc., which inevitably change their contents and
their way of combination as the result of technical progress. But for Marx,
measurement of productivity by the quantity of the means of production

Table 4.2   Technical and organic composition of capital

The number of means of production $\dfrac{300}{100}$ → $\dfrac{30000}{100}$ or $\dfrac{60000}{200}$
The number of workers employed

Technical composition rises 100 times

Amount of constant capital $\dfrac{100c}{100v}$ → $\dfrac{400c}{100v}$ or $\dfrac{800c}{200v}$
Amount of variable capital

Organic composition rises 4 times

---

was indispensable in order to combine the two kinds of composition of capital, technical and organic. Thus, according to his definition, technical composition is the ratio of the number or quantity of the means of production to the number of workers employed or the quantity of labour applied, and organic composition is that ratio translated into terms of value. This definition involves a confusion of logic. For its exposition quoting Marx's text, see Chapter 5 in this volume (citation, note 59) and the following explanation.]

With 100-fold rise of labour productivity or technical composition of capital, the price level of the means of production must have fallen considerably. Therefore, we assume that 4-fold constant capital would suffice to buy 100-fold means of production. So that the organic composition of capital rises 4 times.

These figures adopted in Table 4.2 have some ground in *Capital*. Marx gives an historical illustration as follows:

If the capital value employed today in spinning is $7/8$ constant and $1/8$ variable, whilst at the beginning of the 18th century it was $1/2$ constant and $1/2$ variable, on the other hand, the mass of raw materials, instruments of labour, etc. that a certain quantity of spinning labour consumes productively today, is many hundred times greater than at the beginning of the 18th century.[16]

In this example, 7 times rise of organic composition of capital reflects many hundred times rise of technical composition of capital. So the figures in Table 4.2 are chosen to show that 4 times rise of organic composition reflects 100 times rise of technical composition.

Now if a society with the same number of workers paid with the same amount of wages attains 100-fold productivity rise, the supply of goods will inevitably far exceed the demand for them. In the process of production expansion the increase of producers' goods is expected to be larger than that of consumers' goods. But under the assumption of 100-fold rise of the productive power of society, we cannot think of a case where increase occurs in producers' goods alone and not at all in consumers' goods. The small model society of Table 4.2 would inevitably be afflicted with the over-production of consumers' goods which leads to an economic crisis. Even if we assume that the number of workers employed were doubled during the process from 100 to 200, that would not improve the situation. 200 workers produce 200-fold products. The severity of over-production remains exactly the same.

This is the skeleton of the development and collapse of the capitalist system described in Chapter 25, Book I of *Capital*. In short, the development of productivity in the capitalist society takes the form of rising composition of organic capital. As the productive power of society increases, more and more goods are produced on the one hand, and the wage-level of the labourers remains fixed on the other. Ever-increasing productivity gives rise to an ever-widening gap between productivity and consuming power, severer economic crises, larger scale of unemployment and more miserable conditions of life for the labourers. If this is the 'natural law' of the capitalist society, its collapse if apparently inevitable.

3   The Law of the Falling Rate of Profit

This argument of the rise of the organic composition of capital is further developed as 'The law of the tendency of the rate of profit to fall' in Part III, Book III of *Capital*. Look at Table 4.3.

This is the same model society with 100 workers as shown in Table 4.2. But now '*s*' (surplus value or surplus labour) is added to the story. In Period 1, 100 workers are supposed to work 200 hours altogether, 100 hours (necessary labour) for themselves, i.e. for gaining their wages, and the remaining 100 hours (surplus labour) for producing surplus value which goes into the hands of capitalists. At first they operate constant capital embodying 100 hours of 'dead' or 'past' labour and expend 200 hours of 'living' labour. So the commodities produced, say, 300 units, have the value of 300 hours, which is expressed in terms of Yen ($1h = Y1$). This amount of value 300 is divided into two parts from the capitalist point of view: total capital $(c+v)$ of 200 and profit (surplus value) of 100. Thus the rate of profit in this case is 50%.

Table 4.3   The illustration of the gist of the law of the falling
rate of profit

Pd_1	$100c + 100v + 100s = 300h$	$(300G)$
Pd_2	$400c + 100v + 100s = 60h$	$(30,000G)$

Notes: The figures are two of the five 'hypothetical series'
shown at the beginning of Ch. 13, Book III of *Capital*,
in a form arranged by me (see Ch. 2, Table 2.3 in the
present volume). h (hours) as a unit of labour-input,
numbers of G (goods), productivity and price of
commodities are supplemented by T.H.

        Technical composition : rises 100 times
        Organic composition   : rises 4 times
        Productivity *   : rises 50 times
        Price of commodities : falls to $1/50$
        Rate of profit   : falls to $1/5$

    * For explanation, see (*Note*) in the following
    subsection 4.

Then in Period 2, as the result of technical progress, the 100 workers
are supposed to be able to operate 100-fold means of production and
therefore produce 100-fold commodities, i.e. 30,000 units. In other
words, the technical composition of capital is now 100 times higher
than that of the previous period. But, as is the case in Table 4.2 the
accompanying rise of organic composition of capital is supposed to be
only 4 times. So 400 hours of 'dead' labour ($400c$) and 200 hours of
'living' labour ($100v$ plus $100s$) are materialised in 30,000 commodities.
Moreover, the rate of profit falls to 20%, as total capital of 500 value
($400c$ plus $100v$) produces profit of 100 value ($100s$).

The fall of the rate of profit from Period 1 to 2 needs more
explanation. Suppose in Period 1 average firms invest 100 Yen in
constant capital and 100 Yen in variable capital and employ 100
workers who produce 300 products which are sold at 300 Yen, thus
leaving 100 Yen profit (surplus value) to the capitalists, the rate of
profit being 50%.

If one firm adopts a new technique by investing 400 Yen in constant
capital and succeeds in producing 100-fold commodities with 100
workers who are paid 100 Yen as before, this firm can obtain an

enormous amount of super-profit even if it makes a substantial price-cut.

But competitors will follow suit. As time goes by the new technique spreads generally and the superior firms of yesterday become average firms of today. Then super-profit vanishes and the products are sold at the price level reflecting the amount of value (labour) embodied in them. So 30,000 products made with 500 Yen total capital *(400c + 100v)* are now sold at 600 Yen $(400c + 100v + 100s)$. Thus the profit rate falls to 20%.

The drive of individual capitalists for higher profit rates brings on technical progress which, once popularised, lowers the average rate of profit, contrary to the capitalists' wishes. This is understood to be the dialectics of the law of the falling rate of profit.

It is to be noted that this law means the death sentence of capitalism. Investment is the driving force of capitalist development. The funds for investment are drawn from profit. If the rate of profit falls, the rate of investment must also fall and the rate of economic growth must be slackened. So the law of the falling rate of profit is in modern terminology the law of the falling rate of economic growth.

[*Note:* This one-sided law, apparently incompatible with historic developments, comes from Marx's assumption that the productivity rise in the capitalist society inevitably takes the form of heightening of the organic composition of capital. In the terminology of contemporary economics, technical progress always heightens the capital-coefficient, which, of course, is not in accord with facts. On this point detailed explanation is given in Chapter 5, Section III, 3, in the present volume.

In capitalist society, the more productive power develops, the nearer the rate of economic growth draws to absolute stagnation. According to Marx's words, 'the development of the productivity of labour creates out of the falling rate of profit a law which at a certain point comes into antagonistic conflict with this development'[17] and must be finally overcome by the overthrow of capitalism itself.

4 Self-contradiction involved in the law

This law, 'inherent' in the capitalist system and 'discovered' by Marx, however, involves self-contradiction in itself. First, pay attention to the value-price structure of economics in *Capital*. Marx writes in Chapter 10, Book 1 that 'the value of commodities is in inverse ratio to the productiveness of labour'.[18] (For exact understanding of this thesis, see Table 1.1 and Chapter 2, Section II, subsection 1 in the present volume.)

Let us re-examine the figures shown in Table 4.3 with this price structure in mind. In period 1, 300 commodities embodying 300 hours of labour (value) are sold at 300 Yen, so the price of one commodity is one Yen. In Period 2, owing to a 100-fold rise of productivity caused by the increase of constant capital from 100 Yen to 400 Yen, 30,000 commodities are made with 600 hours of labour (value). So one commodity now embodies only $1/50$ hour of labour (value), which is $1/50$ Yen.

[*Note:*   Here we must distinguish between two kinds of productivity. The rise of productivity of 100 workers is 100 times. This is related only to the living labour: $100v$ (hours) plus $100s$ (hours). But productivity or 'productiveness of labour' which is 'in inverse ratio to the value (price)' is a different thing. The labour in this context involves both dead labour (c) and living labour (v plus s). So the unit price of the commodities drops to $1/50$ from Period 1 to 2. But Marx fails to notice this clear distinction and calls both simply 'productivity (or productiveness) of labour'.

Now 100 workers receiving wages of 100 Yen in Period 1 get 100 commodities because they are sold at 1 Yen per unit. But the same number of workers receiving the same amount of wages in Period 2 should be able to buy 5,000 commodities because they now cost only $1/50$ Yen per unit. Nominal wages of 100 workers are unchanged through Periods 1 and 2. Real wages, however, increase in proportion to the rate of productivity rise.

Marx could not have thought of such a kind of capitalist society. Figures in Table 4.3 are those used by Marx himself as the illustration of the law of the falling rate of profit. In introducing these 'hypothetical series', Marx writes:

Assuming *a given wage* and working-day, a variable capital, for instance of 100, represents a certain number of employed labourers. It is the index of this number. Suppose 100 are the wages of 100 labourers for, say, one week.[19] (emphasis – T.H.)

Marx assumed a given wage because, he thought, capitalists as a rule pay the same amount of wages for the same amount of labour irrespective of its productivity. Increase of earnings due to productivity rise is the fruit of successful entrepreneurship and has nothing to do with the labourers from the capitalists' viewpoint. So for Marx the 'hypothetical series' of Table 4.3 must have been an unmistakable demonstration of the aggravating contradiction between productive power and consumer power. He describes the situation as follows in Chapter 15, Book III, 'Internal contradictions of the law": 'The more productiveness develops, the more it finds itself at variance with the narrow basis on which the conditions of consumption rest.'[20]

100 Yen wages of 100 workers must be 'given' (must have the same purchasing power) throughout Periods 1 and 2 along the line of thought developed in the chapters explaining the law, but at the same time 100 workers getting 100 Yen wages in Period 2 are in fact able to buy 50-fold goods as a logical corollary of the labour-value pricing theory formulated by Marx himself. This is an obvious self-contradiction. Marx might have been vaguely aware of this fatal error. A passage which is found several pages after the 'hypothetical series' gives us a clue:

> We shall entirely ignore here that with the advance of capitalist production and the attendant development of the productiveness of labour and multiplication of production branches, hence products, the same amount of value represents a progressively increasing mass of use-values and enjoyments.[21]

'Development of productiveness of labour' means that 'the same amount of value represents a progressively increasing mass of use-values and enjoyments.' Paraphrased in modern terminology, it means that when the productivity of labour rises, the same amount of labour produces more goods and services. If we 'entirely ignore' that 'the same amount of value represents a progressively increasing mass of use-values and enjoyments' when 'the development of the productiveness of labour' occurs, we have to deny that the same amount of labour produces more goods and services when labour productivity rises. That boils down to the self-contradictory thesis that labour productivity does not rise when it rises. This fallacy originates from another fallacy of entirely ignoring, or rather forgetting, the fall in prices in inverse ratio to productivity-rise. (How Marx came to 'forget' the price-fall in Ch. 13, Book III of *Capital* is analysed in detail in Sec. I, Ch. 7 of the present book.)

If we admit this inadmissible thesis, we can 'entirely ignore' in Period 2 of Table 4.3 that 100-fold commodities are produced with 50-fold rise of productivity and 100 workers buy 50-fold consumer goods with the same wages. They are assumed to buy just the same amount of goods as in Period 1 and the gap between the developing productivity and the restricted consuming power of the masses clearly appears in the hypothetical small society of Table 4.3.

But, evidently, this line of thinking of a violation of Aristotle's law of contradiction. Here we would like to confirm that the law of the falling rate of profit, which is the most fundamental of the laws included in the system of economic theory of *Capital*, not only fails to correspond with historical reality but holds within itself a fatal error in its logical construction. Then, if this law constitutes the theoretical ground for the predicted collapse of capitalism and the proletarian revolution, an overall re-examination of these events must follow from the very nature of the matter.

5 The law, impoverishment and revolution

As I explained above, Marx took the same view as Hegel in regard to the prospect of modern bourgeois society and thought that the development of capitalism inevitably causes the worsening of the living conditions or the 'absolute impoverishment' of the working class. This view was theoretically refined in the laws of the rise of organic composition of capital and the falling rate of profit in *Capital*. I will summarise his argument in Chapter 25, Book I of *Capital*, adding one factor, the relation between the quantity of employment and the working population. In capitalist society, 'the absolute size of the families stands in inverse proportion to the height of wages, and therefore to the amount of means of subsistence of which the different categories of labourers dispose'.[22] In short: 'Poor people have more children.' So that the rapid growth of the working population is the rule. But the quantity of employment increases only in proportion to the increase of variable capital. Accordingly, as an historical trend, the unemployment rate goes up in the process of capitalist development. In Marx's own words: 'The greater the social wealth, the functioning of capital . . . . and, therefore, also the absolute mass of the proletariat and the productiveness of its labour, the greater is the industrial reserve army . . . The relative mass of the industrial reserve army increases therefore with the potential energy of wealth.'[23]

Table 4.4 is a variant of the figures in Table 4.3, which illustrate the law of the falling rate of profit, supplemented with hypothetical figures expressing the relation between the quantity of unemployment and working population.

In Period 1 this small model society of Table 4.4 is supposed to operate with constant capital of 100 Yen, and employs 100 workers with 100 Yen variable capital and produces 300 units of commodities

Table 4.4   Productivity rise → impoverishment → revolution

Pd_1	$100c + 100v + 100s$	working population = 100
		number of employed = 100
		rate of unemployment = 0%
Pd_2	$800c + 200v + 200s$	working population = 300
		number of employed = 200
		rate of unemployment = 33.3%
	(Assumption)	Productivity rises 50 times.
		Commodity prices fall to 1/50
	(Question)	Living standard of workers
		drops to $2/3$? or
		rises to $2/3 \times 50 = 33.3$ times?

amounting to 300 Yen. For simplicity, the number of the working population is also assumed to be 100. Therefore, the rate of unemployment is 0%.

After some years in Period 2, constant capital is increased to 800 Yen and variable capital is doubled to 200 Yen, and the society employs 200 workers. Suppose productivity with regard to 'living labour' $(v+s)$ is raised 100 times and 200 workers produce 200-fold, i.e. 60,000 commodities. But in this case, as constant capital (dead labour) is increased to 8 times, 800 Yen, the rise of productivity with regard to 'dead and living labour' $(c+v+s)$ must be 50 times. In consequence, the commodity prices must have fallen to $1/50$.

Now, if we forget or 'ignore' the increase of commodities and the fall of their prices as Marx did above, the real wages of workers are thought to be exactly the same as those of 100 workers in Period 1. Taking into consideration the increase of the whole working population to 300, the existence of 100 unemployed workers must pull down the living standard of the working population as a whole to $2/3$. As capitalism develops, as more goods are produced, the life of workers gets worse. If this is the inevitable law of capitalist development, it must also be inevitable that the proletariat cannot find any other way to survive than to overthrow capitalism by means of revolution.

But in the model society of Table 4.4, the price level of period 2 must have fallen to $1/50$ of that of Period 1 according to Marx's own

argument developed in Chapter 10, Book I. Therefore, the real-wage
level of 200 employed workers in Period 2 must have risen to 50 times
and the average living standard of the whole working population (200
employed plus 100 unemployed) must have risen to 33.3 times.

Thus, we find that Marx's grand dynamics – the rise of productivity
in capitalist society, the heightening of organic composition of capital,
the absolute impoverishment of the proletariat, and the end of
capitalism through revolution – is now shaken from its foundation
by the application of the thesis established by Marx himself on
productivity and price level. We return to this later, in Chapter 5 of the
present volume (Section III, 3).

III COMMUNISM AND HUMANISM

The necessity of emancipation from dogmatic belief in Marxism does
not end in the spheres of economics and political science. It covers the
ideal aspect of human life.

Marxists very often make assertions to the effect that Marxism is the
highest form of humanism. The logic runs as follows: Capitalism brings
about dehumanisation (in Hegelian terminology '*Selbstentfremdung*')
of man. Man can restore the humanity stripped from him only in a
communist society. So, Marxism, which aims at the overthrow of
capitalism and establishment of communism, is the highest form of
humanism of our times.

Here is one example. A British Marxist philosopher, John Lewis,
writes in his collected essays *Marxism and the Open Mind*:

> Marxism is the highest development of humanism, it is the form in which the
> age-long contradiction between human advance and human subjection is
> resolved; it is the last rebellion of the oppressed, and the only one in which
> success is possible. It takes origin from the rebellion of man against inhuman
> conditions and its single aim is the recovery of man's lost humanity. This is
> the very essence of humanism, and Marx is humanism in its contemporary
> form.[24]

The origin of this type of thought by Lewis is presumed to be in the
following passage written by Marx in *Economic and Philosophic
Manuscripts of 1844*:

> Communism as the positive transcendence of private property and human
> self-estrangement, and therefore as the real appropriation of the human
> essence by and for man; communism therefore as the complete return of man

to himself as a social (i.e. human) being – a return become conscious, and accomplished within the entire wealth of previous development. This communism, as fully-developed naturalism, equals humanism equals naturalism.[25]

Is the following simple formula – capitalism causes perfect deprivation of humanity and communism brings about perfect restoration of it – adequate to explain historic realities? 'Perfect deprivation of humanity' might have been a vivid expression of actual living conditions of the proletariat in the England of the nineteenth century. However, one can hardly deny the contemporary capitalism, with all its defects and faults, is far more advanced than the British capitalism which offered materials for Marx's *Capital*, in physical living conditions, political rights, spiritual freedom, etc. of the working class. Without closing one's eyes to historical facts, one cannot assert that dehumanisation has been steadily going on.

How about, then, the actual situation in communist societies which ought to have been established with the ideal of perfect recovery of humanity? It is true that evils originating from the very nature of the capitalist system have been stamped out in communist societies. But the people of Soviet Russia groaned under the tyranny of Stalin. We know the uprising in Hungary in 1956 and its suppression by the Soviet Army. The Berlin Wall still stands. Communist societies also have their own serious troubles. It is clear that they cannot claim to have achieved their object of 'recovery of man's lost humanity'.

[*Note:* This chapter was written in 1962. Now in 1989 the list of the dehumanising events should be supplemented with the crushing of 'the spring in Prague' and others enumerated in the beginning part of the Preface. And in the communist world attempts to recover 'lost humanity' seem to be under way in various forms and degrees, including a back current in China of suppressing the democratisation movement by guns and tanks of the People's 'Liberation' army.

IV EPILOGUE

Now, how ought we to evaluate Marx and his theory? Arnold Toynbee once wrote in correspondence with John Strachey:

Don't take Marx as either an inspired and infallible prophet on the one hand. Nor on the other hand dismiss him as one more out-of-date 19th-century sociologist. No, Marx was just an ordinary man of genius.[26]

So the fatal defect in Marx's argument pointed out here only means that Marx was also an ordinary human being. Marx was born in 1818. I was born nearly one hundred years later, in 1913. It should be quite natural that I can criticise Marx and find faults in his works. Bernard Shaw once said, 'Shakespeare was taller than I am, but I am standing on his shoulder.' One who studies Marx today should be standing on the latter's shoulder, and, therefore, able to command a better view.

What we ought to learn from Marx are not the 'infallible' laws he 'discovered', but his ideals of the emancipation of man, and of constructing materially affluent and spiritually free societies in the full meaning of the words.

5 The Materialist Concept of History and the Structure of *Capital*: Historical Necessity vs. Man's Responsibility

I *CAPITAL* AS A CORNERSTONE OF MARXIAN IDEOLOGY

Nowadays few people would be so naive as to believe that 'the Marxist doctrine is omnipotent, because it is true', although this is a statement by Lenin in his famous short essay *Three Origins and Three Component parts of Marxism*[1] In the light of the latter half of the twentieth century, Marx's argument for the inevitable collapse of capitalism and the coming of communism sounds strongly deterministic.

[*Note:* This part was written in 1967. Marx's determinism sounds quite hollow in 1989.]

Of course, Marx himself did not feel that way. He was full of confidence in 'the discovery of the natural laws[2] of the motion of bourgeois society. He wrote in his preface to the first German edition of *Capital*:

It is not a question of the higher or lower degree of development of the social antagonisms that result from the natural laws of capitalist production. It is a question of these laws themselves, of these tendencies working with iron necessity towards inevitable results. The country that is more developed industrially only shows, to the less developed, the image of its future . . . . In England the progress of social disintegration is palpable. When it has reached a certain point, it must re-act on the Continent.[3]

For him it was not that he was subjectively deterministic but rather that the laws determining the course of development of society had objective existence, and they were reflected upon his consciousness.

On the higher form of society superseding the capitalist one, he says in Chapter 48, Book III of *Capital*:

> Beyond it (the realm of necessity) begins that development of human energy which is an end itself, the true realm of freedom, which, however, can blossom forth only with this realm of necessity as its basis. The shortening of the working-day is its basic prerequisite.[4]

Thus the ascent of man from the realm of necessity to the realm of freedom takes place in accordance with social laws working with iron necessity. Although Marx maintains in the eleventh thesis on Feuerbach that 'the philosophers have only *interpreted* the world, in various ways; the point, however, is to *change* it',[5] the active role of man in this change is fundamentally restricted by the laws regulating the process. It might be called a materialist version of Hegel's 'cunning of reason'.[6]

But we know now, through historical facts Marx did not know, that he was too optimistic to have expected the advent of 'the true realm of freedom' through a communist revolution. On the other hand, Gunnar Myrdal of Sweden, 'a realm of necessity' by Marx's nineteenth century classification, tells of 'the very idea of introducing, in the capitalist state, peacefully and without revolution . . . coordinated public policies of such a far-reaching consequence that they could gradually bring the economy of a country to function in accordance with the essential idea of economic planning'.[7]

Under these circumstances it seems especially necessary for me to inquire into the inner connection between dialectical philosophy and economics in *Capital*. According to Lenin: 'If Marx did not leave behind him a '*Logic*' (with a capital letter), he did leave the *Logic of Capital* . . . In *Capital*, Marx applied to a single science logic, dialectics and the theory of knowledge of materialism (three words are not needed: it is one and the same thing) which has taken everything valuable in Hegel and developed it further.'[8] And: 'Since the appearance of *Capital*, the materialist conception of history is no longer a hypothesis, but a scientifically proven proposition.'[9] In a word, *Capital* is the cornerstone of the whole ideological edifice of Marxism.

II   METHOD OF MARX: ITS HISTORICAL BACKGROUND AND DIALECTICS

1   'Natural laws' of society

Marx was not the only social scientist who propounded 'natural laws' of society. E. H. Carr in his *What is History?* enumerates Gresham's law, Adam Smith's law of the market, Malthus' law of population, Lassalle's iron law of wages, Edmund Burke's 'laws of commerce, which are the laws of nature, and consequently the Laws of God', and Henry Thomas Buckle's 'one glorious principle of universal and undeviating regularity', which permeates the course of human affairs.[10]

What influenced these political economists and historians was the remarkable progress of natural science since the seventeenth century. Galilei's astronomical discovery, Boyle's law on the volume of gases, Newton's law of gravity and so forth, fostered a conviction that unshakable laws of nature had been discovered and established. Engels, in his speech at the graveside of Marx, had this to say: 'Just as Darwin discovered the law of development of organic nature, so Marx discovered the law of development of human history.'[11] In fact it is true that, *The Origin of Species* by Darwin and *A Contribution to the Critique of political Economy* by Marx happened to be published in the same year, 1859.

In this connection, Carr writes: 'Students of society, consciously or unconsciously desiring to assert the scientific status of their studies, adopted the same languages and believed themselves to be following the same procedure.'[12] Marx had the conviction that the laws of society he thought he had discovered carried the same degree of strict necessity and causality as the laws of nature proper. It was the standpoint of Marx himself to view 'the evolution of the economic formation of society as a process of natural history', as shown in the preface to the first German edition of *Capital*.[13] But, at the same time he stressed the difference between his social laws and the laws of nature in one aspect. In the Afterword to the second German edition of *Capital*, he cites a friendly comment by Professor Kaufman in which we read:

It will be said, the general laws of economic life are one and the same, no matter whether they are applied to the present or the past. This Marx directly denies. According to him, such abstract laws do not exist. On the contrary, in his opinion every historical period has laws of its own . . . As soon as society has outlived a given period of development, and is passing over from one given stage to another, it begins to be subject also to other laws. In a word, economic life offers us a phenomenon analogous to the history of evolution in other branches of biology. The old economists misunderstood the nature of economic laws when they likened them to the laws of physics and chemistry.[14]

This interpretation of Marx's method is evaluated by Marx himself as 'what else is he picturing but the dialectic method?'[15]

2   Obligatory correspondence of production: relations to the productive forces

(1) Crux of the materialist concept of history

In order to understand what Marx means by 'dialectic method' in this case, we need to proceed to the fundamental law of historical materialism underlying the respective economic laws governing societies in their various stages of development. Marx writes in *Wage Labour and Capital*:

> These social relations into which the producers enter with one another . . . will naturally vary according to the character of the means of production. With the invention of a new instrument of warfare, firearms, the whole internal organisation of the army necessarily changed . . . the social relations of production, change, are transformed, with the change and development of the material means of production, the productive forces.[16]

In the preface to *A Contribution to the Critique of Political Economy*:

> In the social production of their existence, men inevitably enter into definite relations, which are independent of their will, namely relations of production appropriate to a given stage in the development of their material forces of production. The totality of these relations of production constitutes the economic structure of society, the real foundation, on which arises a legal and political superstructure and to which correspond definite forms of social consciousness. The mode of production of material life conditions the general process of social, political and intellectual life . . . At a certain stage of development, the material productive forces of society come into conflict with the existing relations of production or – this merely expresses the same thing in legal terms – with the property relations . . . From forms of development of the productive forces these relations turn into their fetters. Then begins an era of social revolution . . . It is always necessary to distinguish between the material transformation of the economic conditions of production, which can be determined with the precision of natural science, and the legal, political, religious . . . in short, ideological forms in which men become conscious of this conflict and fight it out . . . No social order is ever destroyed before all the productive forces for which it is sufficient have been developed, and new superior relations of production never replace older ones before the material conditions for their existence have matured within the framework of the old society.[17]

The crux of the formulation is, in Stalin's expression, 'the economic law of the obligatory correspondence of production relations to the nature of the productive forces'.[18] Lenin has the following remark in *What 'the Friends of the People' Are*:

Materialism provided an absolutely objective criterion by singling out 'production relations' as the structure of society, and by making it possible to apply to these relations that general scientific criterion of recurrence . . . another reason why this hypothesis for the first time made a *scientific* sociology possible was that only the reduction of social relations to production relations and of the latter to the level of the productive forces, provided a firm basis for the conception that the development of formation as of society is a process of natural history.[19]

Marx himself attached great importance to the instruments of production among the productive forces. Already in *The German Ideology* (written in 1845–6) we find his statement on the relation between instruments of production and forms of property as follows: 'In big industry the contradiction between the instrument of production and private property appears.'[20] And in *Capital* he maintains:

It is not the articles made, but how they are made, and by what instruments, that enables us to distinguish different economic epochs. Instruments of labour not only supply a standard of the degree of development to which human labour has attained, but they are also indicators of the social conditions under which that labour is carried on.[21]

In short, his line of argument is: When the productive forces come to be developed to the utmost limit within the production relations which hitherto fostered them, the latter turns into their fetters. This starts an era of the transformation from the old production relations into the new ones, which can be determined 'with the precision of natural science'.

(2) The law of the transformation of quantity into quality

Is this simple schema compatible with our present-day knowledge?

The schema is the case in which one of the three main laws of dialectics, the law of the transformation of quantity into quality, is applied.[22] The other two laws are: the law of the interpenetration of opposites (see Sec.III, Ch. 6 in the present volume) and the law of the negation of the negation.[23]

Take, for example, a steam boiler. Beyond a certain extent of steam pressure, it will explode. The strength of the boiler and the steam pressure are both measurable. So the explosion can be predicted 'with the precision of natural science' by dint of Boyle's law. In this case it is not wrong to say that a certain amount of quantitative change causes a qualitative change.[24]

But how about the productive forces and production relations? How can we measure the productive forces, an inexact and sometimes controversial notion in itself? If we make a forecast that when GNP per annum in Japan reaches, for instance, three hundred trillion (3 followed by 14 zeros) Yen, the capitalist relations of production will be blown up and superseded by socialism, it is anything but a scientific prediction. Moreover, what is capitalism? Britain in the middle of the nineteenth century where polarisation of wealth and poverty proceeded, Britain today which is called a welfare state (though a little less so under Premier Thatcher's rule), Germany under the Nazi (national *socialism*) regime, etc., are all usually classified as capitalism. Then, what is socialism? The USSR is generally thought to be an established socialist country. But the Chinese communists in the era of the Great Cultural Revolution called it 'state monopoly capitalism, 'Soviet revisionist Imperialism',[25] and now they say that their market-oriented socialism is the right path. The Yugoslav people claim that they are aiming at the realisation of a truly Marxist socialism, although they have very often been called reformist by other socialist countries.

Capitalism and socialism are, unlike a steam boiler, complicated, fluid and ever-changing social systems. The working 'necessity of transition from capitalism to socialism' cannot mean anything definite. It is sheer nonsense to assert that by the development of an unmeasurable factor, at a certain stage, there occurs the transition from something indefinite to some other thing indefinite and its time is predictable 'with the precision of natural science'.

Next, let us examine the role of the instruments of production, a concrete and definite concept compared with the ambiguous productive forces. Marx writes in the *Poverty of Philosophy*: 'The hand-mill gives you society with the feudal lord; the steam-mill with the industrial capitalist.'[26] But ancient Greece already had a water-wheel-mill that was more advanced than the hand-mill. A socialist revolution occurred in the Russia of the steam-mill age. And now, the capitalist countries of Britain, the US, France, Japan and the socialist countries, the USSR and China, side by side, have attained the technical level capable of controlling atomic energy. There exists no necessary correspondence between the development of instruments of production and the transformation of production relations.

(3) The Law of the negation of the negation

And yet, the hypothesis of 'the obligatory correspondence of production relations to the nature of the productive forces' is said to have been given a scientific demonstration by the economics of *Capital*. Lenin asserts in the above cited essay that 'Marx . . . was the first to put sociology on a scientific basis by establishing the concept of the economic formation of society as the sum-total of given production relations, by establishing the fact that the development of such formation is a process of natural history'.[27]

Let me quote another part of Professor Kaufman's comment on *Capital* quoted by Marx in the Afterword to the second German edition:

> With the varying degree of development of productive power, social conditions and the laws governing them vary too. Whilst Marx sets himself the task of following and explaining from this point of view the economic system established by the sway of capital, he is only formulating, in a strictly scientific manner, the aim that every accurate investigation into economic life must have. The scientific value of such an inquiry lies in the disclosing of the special laws that regulate the origin, existence, development, death of a given social organism and its replacement by another and higher one. And it is this value that, in point of fact, Marx's book has.[28]

Now let us examine the scientific value of the dialectical method applied in *Capital*. For that purpose it will be useful to cite the famous passage in which Marx predicts the advent of Communism.

> The capitalist mode of appropriation, the result of the capitalist mode of production, produces capitalist private property. This is *the first negation* of individual property, as founded on the labour of the proprietor. But capitalist production begets, with the inexorability of a *law of Nature*, its own negation. It is *the negation of the negation*. This does not re-establish private property for the producer, but gives him individual property based on the acquisitions of the capitalist era: i.e. on co-operation and the possession in common of the land and of the means of production.'[29] (emphasis – T.H.)

Here, as we see, the third law of dialectics, that of the negation of the negation, is employed. This use of dialectics was severely criticised by Eugen Dühring as follows:

> This historical sketch (of the genesis of the so-called primitive accumulation of capital in England) is relatively the best part of Marx's book, and would be even better if it had not relied on the dialectical crutch to help out its scholarly crutch. The Hegelian negation of the negation, in default of anything better and clearer has in fact to serve here as the midwife to deliver the future from the womb of the past . . . It would be difficult to convince a sensible man of the necessity of the common ownership of land and capital, on the basis of credence in Hegelian word-juggling such as the negation of the negation . . . The nebulous hybrids of Marx's conceptions will not

however appear strange to anyone who realises what nonsense can be concocted with Hegelian dialectics as the scientific basis, or rather what nonsense must necessarily spring from it.'[30]

Engels believed that he was successful in defending Marx's position as he asserted in Anti-Dühring:

Marx merely shows from history, and here states in a summarised form, that just as formerly petty industry by its very development necessarily created the conditions of its own annihilation, i.e. of the expropriation of the small proprietors, so now the capitalist mode of production has likewise itself created the material conditions from which it must perish. The process is a historical one, and if it is at the same time a dialectical process, this is not Marx's fault . . . By characterising the process as the negation of the negation, Marx does not intend to prove that the process was historically necessary. On the contrary: only after he has proved that in fact the process has partially already occurred, and partially *must occur in the future*, he in addition characterises it as a process which develops in accordance with a definite dialectical law. That is all.[31] (emphasis – T.H.)

Engels emphasises the historical and empirical character of Marx's method and concludes that his dialectical formulation necessarily comes from the dialectical nature of the object of the study itself. But, as a matter of fact, it is not that Marx gave the dialectical formulation after he proved the process historically but that the dialectical prediction on the advent of communism had been repeatedly made years before he wrote *Capital*. Already in *Economic and philosophic Manuscripts of 1844* he stated that 'communism is the position as the negation of the negation, and is hence the *actual* phase necessary for the next stage of historical development in the process of human emancipation and recovery. Communism is the necessary pattern and the dynamic principle of the immediate future.'[32] Then, in *The German Ideology*, written in 1845–6, he stressed:

It is *empirically established* that, by the overthrow of the existing state of society by the communist revolution and the abolition of private property which is identical with it, this power (of the world market) . . . will be dissolved: and that then the liberation of each single individual will be accomplished in the measure in which history becomes transformed into world history.'[33] (emphasis – T.H.)

The conclusion that the fall of capitalism and the rise of communism are both inevitable had been 'empirically' established as early as 1845–6. What a strange empiricism! And in *Capital*, according to

Engels, Marx historically proved the process which must occur in the future. Is it possible at all to prove *historically* the necessity of communist revolution in the future?

Marx might have made his inference in this way: The inherent laws regulating the origin, development and death of capitalist society were empirically at least in part verified by the birth of the capitalist system, the first negation. Then, through his empirical researches in that social system, the inevitability of communist revolution, the negation of the negation, was also somehow historically proved. Now how could the dialectics of this future event be empirically demonstrated?

He must have started from the premise that the dialectical laws of the motion of capitalist society are intrinsic in it, and through the medium of the empirical study of them, arrived at the conclusion that the laws were proved, they surely existed. And he did indeed attempt to offer scientific proof of the inevitable collapse of capitalism by presenting the fundamental laws of motion of capitalist society, the general law of capitalist accumulation and the law of the falling rate of profit. The basic conclusion which results from these two laws combined is, in the terminology of contemporary economics, that technical progress in the capitalist society is inevitably capital-intensive. This conclusion is not justified because the nature of invention can be capital-intensive, neutral or capital-saving depending on different sets of historical conditions which we cannot foretell. Hence the criticism of Marx by Joan Robinson!

> If there is a fundamental defect in capitalism it must have deeper roots than a mere accident of technique.[34]

But since he never did empirically establish any of his points (it would have been impossible since they are not true), his 'proof' of the dialectical laws governing the future of capitalism was nothing but a typical example of circular reasoning or the fallacy of begging the question.

III   THE DIALECTICAL STRUCTURE OF CAPITAL

Contradiction – a unique universal in both Hegelian and Marxian dialectics – appears in the materialist concept of history as that between productive power (forces) and relations of production. Self-movement of this Contradiction takes the form of the well-known triad, affirmation, negation, and negation of the negation, in the description in *Capital* of the natural laws regulating the origin, development and death of the capitalist system.

1 Affirmation: the commodity

'Our investigation must . . . begin with the analysis of a commodity.'[35] This is the sentence we find at the beginning of the first Book of *Capital*. From the methodological, dialectical point of view, this commodity is usually interpreted as the unity of two opposites, use-value and value, concrete-useful-labour and abstract-human-labour. Use-values, produced by useful labour, 'constitute the substance of all wealth, whatever may be the social form of that wealth'.[36]

Value and its bearer the commodity, however, come about only in the social system where 'private individuals or groups of individuals . . . carry on their work independently of each other.'[37]

In other words, use-values become commodities only in societies where anarchical production prevails on the basis of private ownership. The logical corollary for Marx, therefore, is that the abrogation of private ownership must lead to the extinction of value, commodity, and money, i.e. the liberation of man from the 'fetishism' of commodities.[38]

The development of commodity production is the process of the self-movement of the Contradiction inherent in a commodity. The opposition of use-value and value[39] involved in a commodity is objectified, alienated or estranged, and develops into the external opposition of commodities vs. money, and then into the antagonism of labour vs. capital and finally leads to the collapse of the capitalist system and the realisation of communist society.

For instance, D. Rosenberg, a noted Soviet economist, writes in his *Commentary on Capital*:

> To study capitalism in its birth and development – this is what is demanded by dialectics – means to start it from the beginning of its history, i.e . . . from the genesis of the commodity form of products, the genesis of the contradiction[40] between use-value and value. As Lenin taught us,[41] already in this contradiction all the contradictions of capitalist production are included.[42]

However, does the opposition or contradiction between use-value and value really exist? Rosenberg asserts to this effect as follows:

Results obtained through the method of formal logic must be supplemented and processed . . . The answer, 'yes, yes; no, no', must be supplemented by the answer, 'yes, no; no, yes'. Based on formal logic, one cannot contend that even a single element of use-value does not exist in value on the one hand, and, without use-value value does not exist on the other'.[43]

Is this proposition on the relation between use-value and value describable or understandable only with the help of yes–no dialectics? No, it should not be the case. Use-value is the objective utility of a commodity.[44] Value is abstract human labour embodied in a commodity.[45]

They are differentiated by definition. Thus, although they both exist in a commodity, it is self-explanatory that 'even a single element of use-value does not exist in value'. But 'without use-value value does not exist', is an ambiguous statement, lacking the key word, a commodity. Perhaps it means that 'a commodity without use-value does not exist', or 'a thing cannot be commodity without use-value even if it is loaded with abstract human labour', or 'abstract human labour embodied in a thing cannot be value if the thing is useless'.

These three statements, supplemented with the word 'commodity' or 'thing', are self-evident. We do not find any yes-and-no dialectics between them and the first one. When Rosenberg says: 'Use-value does not exist in value on the one hand, and, without use-value value does not exist on the other', then it is surely a no-and-yes type of proposition. But it is not a dialectical contradiction. Value does not contain and at the same time does contain use-value. This is sheer violation of Aristotelian law of contradiction. It does not make sense.

Now we know that Rosenberg fails in his 'dialectical' explanation of the opposition (or contradiction) of use-value and value. It seems dialectical just because of his ambiguous phraseology.[46] If the contradiction in which 'all the contradictions of capitalist production are included' is nothing more than a contradiction in the sense of formal logic, the inevitability of the whole process beginning from the genesis of commodities up to the collapse of capitalist system comes to be unwarranted.

Another fundamental issue still remains: Marx's method of deducing value. An equation 1 quarter corn $= x$ cwt iron, is shown in Section 1, Chapter 1, Book I of *Capital*. 'What does this equation tell us? It tells us that in two different things . . . there exists in equal quantities something common to both. The two things must therefore be equal to a third', [47] which is, according to Marx, the abstract-human-labour embodied in them, i.e. value.

This process of extracting value has been a target of long-standing criticism since Böhm-Bawerk called it 'the most vulnerable point in the Marxian system',[48] because the conclusion is contained in his early work: Marx presupposes that

> there *is* a single substance which inheres in commodities . . . Having granted this premise, all that is required is the examination of various possibilities until, by a process of elimination, the common factor is found. This, of course, turns out to be the labour time expended in the production of the commodity . . . To the Hegelian rationalist [Marx – T.H.] it is no more possible to conceive of the price of commodities being determined by the equilibrium of the multiplicity of historically evolved forces which determine the shape of individual subjective patterns of preference, than it is to imagine any multiplicity of historical causes.[49]

Of course it is true that the vast majority of commodities are the products of human labour. This simple fact, however, should not lead to the ambiguous *dialectical opposition* of use-value and value, the falsity of which I have already explained. This plain truth does not give operationality to the price theory based on labour-value. Nor does it serve as valid justification for the existence of a single *substance*[50] which inheres in commodities.

[*Note:* On 'the contradiction inherent in a commodity' also see 'Contradiction, opposition and anthropomorphism', Ch. 6, Sec. II, subsection 4, in the present volume.]

2　Negation: the transformation of money into capital

Now, we come to the second phase of the triad, negation. Dühring says, as cited above, that Marx's historical sketch of the transition of England from pre-capitalist to capitalist society is 'relatively the best part'. From the theoretical point of view, however, it seems necessary to make a rigorous reappraisal of 'dialectics' as applied in the analysis of this process.

A dialectical formulation of this transformation is found in Chapter 24, '*Conversion of Surplus Value into Capital*', Book I of *Capital*:

> The laws of appropriation or of private property, laws that are based on the production and circulation of commodities, become by their own inner and inexorable dialectic changed into their very opposite.[51]

This dialectical development is explained in Chapters 4-7, Book I of *Capital*, which concern the transformation of money into capital. Marx's argument there is already expounded and criticised in detail by the author in Section III, Chapter 3 of the present book. So here only the gist of the story is presented:

In a society of simple commodity-producers the circulation of commodities is subject to the law of exchange of equivalents. C (commodity) $= M$ (money) $= C$ (commodity).

Now Mr Moneybags begins his exchange with money in the order of $M-C-M$. This must also be $M = C = M$. And yet he needs to acquire *surplus value*. So he submits the famous question:

> His development into a full-grown capitalist must take place, both within the sphere of circulation and without it . . . Hic Rhodus, hic salta![52]

The key to the 'right' answer is a special commodity, labour-power. Mr Moneybags with 27 shillings in hand buys 24 shillings of raw cotton and spindles and expends 3 shillings in hiring a labourer. In the process of turning cotton into yarn the labourer adds new value of 30 shillings, including 3 shillings representing surplus value. Here Marx writes triumphantly:

> 27 shillings have been transformed into 30 shillings: a surplus value of 3 shillings has been created . . . This conversion of money into capital takes place within the sphere of circulation and also outside it; within the circulation, because conditioned by the purchase of the labour-power . . . outside the circulation, because what is done within it is only a stepping-stone to the production of surplus value.[53]

Let us now examine this seeming 'dialectics' of Marx. The ground of his assertion that it takes place within the sphere of circulation is that the purchase of labour-power is an indispensable preparatory act for it. But at the same time he declares that it does *not* take place in circulation because purchasing of labour-power is 'only a stepping-stone (preparation) to the production of surplus value' in the sphere of production. Here Marx confuses preparation and realisation. If such is allowable, we can even contend: 'I have bought a railway-ticket for Osaka. So I am already in Osaka although I am still in Tokyo, because preparation and realisation are one and the same.'

One more word on Marx's confusion regarding the subjects, 'transformation of money into capital' and 'creation of surplus value'. A correct expression of the situation described by Marx here should be, if we adopt the latter as subject: The creation of surplus value is prepared in the sphere of circulation and realised in the sphere of production. If we adopt the former: The transformation of money into capital is realised throughout all the three processes of first act of circulation, production and the second act of circulation. The indiscriminate usage by Marx of these two subjects is one of the reasons for producing his self-contradictory proposition 'within the sphere of circulation and also outside it' – apparent 'logic of dialectical contradiction' but in substance just a case of the *fallacy of amphiboly*.

Marx's more fundamental confusion now follows. The premise of his argument here is that the simple commodity-producers cannot create surplus value. But in Chapter 10, Book III of *Capital* he clearly states that they do create surplus value (for detailed analysis of this point see Sec. I, Ch. 3, present volume):

> The labourers . . . in possession of their respective means of production . . . in their day's work . . . would have created . . . new value . . . This would comprise their wages plus *surplus value* [emphasis T.H.] . . . which would however belong to them.[54]

Which is right of his two contradictory arguments? Unmistakably the latter. For if simple commodity-producers, or in historical terminology, manual workers and peasants in the feudal society, had not produced surplus (value), how could the feudal lords and nobles have lived in extravagance? How could the capitalist society have come out of this society without surplus? This is simply a matter of common sense.

The theoretical origin of all these ambiguities and confusions which are very often mistaken for profundity is the 'inner and inexorable dialectic'. E. H. Carr once wrote in his biography:

> Marx grew up in a school which was saturated through and through with the Hegelian dialectic. The paraphernalia of thesis and antithesis penetrated not only the thought, but the mode of expression of the young Hegelians . . . His early writings are full of strange antithetical conceits, frequently degenerating into meaningless verbal jugglery.[55]

Capital, his *magnum opus*, is not quite out of reach of this comment.

3   Negation of the negation: the rise of the capital-coefficient

Now let us take up the last phase of the historical triad, the one in the controversy between Dühring and Engels. The two fundamental laws 'working with iron necessity' towards the collapse of capitalist society are the general law of capitalist accumulation (the law of the rising organic composition of capital) and the law of the falling rate of profit. On these, Section II, Chapter 4 of the present book has already given a fairly detailed explanation which clarifies the self-contradictions involved in them. I will sketch them very briefly and then develop the argument further. The following simple illustration is the same as that in Table 4.3, Chapter 4.

Pd_1 $100c + 100v + 100s = 300h$ $(300G)$
Pd_2 $400c + 100v + 100s = 600h$ $(30,000G)$

(Assumption: 1 hour = 1 Yen)

In this small model society 100 labourers produce $300G$ in Period 1. They buy $100G$, $1G$ being ¥1.

In Period 2 they produce $30,000G$, owing to the productivity-rise. Their wages remaining 'given',[56] the developed productivity 'finds itself at variance with the narrow basis of consumption'.[57] The ever-widening gap between supply and demand dooms the capitalist system to its downfall.

Here Marx 'forgets' the price-fall 'in inverse ratio to the productiveness of labour',[58] from $1G = ¥1$ to ¥1/50, which raises 100 labourers' *real* wages in inverse ratio to the price-fall. (The theoretical process in which Marx came to 'forget' this price-fall is explained in detail in Sec. I, Ch. 7.)

It must have been beyond Marx's imagination to see real wages rise in proportion to the productivity-rise. If he wants to keep the real wages of 100 labourers constant in Period 2 what should be done is to cut their nominal wages to 1/50, $2v$, and increase surplus value to $198s$. This is what Marx calls the production of *relative* surplus value in Chapter 10, Book I of *Capital*.

By so doing, the self-contradiction of both constant and rising wages is dissolved. But, as Table 5.1 shows, there are two difficulties involved in this solution.

First: In Pd_{2b} although the relative share of labour and capital has changed, $600h$ (600 Yen) will be enough to buy up $30,000G$, just as in Pd_{2a}. There is no necessity for the ever-widening gap between supply and demand which leads the capitalist system to catastrophe.

Second: The law of the rising organic composition becomes invalid. According to the law, the rise of the organic composition should reflect the rise of the technical composition in an approximate way, i.e. in a

Table 5.1   Composition of capital and capital coefficient

Pd_{2a}	$400c + 100v + 100s = 600h$	$(30,000G)$
Pd_{2b}	$400c + 2v + 198s = 600h$	$(30,000G)$

Compared with Pd_1 (in Table 4.3):

Pd_{2a}

Technical composition	:	rises 100 times
Organic composition (c/v)	:	rises 4 times
Capital coefficient ($c/v+s$)	:	rises 4 times

Pd_{2b}

Technical composition	:	rises 100 times
Organic composition (c/v)	:	rises 200 times
Capital coefficient ($c/v+s$)	:	rises 4 times

slower rate of rise. In this illustration, however, the same level of technology or technical composition is reflected by two quite different ratios of organic composition. The technical compositions in Pd_{2a} and Pd_{2b} are both 100 times higher than in Pd_2. The organic composition is, however, 4 times higher in Pd_{2a} and 200 times (!) higher in Pd_{2b}. The rate of rise in the latter case is faster than that of the technical composition. This nullifies the law of the rising organic composition.

Marx should have utilised, instead of organic composition, c/v, the ratio of constant capital to variable capital plus surplus value, $c/v+s$. This may be regarded as a rough equivalent to the ratio of capital stock to net output. So let us call it capital coefficient. This ratio is the same in Pd_{2a} and Pd_{2b}, in both cases being 4 times higher than in Pd_2.

If we adopt the capital coefficient in place of the organic composition (Marx sometimes substantially means this rate when using the term 'organic composition'), the above-mentioned confusion in the general law of capitalist accumulation, and hence in the law of the falling rate of profit, will be successfully removed.

The reason why Marx confuses $c/v+s$ with c/v is as follows. He writes at the beginning of Chapter 25, Book I of *Capital*:

The composition of capital is to be understood in a two-fold sense. On the side of value, it is determined by the proportion in which it is divided into constant capital or value of the means of production, and variable capital or value of labour-power, the sum total of wages. On the side of material, as it functions in the process of production, all capital is divided into means of production and living labour-power. This latter composition is determined by the relation between the mass of the means of production employed, on the one hand, and the mass of labour necessary for their employment on the other, I call the former the *value-composition*, the latter the *technical-composition* of capital. Between the two there is a strict correlation. To express this, I call the value-composition of capital insofar as it is determined by its technical composition and mirrors the changes of the latter, the *organic composition of capital*.[59]

Marx treats the value (organic) composition and the technical composition as the two aspects of one and the same thing, capital – in other words, equipollent, just as the equiangular triangle and the equilateral triangle are equipollent.

Here lies his mistake. The value of the means of production and the mass of it are certainly the two aspects of the same thing, so equipollent. But the value of labour-power (the sum total of wages) and the living labour-power (the mass of labour necessary for the employment of the means of production) are not equipollent, but two different masses, the former being v (necessary labour) and the latter $v+s$ (necessary labour plus surplus labour).

Therefore, the technical composition of capital expressed in terms of value is not c/v, but $c/v+s$, so that it is not equipollent with the value (organic) composition. Marx mistakes $v+s$ for v perhaps because he calls the former 'living labour-power' and the latter 'value of labour power', believing that they are the same thing as they bear the same name.

Marx asserts that the rise of the organic composition 'mirrors the changes' (rises at a slower rate) of the technical composition. However, as I explained above, the organic composition does not necessarily change that way. It is the capital coefficient that does it in the context of Marx's assumption that the constant capital increases always faster. (This assumption is also unwarranted. On this point, see my explanation following Table 5.2.)

Now we come to the crucial point of the latter law. Some economists assert: that if both the organic composition and the rate of surplus value are variable, the direction of the change of the rate of profit becomes indeterminate. For instance, Paul M. Sweezy is famous for this line of argument.[60] But if the rise of the capital coefficient – in other words, the exclusive development of capital-using technology – were the inevitable law of capitalist society, then the direction of the change of the rate of profit would not be indeterminate. It must fall at least in the long run. Table 5.2 shows the upper limit in the indeterminate movement of the rate of profit.

Table 5.2   The limit in the rise of the rate of profit

Pd_1	$100c + 100v + 100s$	: $p' = 1/2$
Pd_{2b}	$400c + 2v + 198s$	: $p' = 198/402$
Pd_{2c}	$400c + 0v + 200s$	: $p' = 1/2$

In Pd_{2b} the rate of surplus value is already exceedingly high. Yet the rate of profit is lower than that of Pd_1. Even if this rate becomes infinitely great, in other words, if the labourers were not paid wages at all, as shown in Pd_{2c}, the rate of profit could not be higher than in Pd_2. It could be higher while $\frac{v+s}{c}$ (inverse of capital coefficient) of Pd_2 is larger than $\frac{s}{c+v}$ of Pd_2 ($\frac{s_1}{c_1+v_1} < \frac{v_2+s_2}{c_2}$). However, if $\frac{v+s}{c}$ of Pd_2 becomes equal to (the illustrated case) (see following *Note*) or smaller than $\frac{s}{c+v}$ of Pd_1 ($\frac{s_1}{c_1+v_1} \geqslant \frac{v_2+s_2}{c_2}$), the rate of profit must inevitably fall.

[*Note:* In Pd_{2c} $v = 0$. This is quite unrealistic. The labourers should at least be given subsistence wages. Therefore, already in Pd_2 the rate of profit should come to be lower than in Pd_1.]

Thus the necessary condition for the validity of the falling rate of profit is the inevitable fall of the inverse of the capital coefficient, i.e. the rise of the capital coefficient or the exclusive development of capital-using technology.

[*Note:* In Table 5.2 $v + s$ remains the same, 200. But take note that the above algebraic rule applies to any numbers of c, v, s. Examine, e.g., the following case: Pd_2 $50c + 30v + 20s$, Pd_2 $600c + 0v + 150s$.]

The types of future inventions, whether they will be capital-using, capital-saving or neutral, will depend on various kinds of conditions. It is useless to try to predict the dominant type of future technique. Historically we know, thanks to the works of J. Steindl,[61] Colin Clark and others, the capital coefficient has been fairly stable in the advanced capitalist countries.

So we reach the conclusion that the general law of capitalist accumulation and the law of the falling rate of profit are both invalid, because the fundamental premise of these laws, the rise of the capital coefficient, has nothing like 'iron necessity'. (On the invalidity of the law also see Appendix, 'The Two Factors Which Nullify the Law of the Falling Rate of Profit'.)

IV   DIALECTICS: AN ILLUSION

Although this has been a very rough and hasty re-examination of the whole development of the historical triad in *Capital*, we found in all the three stages ambiguity, self-contradiction, unqualified premises and so forth in place of dialectical process realising itself 'with the inexorability of a law of Nature'. The dialectical structure of *Capital* was a great illusion. However, this book was, according to Lenin, the one which elevated the materialist concept of history on the level of proven truth and the model case of application of dialectical materialism to a particular sphere of social science.

I do not deny that many propositions in *Capital*, especially the two fundamental laws reviewed above, are in accordance with the historical realities of British capitalism in the mid nineteenth century.

I do not doubt the honesty and sincerity of Marx when he thought he was approaching his object of research with the attitude of a strictly empirical scientist. Marx himself writes in *The German Ideology*:

> When speculation ends – in real life – real, positive science beginnings . . .
> When reality is depicted, philosophy as an independent branch of knowledge
> loses its medium of existence. At the best its place can only be taken by a
> summing-up of the most general results, abstractions which arise from the
> observation of historical development of men . . . they by no means afford a
> recipe or schema, as does philosophy, for nearly trimming the epochs of
> history.[62]

But when Marx tells us that dialectics is 'in its essence critical and revolutionary',[63] I cannot help feeling the error of assuming what it is required to prove. Marx (and Engels) honestly thought that he showed 'from history . . . that . . . the capitalist mode of production has . . . itself created the material conditions from which it must perish.'[64] And the result of this empirical study corresponded with the dialectical schema of development, the negation of the negation, because the movement of society necessarily follows the inherent laws of dialectics. So the course of history should match and really matches with the dialectical schema. Is this not the fallacy of containing the conclusion in the method?

> History is man-made, and therefore not a blind destiny but our
> responsibility. (Gunnar Myrdal)[65]

124 *Marx's* Capital *and One Free World*

History does nothing, it possesses no immense wealth, fights no battles. It is rather man, real living man who does everything, who possesses and fights. (Karl Marx)[66]

Carelessly read, these two statements may be taken as telling us substantially the same thing. But man, for Marx, is fundamentally a fatalistic figure subject to the dialectical 'necessity' of the nineteenth century, and man for Myrdal is a figure in an age of planning in which he moulds his own destiny in the face of multiple possibilities.

It happens to be the centennial of the publication of the first edition of the first Book of *Capital*. (This part was written in 1967.) The time is long overdue for a valediction to the dialectical 'realm of necessity'.

6 Hegelian Fallacy in Marxian Philosophy: An Inquiry into the Roots of Ambiguity Mistaken for Profundity

The foregoing chapters have examined the skeleton of Marx's economics; the labour value and surplus value theory, the transformation of money into capital and the primitive accumulation, the general law of capitalist accumulation, the law of the falling rate of profit, and the law of the obligatory correspondence of production relations to the productive forces. As a result of all these studies I strongly feel the necessity of proving in a rigorous manner the fallacious character of Marxian dialectical philosophy itself originating from the Hegelian fallacy. The methodological stand based on this demonstration is, I believe, indispensable for a scientific, comprehensive reappraisal and a correct, historical evaluation of Marxian economics and Marxism in general on the one hand, and for an appropriate access to the contemporary problems concerning the two systems and those beyond them, on the other

I DIALECTICS AS THE NEGATION OF ARISTOTELIAN LAW OF CONTRADICTION

Dialectics in the Hegelian and Marxian sense is generally understood as a 'Logic of Contradiction (*Widerspruch*)', i.e. a system of logic which supersedes the Aristotelian Law of Contradiction.

In ancient Greece the word 'dialectics' meant only the art of discussion or polemic and its main theoretical weapon was the Law of Contradiction itself. Zeno of Alea, whom Aristotle called the founder of dialectics, became famous for his paradoxes such as – 'The flying arrow is at a standstill', 'Achilles can never overtake the tortoise crawling in front of him', etc. – on the strength of the Law of Contradiction.[1]

1   The negation of the Law of Contradiction by Hegel

It is since Hegel established his peculiar system of logic that dialectics came to be thought of as a logic built on the negation of the Law of Contradiction. Hegel writes in his 'Small Logic':

> The maxim of identity reads: Everything is identical with itself, A = A: and, negatively, A cannot at the same time be A and not A – This maxim, instead of being a true law of thought, is nothing but the law of abstract understanding . . . Utterances after the fashion of this pretended law (A planet is – a planet; Magnetism is – magnetism; Mind is – mind) are, as they deserve to be, reputed silly.[2]

> Instead of speaking by the maxim of Excluded Middle (which is the maxim of abstract understanding) we should rather say: Everything is opposite. Neither in heaven nor in earth, neither in the world of mind nor of nature, is there anywhere such an abstract 'Either – or' as the understanding maintains . . . Contradiction is the very moving principle of the world: and it is ridiculous to say that contradiction is unthinkable.[3]

We do not need Hegel's teachings to know that statements like 'A planet is a planet', 'Dialectics is dialectics', etc. are nothing but meaningless tautologies. The Law of Contradiction in its general form is that 'A (subject) cannot be at the same time, and in the same respect, both B (predicate) and not B.'

Note that the Law in this broad sense is also denied by Hegel in connection with his criticism of Zeno's negation of motion. Zeno asserted, in essence, that a flying arrow must be at a standstill, if logic should be non-contradictory, because it must be at some point in space at any and every point of time and if it *is* at some point of space it must be at a standstill, and an aggregation of standstills does not make motion. Hegel in his 'Large Logic' refuted Zeno's argument with his 'Logic of Contradiction' as follows:

> Something moves, not because it is here at one point of time and there at another, but because at one and the same point of time it is here and not here, and in this here both is and is not. We must grant the old dialecticians the contradictions which they approve in motion; but what follows is not that is no motion, but rather that motion is existent Contradiction itself.[4]

2   Marx and Engels' acceptance of the 'Contradiction' by Hegel

Marx and Engels 'turned right side up'[5] Hegel's mystical dialectics, but accepted his negation of the Law of Contradiction. Engels writes in *Anti-Dühring*:

To the metaphysician, things and their mental reflexes, ideas, are isolated, are to be considered one after the other and apart from each other, are objects of investigation fixed, rigid, given once for all. He thinks in absolutely irreconcilable antitheses, 'His communication is, 'yea, yea; nay, nay'; for whatsoever is more than these cometh of evil.' For him a thing either exists or does not exist; a thing cannot at the same time be itself and something else. Positive and negative absolutely exclude one another.[6]

According to Engels, in order to have a correct grasp of changes and developments in nature and in human societies, one must supersede the formal logic abiding by the Law of Contradiction with the dialectical logic which holds that a thing can be and not be and A can be both B and not B. Thus, of the motion of a body he thinks just as Hegel does:

> Motion itself is a contradiction: even simple mechanical change of position can only come about through a body being at one and the same moment of time both in one place and in another place, being in one and the same place and also not in it. And the continuous origination and simultaneous solution of this contradiction is precisely what motion is.[7]

These views of Engels on contradiction must have been fully shared by Marx, because in one of the prefaces to *Anti-Dühring* Engels gave notice that 'it was self-understood between us (Engels and Marx) that this exposition of mine should not be issued without his knowledge. I read the whole manuscript to him before it was printed.'[8]

Now let us examine whether the motion of a body can be described without using 'Logic of Contradiction' as Hegel and Engels did. It is an obvious violation of the Law of Contradiction that a thing is in one place and is not there at the same moment. In the wrong, however, are both Zeno who denies motion adhering to the Law and Hegel and Engels who defy the Law to describe motion. The real point of argument is hidden in the premise of the statement in question and it has no connection whatsoever with the Law of Contradiction. The copula 'is' in this case is used in a context implicitly assuming the situation of standstill and therefore the state of motion is excluded beforehand from the premise. This is, using logician's terminology, a fallacy of insufficient disjunction and it gives rise to an unnecessary, seeming violation of the Law of Contradiction. What is under discussion is related to the state of motion. So, use the terms expressing motion and just say: 'The arrow is flying.' 'This body is in motion.' That's all. We have non-contradictory propositions giving a correct description of the events. Only we should not make such nonsensical statements as 'The arrow is flying and is not flying'. 'This body is in motion and is not in motion', because these are true and substantial violations of the Law of Contradiction.

For those who may feel this explanation of mine too handy and therefore untrustworthy, let me present a more dignified and scientific expression of the same thing: 'Motion, change of position of a body, can be precisely and foreseeably described as a function of the space–distance between assumed fixed points (having only position and occupying no space) and the time-interval needed for moving along this distance . . . to say 'be and not be at the same time' in expressing this movement of a body is . . . superfluous.'[9]

Moreover, it is of no use to make an absolute distinction between standstill and motion. When we speak in physics of the motion of a body, we just imply the change of its position *relative* to some other body. If body A is taken as a datum point in measuring the movement of body B, body A is assumed to be at a standstill and B is in motion, and if Body B is taken as a datum point, vice versa.

3   Marx's fallacy of amphiboly mistaken as dialectics

We should take up now the illustrations by Marx himself in *Capital*. In the opening paragraph of Section 2, Chapter 3, Book I he maintains:

> For instance, it is a contradiction to depict one body as constantly falling towards another, and as, at the same time, constantly flying away from it. The ellipse is a form which, while allowing this contradiction to go on, at the same time reconciles it.[10]

'One body falling towards another and at the same time flying away from it.' Unmistakably written so here. But is it possible for one and the same body, without being split into two, to fall towards another body and at the same time fly away from it? If we could suppose that it somehow occurred, it might deserve to be named contradiction. Yet it is not the real contradiction Marx thought of, but an imaginary and unreal contradiction, because it can never happen in reality.

It goes without saying that a real elliptical motion of a planet is *one* motion explained by the balance of a centripetal and a centrifugal force, not two motions of falling and flying away at the same time. Dynamical formulation of elliptical motion was, as is well known, Newton's achievement. A locus of elliptical motion is, in a general form, described as a curve $Ax^2 + By^2 = C$ ($A > 0$, $B > 0$, $C > 0$). In the dynamics and locus of elliptical motion, there is no room for 'real contradiction'. Marx mistook a product of his unreal imagination for a 'real contradiction', confused by his own ambiguous rhetoric. That was after all just a paralogism.[11]

The second example is when Marx gives a series of propositions clearly violating the Law of Contradiction in his explanation of 'conversion of money into capital' in Chapters 4 and 5 in Book I of *Capital*. For these see the argument developed in Chapter 5, Section III, subsection 2, in the present book. There we introduced Marx's famous question put to himself: '. . . Hic Rhodus, hic salta!' and his own answer to that, with my criticism to the effect that if Marx's reasoning is permissible we can even assert: 'I am already in Osaka although I am still in Tokyo as I have bought the railway ticket for Osaka, because the preparation and realisation are one and the same.'

Here again we know that what Marx thinks to be 'dialectical contradiction' is just an apparent, false one brought about by the fallacy involved in his argument.

II CONTRADICTION AND OPPOSITION INTERCHANGED

When dialectics is called 'Logic of Contradiction' it usually means not only the logic which denies the Law of Contradiction, but the logic which regards various kinds of oppositions (*Gegensatze*) as substantially identical with contradictions.

1 Hegel originated the confusion

It was Hegel who extended the denotation of the concept of contradiction by inseparably relating it to the concept of opposition. In 'Doctrine of Essence' in 'Large Logic' he claims:

> Contradiction immediately stands revealed in the determinations of relations (*Verhaltnisbestimmungen*). The most trivial examples above and below, right and left, father and son, and so on without end all contain Opposition (*Gegensatz*) in one term.[12]

In order to have a clear understanding of what Hegel implies by 'opposition', let us see his own explanation in 'Small Logic': 'In opposition, the different is not confronted by any other, but by *its* other.'[13] In plain language it means, for instance, that 'above' and 'below' are different but 'above' does not exist without 'below' and 'below' does not exist without 'above'.

It is quite misleading that this 'opposition' is treated by Hegel as if it were a 'contradiction' i.e. negation of the Law of Contradiction. In 'Large Logic' we find the following passage: 'Positive and negative are the sides, now independent, of opposition . . . in general each is, first, only in so far as the other is . . . Secondly, it is in so far as the other is not.'[14] One side of the opposition *is*, in so far as the other *is*, and at the same time in so far as the other *is not*. This is an evident violation of the Law of Contradiction. If this proposition were meaningful, the 'Logic of Contradiction' called 'dialectics' would be indispensable to a full understanding of the concept of 'opposition'. However, it is meaningless as we now show. Let us apply two concrete terms used by Hegel in this connection to the above propositions: 'Above' is in so far as 'below' is, and at the same time in so far as 'below' is not. This is also an evident violation of the Law of Contradiction. And the latter part of this statement is an absurdity, because 'above' without 'below' does not make sense. What Hegel is really thinking of in the example shown in 'Large Logic' is that 'above' is in so far as there is 'below', and at the same time 'above' is, not *without* 'below', but determined as *not being* *'below'*. (15) We see no 'contradiction', no violation of the Law of Contradiction, in this illustration. But in Hegel's shady, rhetorical language the clear distinction between 'without' and 'not being' is obscured and disappears and opposition comes to be identified with contradiction. Such is an apparent, false 'contradiction' resulting from the fallacy of amphiboly in Hegel's inference.

2   Anthropomorphism and 'real' opposition in Hegel

In Hegelian terminology, this concept of contradiction, mixed up with logical opposition such as above and below, father and son,[16] further implies what is thought to be 'real' opposition (antagonism, struggle). In 'Observation I' to 'Contradiction' in 'Large Logic' Hegel gives the following example:

> Virtue does not exist without struggle . . . and it is virtue not only as compared with vice, but is opposition (*Entgegensetzung*) and struggle in itself.[17]

According to a Marxist philosopher Kazuto Matsumura: 'It goes without saying that the example shown by Hegel (of the struggle of virtue) is an actual opposition and a real contradiction.'[18] But his interpretation is wrong. The 'struggle' of 'virtue' is no more than an anthropomorphism, the assignment of human qualities to other things, very often seen in Hegelian (and Marxian) dialectical statements. In this way, virtue and vice, just ordinary contrary concepts, are vividly impressed on readers' minds as if they were engaged in real struggle. Let me quote here Reichenbach's view on the relation between anthropomorphism and philosophy:

> Where scientific explanation failed because the knowledge of the time was insufficient to provide the right generalisation, imagination took its place . . . Superficial analogies, particularly analogies with human experiences, were confused with generalisation and taken to be explanations . . . It is from this ground that philosophy sprang . . . Many a philosophical system is like the Bible, a masterpiece of poetry, abundant in pictures that stimulate our imagination, but devoid of clarification that issues from scientific explanation.[19]

With regard to *real* opposition, we find Hegel's dialectical argument on the Diet and the government in his *Philosophy of Right*:

> It is one of the fundamental principles of logic, that a definite element, which, when standing in opposition, has the bearing of an extreme, ceases to be in opposition and becomes an organic element, when it is observed to be at the same time a mean (*Mitte*)[20] In this present question it is all the more important to make prominent this principle, since the prejudice is as common as it is dangerous, which presents the Diet (*Stände*) as essentially in opposition to the government. Taken organically, that is, in its totality, the element of the Diet proves its right only through its office of mediation.[21]

Thus, the Logic (denying the Law) of Contradiction, logical opposition (contrary concepts, relative concepts, etc.), the apparent 'opposition' (mistaken through anthropomorphism for 'real' struggle), and the actual opposition (antagonism, struggle) in social life – all these are tied together and called dialectical contradictions (= oppositions).

3 Contradiction set on a pedestal as *causa finalis*

Hegel's next step is to elevate Contradiction to a universal entity which is the prime cause of all the changes and developments in the world. I have already cited in the early part of this chapter a passage in 'Small Logic' which reads: 'Contradiction is the very moving principle of the world.'[22] Here I add some typical statements from 'Large Logic':

Contradiction is the root of all movement and life (*Lebendigkeit*), and it is only in so far as it contains a Contradiction that anything moves and has impulse and activity . . . It must further not be taken only as an abnormality which occurs just here and there: it is the Negative in its essential determination, the principle of all self-movement, which consists of nothing else but an exhibition of Contradiction.[23]

Lenin, in his *Notebooks on Philosophy*, after copying these sentences and those surrounding them, gives the following appraisal:

Movement and '*self-movement*' (this NB! arbitrary (independent), spontaneous, *internally-necessary* movement), 'change', 'movement and vitality', 'the principle of all self-movement', 'impulse' (*Trieb*) to 'movement' and to 'activity' – *the opposite to 'dead Being*' – who would believe that this is the core of 'Hegelianism', of abstract and *abstrusen* (ponderous, absurd?) Hegelianism? This core had to be discovered, understood, *hinuberretten*, laid bare, refined, which is precisely what Marx and Engels did.[24]

The materialists Marx, Engels and Lenin all inherited the idealistic and rationalistic[25] concept of Hegelian Contradiction set on a pedestal as *causa finalis*. And then comes Mao Tse-tung who claims, in his *Essay on Contradiction*, that 'Nothing exists which does not contain contradiction. Without contradiction the world itself does not exist.'[26] It might be admissible, if this were a statement by Hegel who 'has taken the self-development of conceptions or notions to be the medium wherein science really exists'.[27] But when Mao Tse-tung considers contradiction to be the root and origin of the world, we cannot help but say that his dialectics, which should have been Hegelian mystical dialectics 'turned right side up', is still 'standing on its head'.[28]) 'Without the world, contradiction does not exist (the concept of contradiction could not come out).' This ought to be Mao tse tung's statement 'turned right side up again'.

4   Contradiction, opposition and anthropomorphism in Marx

The identification or rather confusion of contradiction with opposition is accepted by Marx in *Capital* from its very beginning and 'contradiction' (opposition) is the prime mover of the capitalist mode of production all through the book. As is well known, the study of bourgeois society in *Capital* starts with the analysis of a commodity.[29] In the process of the exchange of two commodities, 'the opposition or contrast (*Gegensatz*) existing internally in each commodity between use-value and value, is, therefore, made evident externally by two commodities being placed in such relation to each other, that the commodity whose value it is sought to express, figures directly as a mere use-value, while the commodity in which that value is to be expressed, figures directly as mere exchange value.'[30] This external opposition is explained in detail with Hegelian mode of expression:

> The relative form and the equivalent form are two intimately connected, mutually dependent and inseparable elements of the expression of value; but, at the same time, are mutually exclusive, opposite (*entgegengesetzte*) extremes.[31]

In another place this external opposition is called contradiction:

> We saw in a former chapter that the exchange of commodities implies contradictory and mutually exclusive conditions. The differentiation of commodities into commodities and money does not sweep away these contradictions (*Widersprüche*), but develops a *modus vivendi*, a form in which they can exist side by side. This is generally the way in which real contradictions are reconciled.[32]

After all, what Marx wants to tell the readers is this:

> The historical progress and extension of exchanges develops the opposition (*Gegensatz*), sleeping (*schlummernd*) in commodities, between use-value and value. The want (*Bedurfnis*) for giving an external expression to this opposition (*Gegensatz*) for the purpose of commercial intercourse, urges on the establishment of an independent form of value, and finds no rest (*ruht und rastet nicht*) until it is once for all satisfied by the differentiation of commodities into commodities and money.[33]

Thus in Marx's line of argument, contradiction, mixed up with opposition, is inherent in the matter (here, commodity), and it is the root of movement, the driving force in historical development (here, the development of the exchange of commodities and the differentiation of commodities into commodities and money).

Incidentally let us give a look at anthropomorphism in Marx: Opposition 'sleeps', 'wants' and 'finds no rest'. *Capital* in this case might also be qualified as 'a masterpiece of poetry . . . but devoid of clarification . . . like the Bible.'

Returning to the main point, in explaining the genesis of money from commodities, are these dialectical contradictions (opposition) and principles of movement necessary at all? To begin with, does the opposition between use-value and value really exist? The common sense of Marxists tells us that in a society which contains the contradiction between the social nature of production and the private nature of property, concrete useful labour cannot immediately function as social labour. It becomes socially useful through the medium of exchange in the market in the capacity of abstract human labour. This opposition between concrete useful labour and abstract human labour develops into an internal opposition between use-value and value in the body of a commodity.

But the existence of the two aspects, two natures of labour, concrete useful and abstract, is not limited to a society where ownership is private while production is social. They exist, as Marx himself points out, even in the isolated life of Robinson Crusoe.[34] His hunting, fishing, taming goats, etc. is useful labour, and available labour-time, which he apportions between different kinds of work, is nothing but quantitatively measured abstract human labour.

Then again in a socialist society where the contradiction between social production and private property is overcome, all the same, there is a distinction between concrete useful labour and abstract human labour. Here, two different use-values (made by different concrete useful labour) are added up in value (price – abstract human labour materialised, according to Marx) terms as in a capitalist society, just because a summation of, say, ten tons of steel, a bottle of wine, three copies of a book etc. is impossible.

After all, concrete useful labour and abstract human labour, use-value and value are both two aspects of labour and goods in any form of human society as seen from different view-points and have nothing to do with contradictions and oppositions originating from a particular production relation.

In regard to the development of commodity into money, we also see no need of Hegelian dialectical pseudo-explanations such as: the relative form and the equivalent form are two intimately connected, mutually dependent and inseparable elements and, at the same time, are mutually exclusive, opposite extremes; and the external expression of this opposition is the differentiation of commodities into commodities and money. In plain language devoid of dialectical ornamentation, we can give an intelligible explanation of the process. The value (labour-time expended) of a commodity, for instance, linen, cannot be measured directly as such, so it is measured by (a certain quantity of) another commodity, for instance, a coat, through exchange. A coat becomes a measurement of value. In the course of the historical development of exchange, the role of the measurement of value and the medium of exchange come to be fixed to a particular commodity, which is money (in *Capital*, money-commodity is in principle limited to gold).[35]

[*Note:* The aim of my explanation is limited to show that the application of 'dialectic contradiction' is superfluous and wrong in the description of the genesis and development of the commodity–money relation. Therefore, the problem of the economic interpretation of this process is left out here. It was taken up, as is well known, by the so-called Marginal Revolution in the 1870s in which use-value (utility) and value (price) were sophisticatedly combined by the concept of marginal utility.]

III UNITY AND STRUGGLE OF OPPOSITES

Now, we come to the Law of Interpenetration[36] or Unity and Struggle[37] of opposites. This is considered to be most important by Marxists.

1 The rose is red. The individual is universal

Lenin, in his note *On the Question of Dialectics*, refers to 'the method of exposition of dialectics in general' as follows:

To begin with what is the simplest, most ordinary, common, etc., with *any proposition*: The leaves of a tree are green; John is a man; Fido is a dog, etc. Here already we have *dialectics* (as Hegel's genius recognised); the *individual is* the *universal* . . . Consequently, the opposites (the individual is opposed to the universal) are identical: the individual exists only in the connection that leads to the universal. The universal exists only in the individual and through the individual. Every individual is (in one way or another) a universal. Every universal is (a fragment of, or an aspect, or the essence of) an individual. Every universal only approximately embraces all the individual objects. Every individual enters incompletely into the universal, etc., etc.[38] (Here opposition is interpreted as dialectical contradiction. – T.H.)

In this passage Lenin has in mind the dialectical explanation by Hegel of the positive judgements: 'Gaius is learned', 'The rose is red', 'The rose is fragrant', etc. Hegel asserts that they are, in form, illustrations of 'the individual is universal', and, in content, those of 'the universal is individual'.[39]

On closer examination, however, we find that the sophisticated arguments by Hegel and Lenin have, in substance, no relation at all to 'identity of opposites' or 'contradiction'. Let us take up the examples of 'the rose is . . .'. First, if 'the rose is red' means 'this individual rose has a universal property of redness', this latter sentence contains no contradiction. To say, in this case, 'the individual is universal', is, in fact, not a dialectical statement, but a mere fallacy of ambiguous rhetoric. Second, if 'the rose is fragrant' means 'the rose (representing the whole class) has an individual property of fragrance (among many properties it has)', it is again a fallacy of ambiguous rhetoric to say that 'the universal is individual'.

2 Unity and Struggle in economic crises in *Capital*

The above cited remark by Lenin on dialectics in general' is that which comes after and supplements his description as follows on 'a particular case of dialectics' applied by Marx to bourgeois society:

> In his *Capital*, Marx first analyses the simplest, most ordinary and fundamental, most common and everyday *relation* of bourgeois (commodity) society, a relation encountered billions of times, viz. the exchange of commodities. In this very simple phenomonon (in this 'cell' of bourgeois society) analysis reveals *all* the contradictions (or the germs of *all* the contradictions) of modern society. The subsequent exposition shows us the development . . . of these contradictions . . . from its beginning to its end.[40]

Let me here give a sketch of the development of all the contradictions 'from its beginning to its end'. The simplest category at the beginning of *Capital* is a commodity ('cell' of bourgeois society) which is an internal unity of the opposites, use-value and value. The historical development of commodity exchange gives rise to external expressions of this opposition: first, relative form of value vs. equivalent form, then, commodities in general vs. money. Money grows into capital with the appearance of a special commodity, labour-power. Now the opposition takes the form of the struggle between capital and labour. It is driven forward along the historical course set by 'the laws of economic motion' of capitalist society, namely, the general law of capitalist accumulation and the law of the falling rate of profit. With the progress of the productive forces of the society, the gap between production and consumption becomes more widened, the economic crises more explosive, unemployment and absolute impoverishment more serious, and economic growth more stagnant. The capitalist relations of production becomes a fetter upon the productive forces. This fetter is burst asunder. The communist society is born.

Now, can you believe that this long process of the growth and movement of 'all the contradictions' is contained in advance in a 'cell' or a 'germ', a commodity, a contradictory entity, unity of use-value and value which are opposites? As for the contradiction intrinsic in a commodity, we have already seen that use-value and value are neither an opposition nor a contradiction peculiar to the societies of commodity producers, but just two aspects of economic goods observable in any form of society. And the differentiation of commodities and money can be easily explained without dialectics as I did. The contradiction (negation of the Law of Contradiction) in the metamorphosis of money into capital is only a seeming one caused by the fallacy of amphiboly as pointed out in Chapter 3.

Next in the historical order come economic crises, explained by Marx with the schema of 'unity and struggle of opposites'. His argumentation follows:

> Circulation bursts through all restrictions as to time, place, and individuals, imposed by direct barter, and this it effects by splitting up, into the antithesis (*Gegensatz* . . . opposition – T.H.) of a sale and a purchase, the direct identity that in barter does exist between the alienation of one's own and the acquisition of some other man's product. To say that these two independent and antithetical acts have an intrinsic unity (*Einheit*), are essentially one, is the same as to say that this intrinsic oneness (*Einheit*) expresses itself in an external antithesis (*Gegensatz* – T.H.). If the interval in time between the two complementary phases of the complete metamorphosis of a commodity becomes too great, if the split between the sale and the purchase becomes too pronounced, the intimate connexion between them, their oneness (*Einheit*), asserts itself by producing a crisis.[41]

> On the eve of the crisis, the bourgeois, with the self-sufficiency that springs from intoxicating prosperity, declares money to be a vain imagination. Commodities alone are money.But now the cry is everywhere money alone is a commodity! As the hart pants after fresh water, so pants his soul after money, the only wealth. In a crisis, the antithesis (*Gegensatz*) between commodities and their value-form, money, becomes heightened into an absolute contradiction.[42]

> Crisis is the forcible establishment of unity between elements that have become independent and the enforced separation (*Verselbständigung*) from one another of elements which are essentially one.[43]

Crisis is the establishment of unity and an absolute contradiction (opposition) or enforced separation and is at the same time both! At first sight, it looks like a beautifully dialectical and profound demonstration. But we should search into what is really meant underneath this dialectical terminology. 'Direct identity' indicates the perfect correspondence of purchase and sale, demand and supply, in the case of barter. 'External antithesis' stands for the separation of purchase and sale, demand and supply, in the economy with money circulation. 'In crisis, the antithesis between commodities and money becomes heightened to an absolute contradiction' depicts the situation in which the discrepancy between surplus of supply and shortage of demand bursts out and no one wants commodities but seeks only for money needed in payment. 'The forcible establishment of unity' means the recovery of balance between supply and demand in the final stages of a crisis which caused dumping sales, bankruptcy, mass unemployment and so on.

All these things and events can be clearly stated with ordinary language, as I have done. Dialectical conceptions and logic only serve to make the story equivocal. Here again they are superfluous and unwarranted.

[*Note:* Marx's peculiar wording of 'sale' and 'purchase' seems to need some explanation. In a common-sense usage, if there is a purchase there is by definition a sale. For instance, the purchase of a book by A is *at the same time* the sale of it by B *with the transfer of money* from A to B. But when Marx says 'a direct identity' of 'a sale and a purchase' he means barter, e.g., a direct exchange of A's fish for B's stone-arrowhead. A's act of parting with his fish is called 'sale' and obtaining a stone-arrowhead is called 'purchase' These two acts cannot be separated in time. Then, by 'the split between the sale and the purchase' he means the following: A sells his commodity X to B and obtains the price for it (sale). He can keep, and usually keeps, the money for some time. Then, some time later, he buys from C a commodity Y paying the price for it (purchase). A's sale and purchase is separated in time, although A's sale and B's purchase cannot be split in time.]

The last stage is the 'dialectical transition' from capitalism to communism. For this see Chapter 5 in the present book (Section II, subsection 2.

IV DIALECTICS, EMPIRICISM AND VALUE JUDGEMENT

1 The Hegelian fallacy inherited by Marxian economics

We examined, although very roughly, the fallacious character of the economics of *Capital* from its beginning to its end and confirmed that the pivotal conception, moving principle regulating the rise, growth and fall of the capitalist mode of production, was 'contradiction'. This, we saw, originated from the Hegelian fallacy of amphiboly, mistaken for 'Logic of Contradiction'.

There has been a long history of criticism of all kinds of Marxism beginning from Eugen Dühring, Eduard Bernstein, Böhm Bawerk and coming to our near contemporaries and contemporaries, Joseph Schumpeter, Karl Popper, Isaiah Berlin, Hans Reichenbach, E. H. Carr, Joan Robinson, Gunnar Myrdal, Kenneth Boulding, Paul A. Samuelson, etc., as I recollect them almost at random.

But a systematic disclosure has not yet been carried out by anyone of the fallacies common to Hegelian logic and Marxian economics in *Capital*, the corner-stone or rather alpha and omega of Marxism. This is the work I have been engaged in for several years and shown here in brief outline. An inquiry from this angle is indispensable, as I believe, to understand the basic character of Marxian economics.

2 'Cunning of reason' turned into 'necessity'

The next feature common to Hegel and Marx is their fatalistic or deterministic interpretation of historical development. In the case of Hegel, the idealist, the beginning of the world history is *logos* (*das Logische*). Its content 'shows forth God (*die Darstellung Gottes ist*) as he is in his eternal essence before the creation of Nature and of a Finite Spirit'.[44] This essence of God realises itself in the process of world development through the driving force of *contradiction*, and particularly in relation to the human history through the working of the famous *Cunning of Reason* (*List der Vernunft*).[45] The end of the dialectical development is, in his Logic, *The Absolute Idea*,[46] and in the secular world the Germanic nation, or more concretely Prussian state, charged with the task of 'the unity of the divine and the human. By means of it objective truth is *reconciled* with freedom (*die Versöhnung . . . der objektiven Wahrheit und Freiheit*), and that, too, inside of self-consciousness and subjectivity. This new basis, infinite and yet positive, it has been charged upon the northern principle of the Germanic nations to bring to completion'[47] (emphasis - T.H.). Thus, one of the fundamental features of Hegelian dialectical concept of the world is *reconciliation*.

In the materialistic concept of world history of Marx, who 'turned right side up' the Hegelian dialectics and at the same time 'coquetted with the mode of expression peculiar to him',[48] *matter* takes the place of Hegelian *logos* or God, but the prime mover of history is the *same contradiction*, which Marx called the 'rational kernel'[49] of Hegelian dialectics. A decisive difference between his dialectics and that of Hegel is that contradiction is assumed to be irreconcilable. In his *Critique of Hegelian State-Philosophy*, Marx, making a mockery of Hegelian dialectics which places the monarch at an extreme and at the same time at a mean (*Mitte*), says the monarch 'is like the lion in *A Midsummer-Night's Dream* who cries out I am lion, and I am not lion, but Snug'.[50] He disregards the mediating role of either Monarch or the Diet and claims that they 'have come to an opposition worth fighting (*einem Kampf-gerechten Gegensatz*), and an irreconcilable (*unversöhnlich*) contradiction'.[51] Marx's stand of irreconcilable contradiction or struggle had already been established in this early writing of 1843. As a natural sequence, the end of his dialectical development is an inevitable communist revolution. 'The knell of capitalist property sounds. The expropriators are expropriated.'[52] The director of this historical drama, in place of Hegel's 'Reason', is 'the natural laws of capitalist production . . . working with iron necessity'.[53]

3   Inevitability vs. probability

Why and how is Hegelian dialectics conciliatory? For Hegel, an idealist and Christian, all that is needed is to believe, at the starting-point, that the essence of God is harmonious and conciliatory, and that this is so, not because he believes in it, but because it is destined so already before the creation of the terrestrial world. And then 'the self-movement of conceptions'[54] which he himself conceived of leads him to his paradise on earth, the idealised Prussian state.

For Marx, a materialist and as he saw it empiricist, however, there must be some scientific proof of the revolutionary character of his dialectics. He writes in the Afterword to the second German edition of *Capital* that dialectics 'in its rational form . . . includes in its comprehension and affirmative recognition of the existing state of things, at the same time also, the recognition of the negation of that state, of its inevitable breaking-up . . . it is in its essence critical and revolutionary'.[55]

Lenin refers to wrong and right views on movement and asserts that, compared with the first conception which only understands evolutionary development, 'in the second conception the chief attention is directed to knowledge of the *source* of *self*-movement . . . The second alone furnishes the key to the "leaps", to the "break in continuity", to the "transformation into the opposite", to the destruction of the old and the emergence of the new'.[56]

These statements by Marx and Lenin might suffice for staunch Marxist-Leninists as 'empirical' proofs of the revolutionary character 'inherent' in dialectics. But we, the objective observers, cannot find a single fragment of positive verification in them. There is, first, a bit of anthropomorphism in that dialectics is (thinks or acts) 'critical and revolutionary'. Second, we see the fallacy of circular reasoning that dialectics is 'revolutionary' and its vital forms of movement are 'leaps', 'transformation into the opposite..', etc., just because Marx and Lenin assume with the help of the dialectical schema that these are the essential character of dialectics. (Do they offer any other proof?) As a matter of fact, however, changes and developments in Nature and human societies can be gradual, evolutionary, revolutionary, retrogressive or anything. Third, what they think will happen is derived from what they wish to see happen just as in Hegelian dialectics. This is, in a commonplace expression, wishful thinking. Fourth, what is implied by 'revolution', 'transformation into the opposite', 'destruction of the old and emergence of the new', etc., is the transition from capitalism to socialism (communism). This is, as I already pointed out, an obscure transition from something indefinite to some other thing indefinite.

In the contemporary empiricist approach to social phenomena – although there are substantial amounts of rigorous argument on this subject by A. N. Whitehead, Bertrand Russell, Hans Reichenbach, Karl Popper, etc. – generally speaking, we do not believe in absolute certainty guaranteed by natural laws intrinsic to society, but rely on hypotheses set up through the following process: recognition of the problem; formulation of a functional hypothesis; its testing (consequences of deduction tested by additional data); correction and/or improvement of the hypothesis (which we may now call a law or a theory). And as to the complicated and fluid historical or social changes determined by multifarious factors, we do not make predictions 'with the precision of the natural sciences', but are guided by probability criteria on the basis of available information and knowledge.

4 Tools and visions, facts and values

My summary explanation of the functional role of hypotheses may induce some readers to recollect Karl Popper's 'piecemeal engineering',[57] or Lionel Robbins's *pure* definition of economics,[58] and to question the whereabouts of visions and values.

I do not, of course, disregard them. In social issues human strivings are among the most important determinants. In the process of scientific cognition, these elements come into consideration in the first stage, 'recognition of the problem', which is the combined effort of fact-finding and the grip of some vision, or more strictly, the establishment of some 'value premise'[59] in Gunnar Myrdal's terminology.

But in the process of employing hypotheses which take the form of 'If . . . then . . .' statements, visions and values are not included. By saying this I do not mean that I set an absolute line of demarcation between tools and visions, facts and values, *is* and *ought*. For instance, when we make a study of the future economic growth of a country applying some working hypothesis, the concept 'economic growth' itself is already 'value-loaded'.[60] It carries the implication that economic growth is something desirable. This is quite natural and does not do any harm to objective and scientific inquiry into the matter. Only we should always be careful not to forget to ask the radical question 'For what?' and re-examine the value premise itself.

In the Marxian dialectical conception of world history, the prime mover is the contradiction between productive forces and production relations, in which productive forces are the leading factor of the two. Hence Marxists' naive belief in the righteousness of rapid economic growth resulting from advancing productive forces, and their persistent claim on overtaking capitalist countries in economic competition in an age when the survival by harmony and balance without growth is already on the agenda among the most developed economies.

I do not deny that Marx who tried to enforce 'the will of his age'[61] was one of the great men in world history. His grand system of ideology had, still has, and will continue to have a wide and deep influence on the course of history. Not to speak of the communist countries, Japan has many 'progressive' people who think in terms of Marxism, and the western countries see new defenders of Marxian ideology come out one after another. (Written in 1972. Now it is changing.) So the basic fallacies and errors contained in Marxism must be made crystal clear for the establishment of a real free, unrestrained manner of thinking. For those who would miss the absolute certainty and universal validity of Marxian 'laws', Werner Sombart's advice to throw them away, written more than seventy years ago, manifests its validity even today:

> When we lose the comfortable formulas that have hitherto been our guides amid the complexities of existence . . . we feel like drowning in the ocean of facts until we find a new foothold or learn to swim.'[62]

In this historical age of rapid transition it is all the more required to test, improve, if necessary abrogate, old hypotheses, form new ones, and be prepared to make reappraisals of their value foundations.

7 The Law of the Falling Rate of Profit, Reproduction Scheme and Imperialist Expansion: The Self-Contradiction Common to Marx's Law and Lenin's Scheme

I THE FUNDAMENTAL CONTRADICTION INVOLVED IN THE LAW OF THE FALLING RATE OF PROFIT

During the Lent term in 1966 I was staying at Cambridge University. One day Mrs Joan Robinson gave me a copy of her preface, still in manuscript, to the second edition of *An Essay on Marxian Economics*. On reading this I found the following passage:

> The constant rate of exploitation in Volume (Book) III is not explained, and the fact that it entails a rising level of real wages is not noticed. I was much startled when I came upon this in reading *Capital* for the first time. None of the discussions and controversies I have had since have cleared the point up.[1]

There follows my reasoning on how Marx became lost in his theoretical jungle.

1 The pivotal self-contradiction explained in brief

First, the crucial point of Marx's self-contradiction, elucidated in detail in Chapter 4 of the present volume (Section II, subsections 3 and 4), is shown. In the first line of Chapter 13, Book III of *Capital* 'The law (of the tendency of the rate of profit to fall) as such', we read: 'Assuming a given wage'.[2] Then Marx proceeds to develop a 'hypothetical series' demonstrating the law:

Pd_1	$100c + 100v + 100s = 300$	$p' = 50\%$
Pd_2	$400c + 100v + 100s = 600$	$p' = 20\%$

Marx supposes that '£100 are the wages of 100 workers for, say, one week'.[3] But the organic composition of capital rises 4-fold from $100c/100v$ in Pd_1 to $400c/100v$ in Pd_2. This means that productivity rises far more rapidly, say, 50-fold. (This large multiple is based on Marx's own historical example; see Ch. 4, Sec.II, subsection 2, present volume.)

If productivity rises 50-fold, the price of the commodities falls to $1/50$th, because 'the value (=price) of the commodities is in inverse ratio to the productiveness of labour'.[4] (See Ch. 4, Section III, subsection 3, present volume, for a more detailed explanation.) This enables the 100 labourers in Pd_2 receiving the same (nominal) wages of £100 as in Pd_1, to buy 50 times as many goods as the 100 labourers in Pd_1. In other words, the real wage level of the labourers rises 50-fold. Marx overlooked this inevitable discrepancy between nominal wages and real ones. This is what startled Mrs Robinson. But how did Marx come to commit such a self-defeating theoretical error?

2   The confusing explanation of 'relative surplus value' and 'extra surplus value'

The origin of this error is to be found in Chapter 12, 'The concept of relative surplus value'. At the beginning of this chapter Marx gives the definition of relative surplus-value. When the length of a working day is given, if the productivity of the industries related to the production of wage-goods rises, the value of labour-power falls. In other words, the length of the necessary labour-time is shortened, in inverse ratio to the productivity rise. 'The surplus value arising from the curtailment of the necessary labour-time . . . I call relative surplus value'.[5]

This definition is clear-cut, leaving no room for any doubt. But in the following illustration he becomes confused. He begins well enough: 'The cheapened commodity . . . causes only a *pro tanto* fall in the value of labour-power, a fall proportional to the extent of that commodity's employment in the reproduction of labour-power.'[6] Here Marx takes up the instance of shirts, a kind of wage-goods. If shirts are cheapened, 'it causes only a *pro tanto* fall in the value of labour-power'. If wage-goods, 1 . . . n, are cheapened, the aggregation of price curtailments causes *pro tanto* fall in the value of labour-power. 'This general result is treated, here, as if it were the immediate result directly aimed at in each individual case.'[7]

'Each individual case' should be the i-th industry, for instance, shirt manufacturing, out of all wage-goods industries, 1 . . . n. But his illustration (Figure 7.2 below) is the case of an exceptionally advanced enterprise within the i-th industry obtaining an '*extra* surplus value'. In this instance, as is demonstrated in the following section 3, a fall in the value of labour-power *does not occur*. And Marx fails to notice it. Here he begins a chain of confused reasoning.

3 Illustration of extra surplus value by Marx

If one hour's labour is embodied in sixpence, a value of six shillings will be produced in a working-day of 12 hours. Suppose that with the prevailing productiveness of labour, 12 articles are produced in these 12 hours. Let the value of the means of production used up in each article be sixpence. Under these circumstances, each article costs one shilling; sixpence for the value of means of production, and sixpence for the value newly added in working with those means... the price of the labour-power is five shillings.[8]

(So surplus value is one shilling – T.H.)

The above case is shown in an arranged form in Figure 7.1.

$c = 6s$	$v = 5s$	$s = 1s$
12h	10h	2h

per 1 article

$c = 6d$	$v = 5d$	$s = 1d$

The rate of surplus value, $\frac{s}{v} = \frac{1}{5}$

The rate of profit, $\frac{s}{c+v} = \frac{1}{11}$

Figure 7.1   The case of average enterprises: 1 labourer producing 12 articles in a working day

In this case, the rate of surplus value is $\frac{1}{5}$, and the rate of profit is $\frac{1}{11}$. (This latter rate is not perceived by Marx.)

Now let some one capitalist contrive to double the productiveness of labour, and to produce in the working-day of 12 hours, 24, instead of 12 articles. The value of the means of production remaining the same, the value of each article will fall to ninepence, made up of sixpence for the value of the means of production and threepence for the value added by the labour . . . the day's labour creates, as before, a new value of six shillings . . . Of this value each article now has embodied in it $\frac{1}{24}$ th, instead of $\frac{1}{12}$ th, threepence instead of sixpence . . . The individual value of these articles is now below their social value (9 pence) . . . If therefore, the capitalist . . . sells his commodity at its social value of one shilling, he sells it for threepence above its individual value, and thus realises an extra surplus value of threepence . . . If he sells them above their individual but under their social value, say at tenpence each . . . he still squeezes an extra surplus-value of one penny.[9]

This case is shown also in an an arranged form in Figure 7.2.

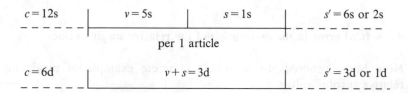

The rate of surplus value, $\frac{s}{v} = \frac{1}{5}$.

The rate of individual surplus-value, $\frac{s+s'}{v} = \frac{1+6}{5}$ or $\frac{1+2}{5}$.

The rate of individual profit, $\frac{s+s'}{c+v} = \frac{1+6}{12+5}$ or $\frac{1+2}{12+5}$.

Note: s' = extra surplus value.

Figure 7.2   The case of an advanced enterprise: 1 labourer producing 24 articles in a working-day

In this case, the (social) rate of surplus value remains at $\frac{1}{5}$, because it is the same society as in Figure 7.1. So if the article is sold for one shilling, the rate of *individual* surplus value (term coined by T.H.) comes to be $\frac{7}{5}$ and the rate of individual profit $\frac{7}{17}$. If he sells it for tenpence, the former rate becomes $\frac{3}{5}$ and the latter $\frac{3}{17}$.

Here Marx mentions, however, that 'the ratio of the necessary labour to the surplus labour, which under average social conditions was 5:1, is now only 5:3'.[10] This passage provides evidence that he does not make a clear distinction between the general or social surplus value, $\frac{s}{v}$, and an individual surplus value, $\frac{s+s'}{v}$. And he refers only to the case of $\frac{s+s'}{v} = \frac{3}{5}$, overlooking $\frac{s+s'}{v} = \frac{7}{5}$. Further, Marx argues that 'he does individually, what the whole body of capitalists engaged in producing relative surplus value, do collectively'.[11] Here comes Marx's confusion into the open. A correct description of the situation should be that the rate of social surplus value, $\frac{s}{v} = \frac{1}{5}$, remains *unchanged*, and only the rate of individual surplus value rises to $\frac{7}{5}$ or $\frac{3}{5}$. If the above could be interpreted as the case of the whole *i*-th industry, for instance shirt-making, instead of an exceptionally advanced enterprise, then the productivity rise of the *i*-th industry would cause *a pro tanto* fall in the value of labour-power, which is transferred to surplus value, thus causing the *rise* of the rate of surplus value. Marx here fails to see the difference of role between an enterprise in the *i*-th industry and the whole body of the *i*-th industry. This ambiguity of his reasoning brings forth another fault in his description of the relative surplus value, as is shown in the following section.

4   A fatal error in the description of the relative surplus value

Now Marx proceeds to present a concrete example of producing relative surplus value:

> The value of commodities is in inverse ratio to the productiveness of labour. And so, too, is the value of labour-power, because it depends on the value of commodities . . . an average social working-day of 12 hours always produces the same new value, six shillings, no matter how this sum may be apportioned between surplus value and wages. But if, in consequence of increased productiveness, the value of the necessaries of life fall, and the value of a day's labour-power be thereby reduced from five shillings to three, the surplus value increases from one shilling to three.[12]

The illustration of this case is shown as Figure 7.3.

In contemporary terminology, when labour productivity rises by $\frac{2}{3}$, from 1 to $\frac{5}{3}$, the price level of wage goods falls in inverse ratio by $\frac{2}{5}$, from 1 to $\frac{3}{5}$, and the nominal wages fall from 5 shillings to 3 shillings, thus producing 2 shillings of relative surplus value and raising the rate of surplus value from 20% to 100%. We see no problem in this lucid illustration. But his remark on 'the particular modes of producing relative surplus value' in the last sentence of this chapter contains an unmistakable self-contradiction as follows:

> The object of all development of the productiveness of labour, within the limits of capitalist production, is to shorten that part of the working-day,

$$P_t = \frac{1}{1+k_1}P_0 \qquad (Pd1)$$

$v = 5s$	$s = 1s$
10h	2h

$$k_1 = \frac{2}{3}$$

If $P_0 = 1$, $\qquad (Pd2)$

$v = 3s$	$s = 3s$
6h	6h

$$P_t = \frac{2}{3}$$

Figure 7.3 An example of production of relative surplus value

When this hypothetical society proceeds from Pd_1 to Pd_2 and
R.W. = const. then N.W. = 5s → 3s and $\frac{s}{v} = \frac{1}{5} \to \frac{3}{3} = 1$.

Note: $P_0 =$ price of commodities at the beginning.
$\quad\quad\ P_t =$ price of commodities after labour
$\quad\quad\quad\quad\quad$ productivity changed.
$\quad\quad\ k_1 =$ the rate of change of productivity in the
$\quad\quad\quad\quad\quad$ production of commodities.
$\quad\ N.W. =$ nominal wages.

during which workman must labour for his own benefit [necessary labour-time, v], and by that very shortening, to lengthen the other part of the day, during which he is at liberty to work gratis for the capitalists [surplus labour-time, s]. How far this result is also attainable, without cheapening commodities, will appear from an examination of the particular modes of producing relative surplus value, to which examination we now proceed.[13]

It is now impossible to curtail v and increase s without cheapening commodities. What can be obtained without cheapening the i-th article in the i-th wage-goods industry is an extra surplus value s' belonging to an exceptionally advanced enterprise, not the relative surplus value (increase of s). If Marx means the production of an extra surplus value by 'the modes of producing relative surplus value', it is an obvious mistake. If he means by that the fall of the value, cheapening, of the i-th articles, as a whole, the relative surplus value will be produced to that extent. But this contradicts the premise of 'without cheapening commodities'. It is clear that Marx confuses the acquisition of an extra surplus value s' by an exceptionally advanced enterprise with the production of relative surplus value s by the fall of value of the i-th articles as a whole.

5   The confusion developed in Chapter 25, Book I

In 'an examination of the particular modes of producing relative surplus value' in Chapters 13, 14, 15 and 25 of Book I, Marx repeats and develops the theoretical error he committed in Chapter 12. I have already disclosed the concrete examples of this confusion in detail in previous work.[14] Here we take up only the last and most significant case in Chapter 25, in which Marx analyses 'the influence of the growth of capital on the lot of the labouring class' and in this case 'the composition of the total social capital . . . with this alone are we . . . concerned'.[15] In section 2 of this chapter he gives a problematical illustration as follows:

> Suppose that a capital-value at first is divided into 50% of constant and 50% of variable. If in the meantime the original capital, say 6,000, has increased to 18,000, its variable capital has also increased. It was 3,000, it is now 3,600. But whereas formerly an increase of capital by 20% would have sufficed to raise the demand for labour 20%, now this latter rise requires a tripling of the original capital.[16]

This story seems to be of an enterprise adopting an exceptionally advanced technology on the one hand, and, at the same time, of the total social capital heightening its average composition as time proceeds on the other. The term 'a capital value' appears to suggest the former case. The theme of this chapter, however, is the total social capital. So 'a capital value' should be a theoretical model of the total social capital. If so interpreted, when the variable capital increases from 3,000 to 3,600 raising employment by 20%, the per capita nominal wage remains constant. And the heightening of the organic composition from $\frac{3000c}{30000v} = 1$ to $\frac{14400c}{3600v} = 4$ means a far more rapid rise in productivity (of expended labour: $c + v + s$), say 50-fold, and a corresponding fall of price level in inverse ratio to $\frac{1}{50}$ th (Refer to Ch. 4, Sec.II, subsections 2 and 3, present volume, here). Accordingly, the real wage level in direct proportion to the rate of productivity-rise is, say, 50-fold. And if we add surplus value to this numerical example, the rate of surplus value should remain constant as is the case of the 'hypothetical series' demonstrating the law of the falling rate of profit. (See the 'series' shown in the beginning of this chapter.) Marx should not have thought of such a capitalist society. This self-contradictory situation can be elucidated step by step by employing Tables 7.1 and 7.2

The case of Table 7.1 is essentially of the same nature as that of Figure 7.2, an advanced enterprise gaining an extra surplus value. But

Table 7.1 The case in Chapter 25, Book I interpreted as the case of an exceptionally advanced enterprise

---

$$(9000G)$$

Average enterprises $3000c + 3000v + 3000s = 9000$ $\frac{s}{c+v} = 50\%$

$$(3000L)$$

$P_t = \frac{1}{1+k_1} P_0$ $\frac{s}{v} = 1$

$(k_1 = 49)$ $1G = \pounds 1$

$$(1080000G)$$

Advanced enterprise $144000c + 3600v + 3600s = 216000$

$$(3600L)$$

$\frac{s}{v} = 1$

$1G = \pounds\frac{1}{50}$ (individual value)

If sold at the price of

$1G = \pounds 1$ (social value)

$s' = \pounds 1058400$ (extra surplus value)

$\therefore \frac{s+s'}{v} = 295$ $\therefore \frac{s+s'}{c+v} = 5{,}900\%$

Note: $G =$ goods, $L =$ labourers

$\pounds 1058400 = \pounds 1080000 - \pounds 21600$

this is out of the question, because the theme of this chapter is the total social capital. In Table 7.2 'a capital value' is regarded as a model of the total social capital. In the period Pd_{2a} the rate of increase of variable capital and that of employment are the same, 20%, as is indicated by Marx. As a logical corollary, the rate of suplus value remains constant and the real wages of the labourers rise in direct proportion to the productivity rise. This might be suitable as a model for contemporary capitalism, but cannot be that of the capitalist society Marx conceived of. To be consistent with 'the lot of the labouring class' Marx foresaw, the model should be arranged as Pd_{2b}, in which real wages remain constant, nominal wages are cut by $\frac{49}{50}$, thus producing 3,528 of relative surplus value and raising the rate of surplus value from 1 to 99. (This case is essentially of the same nature as that of Figure 7.3.)

Table 7.2   The same interpreted as the case of heightening of $\frac{c}{v}$ of the total social capital

---

$$(9000G)$$

Pd_1 $3000c + 3000v + 3000s = 9000$ $\frac{s}{c+v} = 50\%$

$$(3000L)$$

$P_t = \frac{1}{1+k_1} P_0$

$(k_1 = 49)$

$$(1080000G)$$

Pd_{2a} $144000c + 3600v + 3600s = 216000$ $\frac{s}{c+v} = 20\%$

$$(3600L)$$

$\frac{s}{v} = 1$

$1G = £\frac{1}{50}$ (social value)

$N.W. = $ const. $1L = £1$

$R.W._{\cdot t} = (1+k_1)R.W._{\cdot 0}$ (50-fold)

$$(1080000G)$$

Pd_{2b} $144000c + \ \ \ 72v + 7128s = 216000$ $\frac{s}{c+v} = 49.3\%$

$$(3600L)$$

$\frac{s}{v} = 99$

$R.W. = $ const.

$N.W._{\cdot t} = \frac{1}{1+k_1} N.W._{\cdot 0}$ $1L = £\frac{1}{50}$

Thus it is exposed that this numerical example in Chapter 25 inherits the self-contradiction of 'particular modes of producing relative surplus value without cheapening commodities' in Chapter 12: in other words, the confusion of an exceptionally advanced enterprise obtaining an extra surplus value with the total social capital gaining relative surplus value as technology progresses.

6   The accomplishment of the confusion in Chapter 13, Book III

Let us begin with a very simple but interesting computation. If we divide all the terms of the expression Pd_1 in Table 7.2 by 30 and the expression Pd_{2a} by 36, we get the 'hypothetical series' shown in the beginning of this chapter illustrating the law of the falling rate of profit.

At a glance we know that 'a capital value' (plus surplus value, s) in Chapter 25, Book I, and 'a hypothetical series' in Chapter 13, Book III showing the falling rate of profit are of just the same nature (see Table 7.3). And it goes without saying that the law of the falling rate of profit is that of the average rate of the total social capital. This law should be a combination of the production of relative surplus value: in other words, the rise of the average rate of surplus value of the total social capital, $\frac{s}{v}$, in Chapter 12, Book I (where the heightening of the organic composition of capital, $\frac{c}{v}$, is not directly referred to) on the one hand, and the heightening of the organic composition of capital, $\frac{c}{v}$, reflecting the productivity rise in the total social capital in Chapter 25, Book I (where surplus value, s, does not directly come into consideration) on the other.

Now we can confirm that a fundamental premise of the propositions through these three chapters is a productivity-rise from Pd_1 to Pd_2, $k_1 > 0$; respectively $K_1 = 49$ in the 'hypothetical series', $k_1 = \frac{2}{3}$ in Figure 7.3, $k_1 = 49$ in Tables 7.1, 7.2 and 7.3. As 'the value of commodities is in inverse ratio to the productiveness of labour',[17] $P_t = \frac{1}{1+k_1} P_0$, $K_1 > 0$; respectively, $P_t = \frac{1}{50} P_0$ in the 'series', $P_t = \frac{3}{50} P_0$ in Figure 7.3, $P_t = \frac{1}{50} P_0$ in Tables 7.1, 7.2 and 7.3. Another premise in the production of relative surplus value being real wages = const., the productivity-rise causes the reduction of nominal wages in inverse ratio to it: respectively, $\frac{3}{5}v = \sigma L$, (σ = constant) in Figure 7.3 (Pd_2, $= \frac{1}{50}v = \sigma L$ in Tables 7.2 (Pd_{2b}) and 7.3 (Pd_{2b}). Thus we find that in the 'series' (Pd_{2b}) $\frac{1}{50}v = aL$ should be the case, but in fact it is $v = aL$. In plain words nominal wages of 100 labourers in Pd_2 of the 'series' should be reduced to $\frac{1}{50}$-th of the sum which they received in Pd_1. But instead of it they receive the same amount as in Pd_1, therefore enjoying a 50-fold rise in real wages. This conflicts with the labour conditions in a capitalist society Marx assumed. What caused this incompatibility is the beginning sentence of Chapter 13, Book III:

Assuming a *given wage* [emphasis – T.H.] and working-day, a variable capital, for instance of 100, represents a certain number of employed labourers. It is the index of this number.'[18]

A wage level canmnot be given, unchanged in the 'series', when the model society makes technical progress from Pd_1 to Pd_2. If nominal wages remain unchanged, then real wages inevitably rise. So Marx

Table 7.3   The numerical example in Chapter 25, Book I leads to the hypothetical series in Chapter 13, Book III

$$(9000G)$$

Pd_1 $3000c + 3000v + 3000s = 9000$ $\frac{s}{c+v} = 50\%$

        $\div 30$ $(3000L)$ $\div 30$ $\div 30$

                $\div 30$

$P_t = \frac{1}{1+k_1} P_0$

$(k_1 = 49)$

$$(300G)$$

Pd_1 $100c + 100v + 100s = 300$

        $(100L)$

$$(1080000G)$$

Pd_{2a} $144000c + 3600v + 3600s = 216000$ $\frac{s}{c+v} = 20\%$

        $\div 36$ $(3000L)$ $\div 36$ $\div 36$

                $\div 36$

$$(30000G)$$

        $400c + 100v + 100s = 600$

        $(100L)$

$$(1080000G)$$

Pd_{2b} $144000c + 72v + 7128s = 216000$ $\frac{s}{c+v} = 46.3\%$

        $\div 36$ $(3600L)$ $\div 36$ $\div 36$

                $\div 36$

$$(30000G)$$

        $400c + 2v + 198s = 600$

        $(100L)$

should have adopted $400c + 2v + 198s = 600$ (Pd_{2b}, Table 7.3) in place of $400s + 100v + 100s = 600$ (Pd_2, the 'series'). This is Marx's self-contradiction which 'much startled' Mrs Robinson. Its main points are set forth in Table 7.4.

Table 7.4 Self-contradiction involved in the 'series' illustrating the falling rate of profit

Logically consistent premises Marx should have set forth:

$K_1 > 0$, $P_t = \frac{1}{1+k_1} P_0$. In P_t, $\frac{1}{1+k_1} v = \sigma L$

Premises Marx really set forth:

$k_1 > 0$, $P_t = P_0$. In P_t, $v = \sigma L$

Self-contradiction of Marx:

$K_1 > 0$ is contradictory to $P_t = P_0$ and

$v = \sigma L$ which require the premise $K_1 = 0$

Fundamental contradiction:

$k_1 > 0$ and $k_1 = 0$ at the same time.

II MARX'S LAW OF THE FALLING RATE OF PROFIT AND LENIN'S SCHEME OF EXPANDING REPRODUCTION

It is customary to treat the law of the falling rate of profit and the reproduction scheme as separate subjects. In this way, however, it is impossible to form an integral understanding of a series of propositions composing the root and stem of Marxian economics. Development of productive power → heightening of the organic composition of capital → widening gap (contradiction) between production and consumption, priority growth of the department of the means of production, ever aggravating depressions → catastrophe → communist revolution. The demonstration of the 'inevitability' of this historic process 'inherent' in the capitalist society is mainly presented in Chapter 25, 'The general law of capitalist accumulation', Book I; and in Part 3, 'The law of the tendency of the rate of profit to fall', Book III. And substantially the same thing is contained in Lenin's reproduction scheme of an extended scale. Moreover, Lenin's interpretation of it inherits the self-contradiction immanent in the law of the falling rate of profit. How did this come about?

1 Defects in Marx's reproduction schemes on an extended scale

First, let us examine Marx's reproduction schemes. We note that the expression $400c + 100v + 100s = 600$ ('series', Pd_2) has the nature of a one-sector macro-model of a hypothetical society. We can easily change it to a two-sector model as Table 7.5 shows.

Table 7.5   The relation between the law of the falling rate of profit and the reproduction scheme

$$400c + 100v + 100s = 600$$

multiplied by 15

$$6000c + 1500v + 1500s = 9000$$

divided in a ratio of 2 to 1

$$4000c + 1000v + 1000s = 6000$$

$$2000c + 500v + 500s = 3000$$

The last two expressions in Table 7.5 are nothing but the first figures of the two-sector simple reproduction scheme in Chapter 20, Book II of *Capital*.

(1) The 'Initial scheme' contradicting the assumption of perfect competition

As is well known, with a little change in the above expressions, Marx obtained the first year figures of the so-called 'Initial scheme for accumulation on an extended scale',[19] which is introduced in an arranged form in Table 7.6.

This scheme has, however, the inadmissible theoretical defects shown in Table 7.7.

Here Marx still thinks in terms of value-price system in which no discrepancy between value and price exists. This requires (1) demand and supply are always balanced through competition, $S = D$; (2) $\frac{c}{v}$, $\frac{s}{c+v}$, $\frac{\Delta c + \Delta v}{c+v}$ etc. in the two departments are equal and the ratio of the two departments is fixed. These two conditions may be called 'Marxian style golden-age path'. ('The price of production' appears in Part II, Book II of *Capital*. See 'The transformation problem' in Sec.III, Ch.2 of the present volume).

Marx is clearly aware of the first condition, but is not sure of the second condition. This gives rise to the inconsistencies in the schedule as shown in Table 7.6.

Table 7.6   Marx's 'initial' expanding reproduction scheme

Y_1	$4000c_1 + 1000v_1 + 1000s_1 = 6000$ $1500c_2 + 750v_2 + 750s_2 = 3000$

Y_1 $4000c_1 + 1000v_1 + 1000s_1 = 6000$ $1500c_2 + 750v_2 + 750s_2 = 3000$

$\qquad\quad \underbrace{400\Delta c_1 + 100\Delta v_1 + 500\overline{s_1}}\qquad\qquad \underbrace{100\Delta c_2 + 50\Delta v_2 + 600\overline{s_2}}$

Equilibrium condition of expanding reproduction:

$\qquad 1000v_1 + 1000s_1 > 1500c_2$

$\qquad 1000v_1 + 100\Delta v_1 + 500\overline{s_1} = 1500c_2 + 100\Delta c_2$

in algebraic expression

$\qquad v_1 + s_1 > c_2$

$\qquad v_1 + \Delta v_1 + \overline{s_1} = c_2 + \Delta c_2$

Y_2 $4400c_1 + 1100v_1 + 1100s_1 = 6600$ $1600c_2 + 800v_2 + 800s_2 = 3200$

$\qquad\quad \underbrace{440\Delta c_1 + 110\Delta v_1 + 550\overline{s_1}}\qquad\qquad \underbrace{160\Delta c_2 + 80\Delta v_2 + 560\overline{s_2}}$

Y_3 $4840c_1 + 1210v_1 + 1210s_1 = 7260$ $1760c_2 + 880v_2 + 880s_2 = 3520$

$\qquad\quad \underbrace{484\Delta c_1 + 121\Delta v_1 + 605\overline{s_1}}\qquad\qquad \underbrace{176\Delta c_2 + 88\Delta v_2 + 616\overline{s_2}}$

Y_4 $5324c_1 + 1331v_1 + 1331s_1 = 7986$ $1936c_2 + 968v_2 + 968s_2 = 3872$

$\qquad\quad \underbrace{4532\Delta c_1 + 133\Delta v_1 + 666s_1}\qquad\qquad \underbrace{193\Delta c_2 + 97\Delta v_2 + 678\overline{s_2}}$

(*Y_5* and *Y_6* are omitted)

Note: $\overline{s}$ = surplus value for consumption.

       $\frac{c}{v} = \frac{\Delta c}{\Delta v}$ ∴ technology unchanged.

       Y = year.

First, the organic composition of capital, c, and the rate of profit, $\frac{s}{c+v}$, are different in the two departments. Then the transfer of capital from Department 1 (means of production) to Department 2 (means of consumption) is inevitable. Therefore, commodities are to be exchanged not at value-price, but at 'the price of production'.

Second, the rate of accumulation, $\frac{\Delta c + \Delta v}{s}$, is larger in Department 1 than in Department 2.

Third, the capital-growth rate, $\frac{\Delta c + \Delta v}{c+v}$, in the first year of Department 1 is larger than that of Department 2. This causes the priority growth of Department 1 in the transition process from the first year to the second year.

158   *Marx's* Capital *and One Free World*

Table 7.7   Theoretical defects in Marx's 'initial' scheme

% except $\frac{c}{v}$	$\frac{c}{v}$		$\frac{s}{c+v}$		$\frac{\Delta c + \Delta v}{s}$		$\frac{\Delta c + \Delta v}{c+v}$		$\frac{c_2+v_2+s_2}{c_1+v_1+s_1}$
$\frac{c}{v}$	I	II	I	II	I	II	I	II	
Y_1	4	2	20	33.3	50	20	10	6.6	50
Y_2	4	2	20	33.3	50	30	10	10	48
Y_3	4	2	20	33.3	50	30	10	10	48
Y_4	4	2	20	33.3	50	30	10	10	48

Defects:
1. $\frac{c}{v}$, $\frac{s}{c+v}$ between two departments are different
2. In Y_1 $\frac{\Delta c + \Delta v}{c+v}$ is larger in department 1 than in department 2.

Note: This table is calculated from Table 7.6.

(2) The 'Scheme a' abandoned by Marx unaccomplished

All these points runs counter to the 'golden-age path' at value-price. Why did it happen? The answer will be obtained by analysing his 'Scheme a' and 'Second illustration'[20] which involve the defects closely related to those found in the 'Initial scheme'. In Section 3, Chapter 20, Book II of *Capital* Marx first presents the 'Scheme a' as shown in the Table 7.8 in an arranged form.

In this 'Scheme a' the conditions of the 'golden-age path' at value-price are mostly fulfilled because both Department 1 and Department 2 have the same ratios in the organic composition of capital (4%), the rate of profit (20%), the rate of accumulation (50%), and the rate of capital-growth (10%).

However, as regards the half of the surplus value allotted to accumulation, there are evident mistakes. First, in Department 1 the additional investment is $500\Delta c_1 + 0\Delta v_1$. Thus we cannot find the wages needed to employ the additional labourers for operating the additional means of production purchased by $500\Delta c_1$. In the expanding reproduction under the assumption of a given technique, the right allocation should be $400\Delta c_1 + 100\Delta v_1$. Second, in Department 2 the additional investment is $140\Delta c_2 + 48\Delta v_2$. Thus the organic composition is 3, which signifies that the technical level of the newly invested capital

Table 7.8 Unaccomplished reproduction 'Scheme a'

$4000c_1 + 1000v_1 + 1000s_1 = 6000$	$1500c_2 + 376v_2 + 376s_2 = 2252$
$500\Delta c_1 + 500\overline{s_1}$	$140\Delta c_2 + 48\Delta v_2 + 188\overline{s_2}$
$(400\Delta c_1 + 100\Delta v_1)$	$(150\Delta c_2 + 38\Delta v_2)$

Note: $\overline{s} = s$ for consumption

$\dfrac{c}{v}$	$\dfrac{s}{c+v}$	$\dfrac{\Delta c + \Delta v}{s}$	$\dfrac{\Delta c + \Delta v}{c+v}$
4	20	50	10

Note: % except $\dfrac{c}{v}$

is lower than that of the existing capital. This must be corrected as follows: $150\Delta c_2 + 38\Delta v_2$.

Now let us examine whether the equilibrium condition of reproduction on an extended scale, $v_1 + \Delta v_1 + \overline{s} = c_2 + \Delta c_2$, is fulfilled in this 'Scheme a'. First, if we apply Marx's figures involving mistakes, we obtain $1000v_1 + 500\overline{s_1} < 1500c_2 + 140\Delta c_2$. This inequality means that $140mp$ (means of production) which should be exchanged with $140\Delta c_2 \, mc$ (means of consumption) is lacking. Second, if we apply the figures corrected by the author, we obtain $1000v_1 + 100\Delta v_1 + 500\overline{s_1} < 1500c_2 + 150\Delta c_2$. In this case only $100mp$ exists for the exchange with $150\Delta c_2 \, mc$, i.e. $50mp$ is lacking

The reason why Marx could not proceed to the second year and after is now clear. With the figures he had adopted the equilibrium condition of expanding reproduction could not be fulfilled. So that he abandoned the 'Scheme a' unaccomplished and moved to the 'Initial scheme for accumulation on an extended scale', which is already shown as Table 7.9. This scheme fulfills the equilibrium condition, $1000v_1 + 100\Delta v_1 + 500\overline{s_1} = 1500c_2 + 100\Delta c_2$, but it violates the assumption in the course of his efforts to seek out numbers which satisfy the above equation.

(3) The 'second illustration' with the 'priority growth of Department 2'

Then Marx presents the 'second illustration', as shown in Table 7.9, in which 'the general average ratio of the variable to the constant capital is that of 1:5', presupposing 'a considerable development of capitalist production and accordingly of the productivity of social labour'[21] compared with the state of the 'Initial scheme'.

Table 7.9 *'Second illustration' with the 'priority growth of Department 2'*[22]

Y_1 $5000c_1 + 1000v_1 + 1000s_1 = 7000$ $1430c_2 + 285v_2 + 285s_2 = 2000$

$417\Delta c_1 + 83\Delta v_1 + 500\bar{s}$ $153\Delta c_2 + 31\Delta v_2 + 101\bar{s}$

Y_2 $5417c_1 + 1083v_1 + 1083s_1 = 7583$ $1583c_2 + 316v_2 + 316s_2 = 2215$

$452\Delta c_1 + 90\Delta v_1 + 541\bar{s}$ $132\Delta c_2 + 26\Delta v_2 + 158\bar{s}$

Y_3 $5869c_1 + 1173v_1 + 1173s_1 = 8215$ $1715c_2 + 342v_2 + 342s_2 = 2399$

$489\Delta c_1 + 98\Delta v_1 + 586\bar{s}$ $143\Delta c_2 + 29\Delta v_2 + 170\bar{s}$

Y_4 $6358c_1 + 1271v_1 + 1271s_1 = 8900$ $1858c_2 + 371v_2 + 371s_2 = 2600$

	$\frac{c}{v}$		$\frac{s}{c+v}$		$\frac{\Delta c + \Delta v}{s}$		$\frac{\Delta c + \Delta v}{c+v}$		$\frac{c_2+v_2+s_2}{c_1+v_1+s_1}$
	I	II	I	II	I	II	I	II	
Y_1	5	5	16.6	16.6	50	65	8.3	10.7	28.6
Y_2	5	5	16.6	16.6	50	50	8.3	8.3	29.2
Y_3	5	5	16.6	16.6	50	50	8.3	8.3	29.2
Y_4	5	5	16.6	16.6	50	50	8.3	8.3	29.2

Note: % except $\frac{c}{v}$.

The 'Second illustration' is better than the 'Initial scheme' in that its Departments 1 and 2 have the same ratios in the organic composition of capital (5) and the rate of profit (16.6). But still one theoretical defect is left. The capital-growth rate of Department 2 in the first year (65%) is larger than that of Department 1 (50%). This causes the 'priority growth of Department 2' (from 28.6% to 29.2%) in the process of the transition from the first year to the second. Here again Marx failed to reach a 'golden-age path' model in his attempt to satisfy the equilibrium condition of expanding reproduction in the case of two-sector model, $v_1 + \Delta v_1 + \overline{s_1} = c_2 + \Delta c_2$.

(4) An expanding reproduction scheme Marx should have composed

Thus all through the three schemes of expanding reproduction shown above, Marx failed to construct the 'golden-age path' model, which at the same time satisfies $v_1 + \Delta v_1 + \overline{s_1} = c_2 + \Delta c_2$. The scheme he was subconsciously seeking after and almost attained should have been that of Table 7.10 which the author worked out.

In this scheme the organic composition of capital, the rate of profit, the rate of accumulation and the rate of capital-growth are all equal in Departments 1 and 2. So that the assumption of the 'golden-age path' at value-price is satisfied and, therefore, the two departments grow with the same rate from the beginning, fulfilling the equilibrium condition of $v_1 + \Delta v_1 + \overline{s_1} = c_2 + \Delta c_2$.

2   Lenin's expanding reproduction scheme inheriting the contradiction involved in the law of the falling rate of profit

Marx's 'initial' expanding reproduction scheme is composed on the premise of unchanging technology. Therefore, Lenin points out, in his article, *On the So-called Market Question*, that 'from Marx's scheme . . . the conclusion cannot be drawn that Department 1 predominates over Department 2: both develop on parallel lines'.[23] And he makes one change in the premise of Marx's scheme that technology makes progress, i.e. $\frac{c}{v}$ heightens, in order to clarify that 'there will be a relatively more rapid increase in means of production than in articles of consumption'.[24]

Lenin's expanding reproduction scheme thus composed is shown in Table 7.11 in an arranged form. It seems correct in elucidating the priority growth of Department 1 by the gradual percentage decrease of Department 2 year by year (see the chart in Table 7.11).

Table 7.10　An expanding reproduction scheme Marx should have composed

Y_1　$4000c_1 + 1000v_1 + 1000s_1 = 6000$	$1454c_2 + 364v_2 + 364s_2 = 2182$

$$400\Delta c_1 + 100\Delta v_1 + \overline{500s_1}　　　　146\Delta c_2 + 36\Delta v_2 + \overline{182s_2}$$

Condition of balanced reproduction:

$$1000v_1 + 100\Delta v_1 + \overline{500s_1} = 1454c_2 + 146\Delta c_2$$

Y_2　$4400c_1 + 1100v_1 + 1100s_1 = 6600$	$1600c_2 + 400v_2 + 400s_2 = 2400$

$$440\Delta c_1 + 110\Delta v_1 + \overline{550s_1}　　　　160\Delta c_2 + 40\Delta v_2 + \overline{200s_2}$$

Y_3　$4840c_1 + 1210v_1 + 1210s_1 = 7260$	$1760c_2 + 440v_2 + 440s_2 = 2640$

$$484\Delta c_1 + 121\Delta v_1 + \overline{605s_1}　　　　176\Delta c_2 + 44\Delta v_2 + \overline{220s_2}$$

% except $\frac{c}{v}$	$\frac{c}{v}$	$\frac{s}{c+v}$	$\frac{\Delta c + \Delta v}{s}$	$\frac{\Delta c + \Delta v}{c+v}$	$\frac{c_2+v_2+s_2}{c_1+v_1+s_1}$
Y_1	4	20	50	10	36.36
Y_2	4	20	50	10	36.36
Y_3	4	20	50	10	36.36

How to work out this scheme:　In order to find out in Y_1 the numbers which satisfy the expanded reproduction under the limitation that $\frac{\Delta c + \Delta v}{c+v}$ are equally $\frac{1}{10}$ in both departments, the following equation must be solved:

$$1000v_1 + 100\Delta v_1 + \overline{500s_1} = c_2 + \frac{1}{10}c_2$$

And v_2 should be $\frac{1}{4}c_2$ and equal to s_2 by assumption.

Table 7.11   Lenin's expanding reproduction scheme[25]

Y_1	$4000c_1 + 1000v_1 + 1000s_1 = 6000$	$1500c_2 + 750v_2 + 750s_2 = 3000$
	$\overbrace{450\Delta c_1 + 50\Delta v_1 + 500\overline{s_1}}$	$\overbrace{50\Delta c_2 + 10\Delta v_2 + 690\overline{s_2}}$
Y_2	$4450c_1 + 1050v_1 + 1050s_1 = 6550$	$1550c_2 + 760v_2 + 760s_2 = 3070$
	$\overbrace{500\Delta c_1 + 25\Delta v_1 + 525\overline{s_1}}$	$\overbrace{50\Delta c_2 + 6\Delta v_2 + 704\overline{s_1}}$
		[702]
Y_3	$4950c_1 + 1075v_1 + 1075s_1 = 7100$	$1600c_2 + 766v_2 + 766s_2 = 3132$
	$\overbrace{517.5\Delta c_1 + 20\Delta v_1 + 537.5\overline{s_1}}$	$\overbrace{32.5\Delta c_2 + 3\Delta v_2 + 730.5\overline{s_2}}$
	[1602]	[3134]
Y_4	$5467.5c_1 + 1095v_1 + 1095s_1 = 7657.5$	$1632.5c_2 + 769v_2 + 769s_2 = 3170.5$
	[1634.5]	[3172.5]

Note: Figures in [ ] are those miscalculated by Lenin. The figures above them are the right ones calculated by T.H.

% except $\frac{c}{v}$	$\frac{c}{v}$		$\frac{s}{c+v}$		$\frac{\Delta c + \Delta v}{s}$		$\frac{\Delta c + \Delta v}{c+v}$		$\frac{c_2 + v_2 + s_2}{c_1 + v_1 + s_1}$
	I	II	I	II	I	II	I	II	
Y_1	4.00	2.00	20	33.3	50	8	10.00	2.6	50
Y_2	4.24	2.04	19.1	32.9	50	7.4	9.5	2.4	46.9
Y_3	4.60	2.09	17.8	32.4	50	4.6	8.9	1.5	44.1
Y_4	4.99	2.12	16.7	32.0	–	–	–	–	41.4

Note: The priority growth of Department 1 depends not only on $\frac{c}{v} < \frac{\Delta c}{\Delta v}$ but also on $\frac{\Delta c_1 + \Delta v_1}{c_1 + v_1} > \frac{\Delta c_2 + \Delta v_2}{c_2 + v_2}$.

But in fact it is not. The first year figures of Lenin's scheme are just those of Marx's 'initial' scheme. Accordingly, the defects of Marx's scheme are exactly followed in Lenin's scheme. The existence of differences in and $\frac{c}{v}$ and $\frac{s}{c+v}$, between the two departments is a violation of the assumption of 'golden-age path' at value-price. Larger $\frac{\Delta c + \Delta v}{s}$ and $\frac{\Delta c + \Delta v}{c+v}$ in Department 1 than in Department 2 are also the same kind of violation and makes the growth of Department 1 faster than that of Department 2. Thus, the priority growth of Department 1 in Lenin's scheme is a composite result of technical progress = the heightening of the organic composition of capital, $\frac{c}{v} < \frac{\Delta c}{\Delta v}$, and a larger rate of investment in Department 1 than in Department 2, $\frac{\Delta c_1 + \Delta v_1}{c_1 + v_1} > \frac{\Delta c_2 + \Delta v_2}{c_2 + v_2}$. Lenin should have demonstrated the priority growth of Department 1 under the conditions of $\frac{c}{v} < \frac{\Delta c}{\Delta v}$, $\frac{\Delta c_1 + \Delta v_1}{c_1 + v_1} = \frac{\Delta c_2 + \Delta v_2}{c_2 + v_2}$. Thus Lenin's scheme involves a failure derived from that of Marx's scheme.

Now let us proceed to the most problematical point in his scheme, which he did not intend, nor did he presumably notice. This scheme, composed on the basis of the heightening of the organic composition of capital in Chapter 25, Book I of *Capital*, and the constant rate of surplus value in the 'series' illustrating the law of the falling rate of profit in Chapter 13, Book III, logically comes to be another illustration of the law itself. The rate of profit falls year by year as shown above (see $\frac{s}{c+v}$ in Table 7.11). This is just as it should be and at the same time it should not be. For Marx the law of the falling rate of profit is the logical demonstration of the inevitable gap between supply and demand, $S > D$, caused by the 'contradiction' between the ever-expanding productive power of capitalist society and 'the consumer power based on the antagonistic conditions of distribution which reduce the consumption to a minimum'.[26] On the other hand, Lenin's scheme, a demonstration of the equilibrium conditions of reproduction, unmistakably assumes a balanced relation between supply and demand, $S = D$. Marx's law of the falling rate of profit, which 'is' a demonstration of $S > D$, is exemplified by Lenin's reproduction scheme which strictly holds to the premise of $S = D$!

The origin of this antinomy lies in Marx's self-contradictory composition of arguments on his law of the falling rate of profit. As already explained at the beginning of this chapter, Marx sets forth a wrong premise that the wage level is 'given' (constant) and reaches a mistaken conclusion of $S > D$. But at the same time his own value-price theory, $P_t = \frac{1}{1+k_1} P_0$, tells that, when nominal wages are constant, real wages must rise in direct proportion to the productivity rise, thus exactly maintaining the state of $S = D$. The law taken by Marx for a verification of $S > D$ is proven to be $S = D$ by his own value-price theory.

This contradiction is inevitably involved in Lenin's scheme in a latent state and influences his later theoretical works on the reproduction process and 'realization'. Let me pick up a typical example of that from his article, *Reply to Mr. Nezhdanov*:

> Even with fully proportional, ideally smooth realisation [Lenin's scheme is an ideal example of it – T.H.] we cannot imagine capitalism without a contradiction between production and consumption, without the tremendous growth of production being accompanied by an extremely slow growth (or even stagnation and worsening) of consumption by the people. Realisation is due more to means of production than to articles of consumption – this is obvious from Marx's schemes; and from this, in turn, it follows inevitably that 'the more productiveness develops, the more it finds itself at variance with the narrow basis on which the conditions of consumption rest' (Marx).[27] It is obvious from all the passages in *Capital* devoted to the contradiction between production and consumption that it is only in this sense that Marx understood the contradiction between production and consumption.[28]

In the case of 'fully proportional, ideally smooth realisation', in which $S = D$ is unquestionable, Lenin emphasises that 'we cannot imagine capitalism without contradiction between production and consumption', citing from *Capital* the passage: 'the more productiveness develops, the more it finds itself at variance with the narrow basis . . . of consumption', an explanation of the widening $S > D$, the final cause of economic crises based on the 'internal contradiction' of the law of the falling rate of profit.

The background of Lenin's self-contradictory statement quoted above can be traced in his scheme as shown in Table 7.12.

Table 7.12   Lenin's contradiction of $S = D$ and $S > D$ in his scheme

---

$$(6000G: 1G = £1)$$

Y_1 $4000c + 1000v + 1000s = 6000$

$\frac{c}{v} = 4 \to 4.24$ $P_t = \frac{1}{1 + k_1} P_0$, $K_1 = 1$

$$(2100G) \qquad\qquad (13100G: 1G = £\tfrac{1}{2})$$

Y_2 $4450c + 1050v + 1050s = 6550$

[*Note*: Lenin's premise: $S = D$. But if $P_t = P_0$, $1G = £1$, then $S > D$.]

The figures in the table are those of Department 1 in the first and second year in Lenin's reproduction scheme. $S = D$ is the basic premise. The organic composition of capital, $\frac{c}{v}$, rises from 4 in the first year to 4.24 in the second year. It is the reflection of the far more rapid rise of productivity, say, 2-fold.

[*Note*:   The reason why I chose the figure '2'-fold for expressing 'the far more rapid rise of productivity' is this: Marx himself gives an historical example of 7-fold rise of organic composition reflecting 'many hundred times' rise of technical composition (labour productivity measured in terms of $v + s$) (see note 16, Ch. 4 in this book). Therefore, I chose the 100-fold rise of technical composition and the 50-fold rise of productivity (in terms of $c + v + s$) as the figures corresponding to the 4-fold rise of organic composition in Table 4.3 of Chapter 4. So, a 2-fold rise of productivity (in terms of $c + v + s$) in the case of 4450/4000 ($= 1.1125$)-fold rise of organic composition should be an adequate assumption. (Also see (*Note*) in Sec.IV, Ch.4.)]

Then, price level falls to $\frac{1}{2}$ and the real wages of the labourers rise 2-fold. $13100G$ at $1G = \pounds\frac{1}{2}$ are sold out at a GNP of 6550, i.e. $S = D$. This is 'fully proportional, ideally smooth realisation'. And the growth of Department 1 from Y_1 to Y_2 is faster than $k_1 > k_2$. 'Realisation is due more to means of production than to articles of consumption', $S = D$. $k_1 > k_2$. But Lenin argues that from this it follows inevitably that 'the more productiveness develops, the more it finds itself at variance with the narrow basis of consumption', $S > D$, because Lenin here adopts (unconsciously) Marx's self-contradictory assumption of 'a given wage' and, therefore, of a constant price level, in the law of the falling rate of profit. Then he thinks that 'the tremendous growth of production' is 'accompanied by . . . stagnation', in the concrete figures (added by T.H.) of his scheme; i.e. that the 2-fold increase of production per capita from Y_1 to Y_2 is accompanied by 'a given wages', a constant real wage level, for the labourers, which inevitably gives rise to $S > D$ in the framework of $S = D$. 'It is only in this sense ($S = D$, $k_1 > k_2$) that Marx understood the contradiction between production and consumption ($S > D$, $k_1 > k_2$).' Marx and his faithful disciple Lenin are quite alike in mistaking $S = D$ for $S > D$ and remain unconscious of their inadmissible confusion.

III   THE THEORETICAL LEGACY FROM *CAPITAL* TO *IMPERIALISM*

The opening sentence of *Karl Marx's Capital and the Problem of Contemporary Capitalism* (Moscow, 1968) is the following:

Depending on the theory and method of *Capital*, Lenin established the doctrine of imperialism which arms the proletariat with the theory of socialist revolution under monopoly capitalism.[29]

This is supposed to be a standard interpretation widely acknowledged by Marxists of the successive relation in the theoretical structure between Marx's *Capital* and Lenin's *Imperialism*. But, in practice, it is not necessarily easy to find a theoretical chain linking *Capital* and *Imperialism*. The former is essentially theoretical in its character and the latter is rather of an historical and positive nature. Lenin cites *Capital* in *Imperialism* only twice almost in passing, the contents of the citations being anything but important.[30]

1 The wrong $S > D$ of the law of the falling rate of profit as a common basis

A closer analysis reveals, however, that the hidden elements forming the theoretical backbone common to the two books are the law of the falling rate of profit and the reproduction scheme.

First, let me quote a passage from Chapter 15, 'Internal contradictions of the law [of the falling rate of profit]', Book III:

> The limits within which the preservation and self-expansion of the value of capital resting on the expropriation and pauperisation of the great mass of produces can alone move – these limits come constantly into conflict with the methods of production employed by capital for its purpose, which drive towards unlimited extension of production . . . The capitalist mode of production is, for this reason, a historical means of developing the material forces of production and creating an appropriate world-market and is, at the same time, a continual conflict between this its historical task and its own corresponding relations of social production.'[31]

The economics of *Capital* is in principle that of a closed system. Marx writes: 'In order to examine the object of our investigation in its integrity, free from all disturbing subsidiary circumstances, we must treat the whole world as one nation, and assume that capitalist production is everywhere established.'[32] But in some places he takes up the subjects extending to an open system. The quotation above referring to 'a world-market' is one of them. The 'drive towards unlimited extension of production' continually comes into conflict with 'the pauperisation of the great mass of producers' as illustrated by the 'hypothetical series' exemplifying the law of the falling rate of profit with my interpretation as in Tables 4.3 and 4.4 of Chapter 4, in which production increases 50-fold but labourers' wages remain constant.

This over-production, $S > D$, necessitates an ever-expanding world-market beyond the national boundary.

> [*Note*:   In the Tables referred to above nominal wages remain constant, but real wages rise in direct proportion to the productivity-rise. Marx is unaware of it and simply thinks that 'wages' are 'given'.]

We find a corresponding passage to the one by Marx quoted above in Lenin's *Imperialism*:

> It goes without saying that if capitalism could develop agriculture, which today frightfully lags behind industry everwhere, if it could raise the standard of living of the masses, who are everywhere still half-starved and poverty-stricken, in spite of the amazing technical progress, there could be no talk of a superabundance of capital . . . But if capitalism did these things it would not be capitalism; for both uneven development and a semistarvation level of existence of the masses are fundamental and inevitable conditions and premises of this mode of production. As long as capitalism remains what it is, surplus capital will be utilised not for the purpose of raising the standard of living of the masses in a given country, for this would mean a decline in profits for the capitalists, but for the purpose of increasing profits by exporting capital abroad to the backward countries.[33] The export of capital thus becomes a means for encouraging the export of commodities[34]

Here Lenin strictly follows Marx's line of argument based on the law of the falling rate of profit. The contradiction between ever-increasing production through technical progress (heightening of the organic composition of capital, $\frac{c}{v}$) and stagnant consumption 'based on antagonistic conditions of distribution, which reduce' it 'to a minumum'[35] drives capitalism to the acquisition of ever-extending foreign markets for surplus commodities, colonial conquests, imperialism.

As is well known, Lenin emphasises the importance of capital export in the age of monopoly capitalism mainly on historical grounds. From the theoretical point of view, however, Marx already throws light on the advantages for the capitalist of exporting capital abroad in Chapter 14, 'Counteracting causes', and Chapter 15, 'Internal contradictions' of the law of the falling rate of profit:

> As concerns capitals invested in colonies, etc. . . . they may yield higher rates of profit for the simple reason that the rate of profit is higher there due to backward development, and likewise the exploitation of labour, because of the use of slaves, coolies, etc.[36]

> Over-production of capital is never anything more than over-production of means of production . . . which may serve as capital, i.e. may serve to exploit labour at a given degree of exploitation: a fall in the intensity of exploitation

below a certain point, however, calls forth disturbances, and stoppages in the capitalist production process, crises, and destruction of capital . . . If capital is sent abroad, this is not done because it absolutely could not be applied at home, but because it can be employed at a higher rate of profit in a foreign country.'[37]

We can easily see that Marx gives here a more detailed explanation of capital export than Lenin's remark above to the effect that 'surplus capital will be utilised not in a given country, but for the purpose of increasing profits by exporting capital abroad'.

As for the commodity imports, we find in Chapter 14:

> Since foreign trade partly cheapens the elements of constant capital, and partly the necessities of life for which the variable capital is exchanged, it tends to raise the rate of profit by increasing the rate of surplus value and lowering the value of constant capital.[38]

Lenin did not present any theoretical explanation of commodity imports such as this. What we can find in *Imperialism* is the following description based on his realistic observation:

> Colonial possession alone gives the monopolies complete guarantee against all contingencies in the struggle with competitors . . . the more capitalism is developed, the more strongly the shortage of raw materials is felt, the more intense the competition and the hunt for the sources of raw materials through the whole world, the more desparate the struggle for the acquisition of colonies.[39]

Now we know that the law of the falling rate of profit is the common theoretical backbone bridging the closed system of *Capital* and the open system of *Imperialism*. Technology progresses (the organic composition of capital heightens, i.e. $\frac{c}{v}$ rises), the uneven development of industries proceeds (its simplest model being $k_1 > k_2$; see explanation in Table 7.11), the gap between production and consumption. $(S > D)$ widens, economic crises become intensified, moving closer to the final catastrophe. As preventive or counteracting measures, capitalist states compete for the acquisition of extending foreign markets, building larger colonial empires, to which they export surplus commodities and capital and from where they import cheaper raw materials and food crops. This is imperialism, and the wars among them are imperialist wars.

Here we should come back to the fundamental self-contradiction involved in the law of the falling rate of profit. If the price-fall in inverse ratio to the productivity-rise is the premise of the law, and it must be so, the real wages and the real purchasing power of money in general cannot remain unchanged. They rise in direct proportion to the productivity-rise, keeping the increasing production and consumption perfectly balanced, $S = D$.

Of course, I do not assert that supply and demand are perfectly balanced in the capitalist society, nor do I lose sight of over-production, economic crises, imperialist wars, etc. as historical facts. I only want to clarify the fact that a theoretical model which cannot but suit in $S = D$ has been misinterpreted as that of $S > D$ and applied as such in economic (and political) analysis. This is misleading and harmful.

2   How $S = D$ of the reproduction scheme results in $S > D$

In the case of reproduction schemes, another theoretical link between *Capital* and *Imperialism*, the self-contradiction involved in the process of reasoning comes more clearly to the fore than in the case of the law of the falling rate of profit, because the production schemes are the models strictly built upon the premise of $S = D$ and the explanation of imperialist expansion needs, as its driving force, over-production, $S > D$.

In Chapter 20 'Simple reproduction', Book II of *Capital*, we read:

> Capitalist production does not exist at all without foreign commerce. But when one assumes normal annual reproduction on a given scale one also assumes that foreign commerce only replaces home products by articles of other use or bodily form without affecting value-relations . . . the involvement of foreign commerce in analysing the annually produced value of products can therefore only confuse without contributing any new element of the problem, or of its solution. For this reason it must be entirely discarded.[40]

Lenin, who supportingly quotes Marx's above passage,[41] asserts, in relation to his expanding reproduction scheme with technical progress (heightening organic composition), 'that the product *can* be realised in a capitalist society . . . that it would be incorrect to introduce foreign trade . . . to explain this realisation'.[42] This is also all right because the scheme assumes balanced ($S = D$) growth of Departments 1 and 2 in a closed system. His following contention, however, puts him into a theoretically awkward position:

> I did not say anywhere that this contradiction [between production and consumption, $S = D$, $k_1 > k_2$, – T.H.] should *regularly* produce a surplus-

product . . . I stress *regularly* because the irregular production of surplus-product (crises) is inevitable in capitalist society as a result of the disturbance in proportion between the various branches of industry.[43]

Lenin thinks that in the reproduction process in a capitalist society supply and demand are balanced, $S = D$, in principle and only by irregular disturbances in proportion among various industries this balance is broken, $S > D$, and crises occur. This interpretation of crises contradicts that of crises caused by inevitable, ever-widening $S > D$ 'inherent' in the law of the falling rate of profit. But Lenin in this context fails to notice it and maintains the following:

Capitalism's need of a foreign market is by no means to be explained by the impossibility of realising the product on the home market.[44]

Then, does Lenin think that a foreign market is necessary only when the balance between supply and demand is irregularly broken, only in times of crises? Lenin himself, who maintains 'that the product can be realised in a capitalist society (= home market)', explains, at the same time, the necessity of a foreign market as follows:

It (capitalism) inevitably leads to an unlimited growth of production which overflows the old, narrow limits of earlier economic units. With the unevenness of development inherent in capitalism, one branch of production outstrips the others and strives to transcend the bounds of the old field of economic relations.[45]

The various branches of industry, which serve as 'markets' for one another, do not develop evenly, but outstrip one another, and the more developed industry seeks a foreign market. This does not mean at all 'the impossibility of the capitalist nation realising surplus value'.[46]

The starting point of Lenin's line of argument is that 'the product can be realised' in a home market, $S = D$. On the basis of this thesis he explains the necessity of a foreign market by 'an unlimited' growth of production which 'overflows' the home market and 'the more developed industry' which 'seeks a foreign market'. But why does a foreign market come to be necessary? Undoubtedly because supply cannot find corresponding demand within the home market, $S = D$, the commodities for export ought not to be left over. Nevertheless, he concludes that 'this does not mean at all the impossibility of the capitalist nation realising' the product in the home market, $S = D$.

This evident self-contradiction in Lenin's argument is a reflection of that involved in his reproduction scheme in which $S = D$ according to the premise, but at the same time $S > D$ according to an inadmissible assumption that the wages and prices are constant (see Table 7.12). Thus be finally reaches in *Imperialism* the analysis of 'the amazing progress' on the one hand and the 'half-starved living of the masses' on the other, which gives rise to surplus capital and surplus commodities flooding into the foreign market. Here again it is obviously $S > D$, yet at the same time $S = D$ according to his reproduction and market theory. (See Table 7.12 and related explanation.)

IV   EPILOGUE

It is now beyond doubt that the absolute impoverishment theory of Marx and Lenin cannot be valid in an analysis of the contemporary capitalism in which wasteful 'affluence' is the trouble. But the self-contradictory nature of argumentation inherent in *Capital* and inherited by *Imperialism* is not yet generally recognised.

This erroneous theory might have played a certain historical role as a sharp criticism in the age when Cecil Rhodes could boastfully say: 'The Empire is a bread and butter question. If you want to avoid civil war, you must become imperialists.[47] But nowadays, faced with the knotty North-South problem, we are called upon to have 'the awareness that we live in a world village, that we belong to a world community'.[48] In this historical setting we should first confirm the illogicality and outdatedness of the theory of imperialism by Marx and Lenin if we want to make a correct approach to the global task we have to deal with.

8 Marxian Economics in the Contemporary World: Discussions with Chinese, Polish and Russian Economists

We now proceed to the contemporary significance of clarifying the fallacies inherent in Marxian economics and Marxism in general. I acutely feel this need through my direct contact with Marxist economists and politicians and through their writings both in and outside the communist countries.

I THE ECONOMIC GROWTH OF WORLD CAPITALISM VS. THE FORESIGHTS OF MARX AND KEYNES – A LECTURE IN CHINA

In August 1982 I had an opportunity to make a short visit to China, the Beijing and Shanghai Institutes of Economic Research (both under the Academy of Social Science), at the invitation of the Sino-Japanese Friendship Association. We were a small party of Waseda University Scholars representing the fields of nuclear physics, architecture, drama, political science, economics, etc. Our aim was to improve the friendly relationship between the countries through the international exchange of academic knowledge and the first-hand observation of the state of things in China.

I had two anxieties. First, it was doubtful to what extent I could develop my argument for a fundamental reappraisal of Marxian economics. Second, I was wavering whether I should let it be known that I had experience as a soldier in the China theatre of war, although I had no reason to conceal it.

'The textbook issue'[1] suddenly blew away my anxieties. The case was being taken up by the Chinese seriously and extensively, so I decided to deal straightforwardly with the matter on all occasions during my stay in China. The gist of my greetings follows:

> The Chinese people we meet are all so kind as to refrain from referring to the 'textbook issue'. I know, however, as a war-veteran, that the activities of the Japanese army were no less than 'aggression', and we must not quibble by naming it 'advance'. I feel the responsibility of correctly conveying the historical facts to the generations who did not have war experience and through that being of use for the establishment of lasting peace and friendship between our two nations on the basis of truth.
>
> However, as a scholar who wishes to strengthen out friendship through exchange, I must 'explore the facts, seek truth' (Shishijiushi – an old saying, which originated in *Hanshu*, an ancient history book written in the first century), remaining faithful to my scholarly conviction. My argument as a political economist might in some cases contradict generally accepted ideas and norms in your country. I hope you will adopt from my presentation what might be useful and refute what, you think, should be refuted. I believe this is the right way to attain real friendship.

In all instances this candour was agreeably accepted. A high official of Chinese Education Ministry told me:

> Now that you have frankly spoken out on the ticklish question, I will also tell you that I myself was in Bulujun (Eighth-route army – main part of the wartime Chinese communist military force); that I happened to be your enemy. But, of course, I have no grudge against you as an individual. On the contrary, we are now friends making common efforts for consolidating the friendship between our two nations.

He firmly shook hands with me. During my trip I met three more persons who let me know that they had served in the communist army and exchanged a warm handclasp with me.

In such an atmosphere I felt unexpectedly free to express my criticism of Marxian economics in a lecture entitled 'The economic growth of world capitalism vs. the foresights of Marx and Keynes'. The gist of it and the following discussion are given below.

1 The 'prophecies' of Marx, Lenin, Keynes and Stalin

Figure 8.1 illustrates the growth rate of industrial production of world capitalism as a whole from the early part of the nineteenth century until 1982. Although this is a very rough graph it should be sufficient to see a broad trend. Compared with this curve, the theoretical stances of Marx, Lenin, Keynes and Stalin all fell wide of the mark as predictions on a long-term trend.

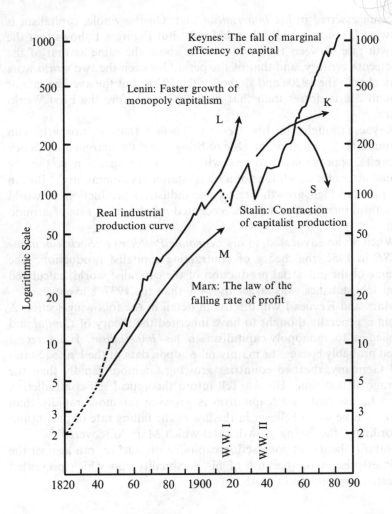

Figure 8.1   The trend of industrial production in the capitalist world[3]

Marx's law of the falling rate of profit amounts, in other words, to a law of the falling rate of economic growth. If this law had been realised as a long term trend, the real industrial curve should have slowed down like the supposed curve of Marx's falling rate of profit. As a matter of fact, however, the real growth rate curve of industrial production from around 1850 through 1913, just before the First World War, shows roughly a fixed slope (growth rate of about 4%) as a trend.

Lenin asserted in his *Imperialism* that 'On the whole, capitalism is growing far more rapidly than before'.[2] But Figure 8.1 shows that the growth rate between 1900 and 1913 is about the same as that of the nineteenth century, and that of the period between the two world wars is quicker in the 1920s and slower in the 1930s, but the average rate of around 2% is slower than that of the period before the First World War.

Keynes thought in his *General Theory* that a 'properly run community . . . ought to be able to bring down the marginal efficiency of capital approximately to zero within a single generation; so that we should attain the conditions of a quasi-stationary community'.[4] But, in the postwar high growth period the industrial production of world capitalism increased at an unprecedented rapid annual rate of around 5%.

When Stalin advocated, in his *Economic Problems of Socialism in the USSR* in 1952, the theory of contracting capitalist production,[5] the volume of the industrial production of the capitalist world, calculated from UN statistics, was larger by 74% than the 1937–8 average.

Marx and Keynes I will discuss in detail in the following section 2. Lenin is generally thought to have inherited the theory of *Capital* and applied it to monopoly-capitalism in his *Imperialism*. His forecast failed probably because he mainly relied upon data of the United States and Germany, the two countries growing far more rapidly than the average at that time. He also fell into a theoretical self-contradiction when he asserted that 'capitalism is growing far more rapidly than before', as he was a believer in the law of the falling rate of profit (and accordingly, the falling growth rate) which Marx 'discovered'.[6]

Stalin's 'theory' of contracting capitalist production ran against the realities presumably because of his personality cult which prevented objective exploration of truth.

2   The rapid economic growth of postwar capitalism and Marx, Keynes, Harrod

In the latter half of the nineteenth century when Britain, the most advanced of the capitalist countries, had been under the pressure of cutthroat competition with the younger and more vigorous ones such as Germany, the United States, and suffering from a slower growth rate, the law of the falling rate of profit in *Capital*, formulated against the historical background of the British economy at that time, might have been accepted with realistic appreciation: both profits and growth did decline. However, if one looked at world capitalism as a whole, the declining trend in the rate of economic growth could not have been found, as shown in Figure 8.1.

In the worldwide Great Depression period of the 1930s, during which Keynes's *General Theory* was published in 1936, investment in new equipment had been almost at a standstill. Thus, the seemingly extreme prerequisite of excluding technical progress so as to obtain a falling marginal efficiency of capital essentially reflected the actual circumstances. The logical consequence of such reasoning is a society of zero growth. It should be self-evident that this theory is of no avail for the explanation of the rapid growth of the postwar capitalism.

Let us here compare Keynes' falling marginal efficiency of capital and Marx's falling rate of profit. As shown in Table 8.1, if we think approximately $c + v \doteqdot K$, $s \doteqdot P$, we can express both the falling marginal efficiency and the falling rate of profit in one and the same formula in which the limit of the rate of return is zero, $\frac{P}{K} \to 0$, accordingly, the economy ceases to grow.

Table 8.1   A foresight common to Keynes and Marx: The trend in capitalism towards stagnation

---

Keynes: the falling marginal efficiency of capital

[K = capital per unit P = expected return
1 . . . . . n = time series of added investment and expected return]
$\frac{P_1}{K_1} > \frac{P_2}{K_2}$ . . . . $\frac{P_n}{K_n} \to 0$

Marx: falling rate of profit

[$c + v \doteqdot K$, $s \doteqdot P$ $\therefore \frac{s}{c+v} \doteqdot \frac{P_1}{K_1}$]
$\frac{P_1}{K_1} > \frac{P_2}{K_2}$ . . . . $\frac{P_n}{K_n} \to 0$

However, this formula representing the two laws of Keynes and Marx is clearly inapplicable to the fast growing postwar capitalism. In the case of Keynesian economics, Harrod and Domar coped with the situation by bringing in technical progress and thus developing the theory towards dynamics. Marx's law of the falling rate of profit also assumes technical progress, indirectly expressed by the rise of organic composition of capital, $\frac{c}{v}$, which, in turn, pulls down the rate of profit and thus the economic growth rate.

There is no necessity, however, that technical progress should cause the rise of organic composition of capital, $\frac{c}{v}$, or the rise of the ratio of the labour time (value) embodied in constant capital to the labour time (value) expended by labourers, $\frac{c}{v+s}$.[7] If so, there is also no necessity for the rate of profit to fall. Even Marx himself admits in *Capital* that 'considered abstractly the rate of profit may remain the same'.[8]

Let us assume that $v + s \doteq Y$, and $c \doteq K$ ('value product' in Marxian economics is approximately the same as 'value added' or 'income' in Keynesian economics and 'constant capital' approximately the same as 'physical capital'). Then, $\frac{c}{v+s} \doteq \frac{K}{Y}$, $\frac{K}{Y}$ is the capital coefficient in the terminology of contemporary economics. Historical experience shows that it can rise, remain unchanged or fall. If, for instance, in the steel industry, labour-saving large-scale technical progress occurs, its capital coefficient $\frac{K}{Y}$ would be rather high. In the communications industry the conversion from wire telegraph to wireless or from vacuum tube to transistor would lower $\frac{K}{Y}$.

In long-term and average observation we find the capital coefficient remains rather stable. According to the classical study by J. Steindl the capital coefficient in American capitalism during 1869–1938 had been between 2.5 and 3.2.[9]

Here let us apply Harrod's fundamental equation, $GC = S$[10] to our case. G denotes growth rate, C capital coefficient and S propensity to save. We can rewrite it as follows:

$$GC = S \rightarrow G = S\frac{1}{C} \rightarrow G = S\frac{1}{K/Y} \rightarrow G = S\frac{1}{c/v+s}$$

[*Note*:   In Harrods's text 'propensity to save' is denoted by '*s*', but here it is denoted by '*S*' in order to distinguish it from '*s*' = 'surplus value'.]

Assuming that S is given, the growth rate G is determined by the value of the capital coefficient $\frac{K}{Y}$ or organic composition of capital.[11] If $\frac{K}{Y}$ or $\frac{c}{v}$ or $\frac{c}{v+s}$ becomes bigger, G must fall and vice versa. If it is unchanged, G also remains constant. All three cases are possible due to the nature of invention. The law of the falling rate of profit is of a one-sided character. It assumes that all (or prevailing) kinds of technical progress raise the capital coefficient. This does not match historical and statistical facts.

3 The law of the falling rate of profit and Lenin's *Imperialism*

Here I take up the self-contradiction involved in the law of the falling rate of profit, the most fundamental defect in Marx's theoretical system (see Table 8.2).

Table 8.2 The self-contradiction in the law of the falling rate of profit

---

Pd_1 $100c + 100v + 100s = \dfrac{300G}{£300}$ (unemployment rate $= 0\%$)

productivity rises 50-fold

$$P_t = \frac{1}{1+k_1}P_0 \rightarrow \therefore \text{price level falls to } \tfrac{1}{50}$$

Pd_2 $400c + 100v + 100s = \dfrac{30000G}{£600}$ (50 unemployed workers unemployment rate $= 33.3\%$)

productivity rises 50-fold

$$P_t = \frac{1}{1+k_1}P_0 \rightarrow \therefore \text{price level falls to } \tfrac{1}{50}$$

(Conclusion by Marx)

(1) $S > D$ (from assumption: wage = const.)

(2)   Rate of profit falls (from 50% to 20%)

(3)   Absolute impoverishment (constant wage level + rising unemployment rate)

(Erroneous points in his argument)

(1) $S = D$ (If nominal wage or income is constant real purchasing power goes up to 50-fold.)

(2)   Fall of profit-rate is due to the assumption of technical progress of capital coefficient rising type.

(3)   The rise of unemployment rate is unwarranted.

[*Note*: Table 8.2 is a condensed presentation of the subject already explained in detail in the present volume (Sec. II, Ch. 4. and 3, Sec. III, Ch. 5). My lecture in China gave some necessary interpretation of the table, but here I proceed straight to three points I want to elucidate in connection with it.]

First, Marx firmly believes that the law of the falling rate of profit is an unmistakable demonstration of the inevitable overproduction, $S > D$, in the capitalist society. In the case shown in Table 8.2, however, the price of a commodity falls to $\frac{1}{50}$. Thus with a given nominal wage of £100, 100 labourers can buy 5,000 goods. The society as a whole with 600 has real purchasing power for 30,000 goods. It is $S = D$. Marx must have forgotten this price fall when he assumed 'a given wage'.[12] As a result, he found $S > D$, the cause of economic crises, in a series which should be $S = D$ by his own value-price system, $P_t = \frac{1}{1 + k_1} P_0$.

By pointing out this contradiction I do not maintain that economic crises do not occur in capitalism. What I want to say is that the law of the falling rate of profit is of no use as an explanatory principle of crises.

On the second point, Marx's conclusion of the falling rate of profit, my criticism is already presented. The capital coefficient may rise, remain neutral, or fall, depending on the nature of technical progress. So the rate of profit and of economic growth may rise, remain unchanged or fall.

On the third point, absolute impoverishment. If the wage of employed workers is 'given' and the unemployment rate increases,[13] the labouring class as a whole suffer absolute impoverishment in the literal sense of the word. In the illustration of Table 8.2 their standard of living is thought to fall to two-thirds. But if we take into consideration the factor forgotten by Marx, a 50-fold rise of real wage, the standard of living of the labouring class as a whole rises 33.3-fold even with the unemployment rate of 33.3%.

Now it is demonstrated that all the three theses have no inevitability; those drawn out of the law of the falling rate of profit, i.e. overproduction → economic crises; the fall of the rate of profit → that of the economic growth rate, and the rise of unemployment rate → absolute impoverishment. Therefore, it is wrong to expect the fall of capitalism and the rise of communism relying on this law 'discovered' by Marx. Lenin seems to have committed this error in connection with the first World War and the revolutionary strength of the European working class. In his *Imperialism* we read:

> If capitalism could raise the standard of living of the masses . . . there could be no talk of a superabundance of capital; . . . But if capitalism did these things it would not be capitalism.'[14]

Lenin, who took over and developed the political economy of *Capital*, was a believer in the theory of absolute impoverishment in the literal sense. In *Imperialism* we cannot find even a single statistic on the real wage of the standard of living of the workers. This fault presumably led Lenin to a mistaken belief in the pauperisation of the workers and the uplift of their revolutionary energy in the period when the real income of the working class of main capitalist countries had been remarkably on the rise as shown in Table 8.3.

Table 8.3   The rising per capita real income of the working population in four major countries (%) [15]

Germany	1877 – 85 = 100	1911 – 13 = 120
France	1870 – 79 = 100	1900 – 19 = 136
Great Britain	1877 – 85 = 100	1911 – 13 = 138
USA	1870 = 100	1913 = 139

This probably gave rise to the following tragicomedy. The German Social Democratic Party, which was believed to be the mainstay of anti-war activities, cast ballots for the Kaiser's war budget on 4 August 1914. Lenin in Zurich read *Vorwärts*, organ of the SDP, which reported it, and cried out.

It is impossible. This copy is certainly a forgery. The bourgeois German canaille must have published a special number.[16]

But it was a genuine one.

4   The gist of the questions and answers

Although very briefly, I have clarified the fundamental faults involved in the edifice of Marx's political economy. I know you ladies and gentlemen present here would certainly raise objection to my arguments from the standpoint of your leading ideology, Marxism, Leninism and Maoism. I would be very glad to answer you and I hope we both can benefit from our discussions. Lastly, let me add one thing. The contents of my criticism on Marxian economics are, I firmly believe, quite clear, like two plus two is not five, but four. If I do not take up these issues here today, someone will some time, somewhere become aware of them and take them up. So it is my sincere desire that you will here now squarely deal with my presentation.

(1) On the law of the falling rate of profit and other laws

Q. – Marx demonstrated the inevitable collapse of capitalism based not only on the sole law of the falling rate of profit but also based on many other laws including the 'general law of capitalist accumulation' in Chapter 25, Book I, *Capital.*

A. – The core of the general law of the capitalist accumulation is the heightening organic composition of capital, the rise of $\frac{c}{v}$. The law of the falling rate of profit is composed of this element plus surplus value, s. Therefore, my criticism of the latter law is simultaneously that of the former. And I presume the discussant has also in mind the law of historic materialism: 'obligatory correspondence of production relations to the productive forces' Marx reduced 'productive forces' further to 'instruments of labour'.[17] But it should be self-evident by now that there is no such correspondence indicating that the social system in the age of tools moved by manpower is feudalism; that in the age of machinery operated by steam or electric power is capitalism; and that in the age of atomic power and electronic computers is communism.

Q. – The law of the falling rate of profit is the law on the long-term 'tendency'. It might be realised or might not be realised even in the long-term.

A. – Marx writes in the 'counteracting influences' (on the law) in Chapter 14, Book III, *Capital* that 'There must be some counteracting influences at work, which cross and annul (*aufheben*) the effect of the general law'[18] and at the same time that the 'counter effects . . . do not do away with (*nicht aufheben*) the law, but impair its effect'.[19] First, it should be pointed out that this sort of self-contradictory statement is not permissible in a scientific work. Second, we know that Marx was not certain whether the law would be realised or not. Consider this law as the demonstration of the inevitable collapse of capitalism. If the realisation of this law is not certain, the inevitable collapse of capitalism inevitably comes to be uncertain too.

Q. – The rapid economic growth in the age of monopoly-capitalism and the falling rate of profit are compatible because 'the mass of profit compensates' for the falling rate of profit.

A. – In *Capital* Marx writes that 'as soon as formation of capital were to fall in the hands of a few established big capitals, for which the mass of profit compensates for the falling rate of profit, the vital flame of production would be altogether extinguished. It would die out'.[20] Marx did not say that the compensation allows high economic growth. On the contrary he anticipated eventual stagnation. Let me explain by an illustration. Suppose in an age of innumerable small capitals the average magnitude of individual capitals and their profits were $10C + 10P$, profit rate being 100%. Then time has passed and now in the age of a few big capitals the average is $10,000C + 100P$. The mass of profit 'compensated for' the rate and grew ten-fold. But the profit rate fell to 1%. In such a case how can one imagine a more rapid growth?

[*Note*: The questioner, eager to defend the falling rate of profit at all costs, reads the passage, 'the mass of profit compensates', in the following way: The increasing absolute mass of profit (under the condition of the falling rate of profit) enables the faster rate of growth of production (which is possible under the rising rate of profit). This is a confusion of *mass* and *rate*. Helped by an ambiguous term 'compensates' he thinks that the enormous absolute increase of profit allows a faster growth rate.]

(2) On the concept of 'absolute impoverishment'

Q. – By the concept 'absolute impoverishment' Marx meant not only the fall of real wage of the workers but also included aggravation in social and moral spheres. The rising real wage of Japanese labourers does not necessarily exclude their impoverishment.

A. – I agree with you in that the real wage is not the sole factor in absolute impoverishment. For instance, Engels talks of 'existential insecurity' (*Existenzunsicherheit*).[21] But it is also true that real wage or physical standard of living is the fundamental factor. The *Manifesto of the Communist Party* declared that 'the modern labourer . . . sinks deeper and deeper below the conditions of existence of his own class . . . the bourgeoisie . . . is incompetent to assure an existence to its slave within his slavery'.[22] This statement unmistakably shows that Marx and Engels were thinking of absolute impoverishment in the literal sense.

Q. – It is true that Lenin said: 'The worker is becoming poorer than before; he is compelled to live worse, to eat worse, to suffer hunger more, and to live in basements and attics.'[23] It was, I think, rather rhetorical than literal. In another instance he stated: 'Poverty grows, not in the physical but in the social sense.'[24]

A. – Lenin's remark 'The worker is becoming poorer . . .' is not a prose poem but a statement by a social scientist. It must be read literally. Lenin asserted absolute impoverishment in the primary sense of the word.

In 1966 in Rome I met Antonio Pesenti, the leading theorist of the Italian Communist Party. He told me as an example of contemporary presence of absolute impoverishment that the workers in Rome are troubled with severe traffic when commuting in their cars and they cannot enjoy wine as freely as their parents' generation because they have to pay instalments for their cars. My comment was that if curtailing wine for buying a car were named 'absolute impoverishment' ordinary workers would surely be confused and the credibility of the Italian Communist Party would be impaired.

[*Note*: Even the 'fact' that the workers in Rome 'cannot enjoy wine as freely as their parents' generation is highly questionable. The population of Italy was 41,177,000 in 1931. It increased to 54,137,000 in 1971 by 31%. On the other hand, the average yearly production of wine in 1926–35 was 42,414,000 hectolitres. It increased to 69,205,000 hectolitres in 1966–75 by 63%.[25]]

Q. – As time proceeds the level of education and physical standard of living rises. Accordingly, the value of labour power increases. The rise of real wage level, however, lags behind the increase of value of labour power. This is what we call absolute impoverishment.

A. – I disagree with the idea. First, it is an abuse to apply the concept, absolute impoverishment, to the case of insufficient rise in real wage. Second, the increase of value of labour power and the rise of the physical standard of living are theoretically mixed up. As time proceeds the level of education rises and, therefore, the value of labour power increases. But technical progress simplifies the labour process which earlier needed higher skill, thus decreasing the value of labour power. For simplicity, let us assume that the two opposite tendencies are counterbalanced, therefore the mass of value produced by a fixed time of labour remains unchanged as in Marx's *Capital*. Now suppose that in Period 1 of Figure 8.2 a labourer works 4 hours of necessary labour and 4 hours of surplus labour, obtains a wage of 4 Yen and buys 4 units of consumer goods. In Period 2 productivity rises 2-fold and, therefore, the price level falls to $\frac{1}{2}$. Then, in Pd_{2a}, the necessary labour time (value of labour power) is cut down to $\frac{3}{4}$, 3 hours and yet the real wage increases 1.5-fold. In Pd_{2b}, necessary labour time is unchanged and the real wage increases 2-fold in proportion to the productivity rise. In Pd_{2c}, the necessary labour time increases to 5 hours and the real wage increases 2.5-fold. In this case the rate of surplus value falls giving rise to the relative impoverishment of the capitalist.

The discussant should not have mentioned case Pd_{2c}. By the expression 'the rise of real wage level lags behind the increase of value of labour power' he is supposed to have meant in substance case Pd_{2a} where the rise of real wage lags behind the rise of productivity because of the reduced value of labour power. Here lies the confusion of the change in the mass of value of labour power and the change in the quantity of use-values bought by that mass of value.

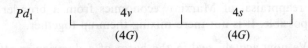

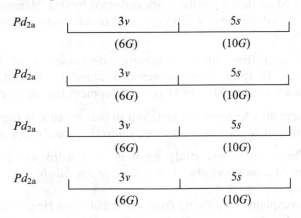

Figure 8.2   The effect of productivity-rise on the value of labour-power and the mass of use-values obtained by a labourer

Now let us examine the last case Pd_{2d}, in which the whole labour day is shortened from 8 hours to 6 hours and both value of labour-power and surplus value are cut down to 3/4. Still both the labourer and the capitalist can enjoy 1.5-fold rise of their real income. This roughly reflects the historical tendency of the capitalist development, which Marx could not foresee.

(3) On methodology, dialectics, etc.

Q. – Is there any significance in criticising *Capital* only in its extremely abstract dimension and discussing Marx, Keynes and Harrod all mixed up together?

A. – I am pointing out that Marx's propositions in the most abstract and therefore most fundamental dimension contain inadmissible faults. If they were let alone and applied to the realities, the faults would unavoidably be amplified. Moreover, I make comparisons and find a relatedness between Marx and Keynes-Harrod. By doing this a reappraisal of Marxian economics from a broader view is made possible. It is not mere mixing them up together.

Q. – We now acutely realise the harm of a doctrinaire attitude in studying Marxian economics. We do not think Marx is infallible. But it is without doubt that *Capital*, the fruit of long years and earnest study by Marx, is a scientific work endorsed by strict demonstration. So that we intend the development of Marxian economics but not its criticism.

A. – I also first intended creative development of Marxian economics. In its process, however, I found fundamental errors and inconsistencies. My effort for development led me to criticism.

Q. – There may be room for criticism in the contents of *Capital*. But the validity of Marx's methodology, dialectics, stands beyond doubt.

A. – The result of my study on it is, in a word: the essence of Hegelian-Marxian dialectics is a *fallacy of amphiboly*.

I tried to explain it beginning from my criticism on Hegel's refutation of Zeno's famous aporia: A flying arrow is at a stand-still. But, evidently, it was not a problem which could be expected to be settled by discussion in a few minutes. So I gave up persuasion on the spot and I presented a book of mine entitled *Benshoho Keizaigaku Hihan* (*The*

Critique of Dialectical Economics),[26] the essence of which is in Chapter 6 here.

[*Note*: About two years after my lecture in China I found an interesting article in *Asahi Shimbun*, 30 September 1984, by its Beijing correspondent entitled '*Shishi-jiushi*' (Explore the facts, and seek truth). A passage of it reads:

An official in the responsible position of the Academy of Social Sciences stated: 'We firmly uphold the standpoint and methodology of Marxism, Leninism and Maoism. However we do not literally believe in their writings.' And a cadre of the Party gave an example as follows: 'Marx's theory of the impoverishment of the labourers in the capitalist countries is not compatible with reality'.

And on 7 December 1984 the *People's Daily (Renmin Ribao)* Party organ declared:

Some of Marx's ideas are not necessarily suited to today's situation . . . We cannot depend on the works of Marx and Lenin to solve our present-day problems.

(The last words were changed the following day to 'all of our present-day problems'.)

Beijing Weekly, No. 49, 10 December 1985, published an essay by Ma Tin, *Ten big changes in the study of economics in China*, in which we read:

Now the main task of Marxian economics is not to criticise capitalism, the old world, but to serve in the construction of socialism, the new world . . . The emphases of our research must be laid on the development of social productive forces, the increase of the wealth of our nation, the steady growth of our economy, etc. . . . In *Capital* we can not find ready-made answers to these problems. (T.H.'s translation from Japanese edition.)

My lectures might have given some impetus to their gradual departure from dogmatism.]

II THE FALLACY OF 'THE LAW COMMON TO ALL SOCIAL SYSTEMS'

1 The law as such and its relation to Lenin's scheme

According to the contemporary Marxists there exists a convenient law by which one can explain both the rapid and balanced economic growth of the socialist countries and the economic stagnation and crisis in the capitalist countries. The popular textbook *Political Economy* of the USSR asserts:

> In any system of society development of the productive forces is expressed in the share of social labour devoted to the production of means of production growing in comparison with the share devoted to the production of consumer goods . . . Under capitalism a more rapid growth of the production of means of production compared with the production of consumer goods is expressed as a more rapid growth of constant capital compared with variable, i.e. a rise in the organic composition of capital.[27]

> A more rapid growth of Department I compared with Department II is a necessary condition for ensuring the uninterrupted advance of socialist production on the basis of higher techniques.[28]

A Course on Political Economy issued by Moscow University maintains:

> The objective tendency of the priority growth of means of production . . . is realised under capitalism in the deformed pattern of the growth of Department I without corresponding growth of Department II . . . Under socialism . . . the main tendency is the rise of technical composition and it demands the more rapid development of Department I.[29]

So they argue as follows: The priority growth of Department I is the law of economic development common to any and all societies. Under capitalism it is realised as the rise of organic composition of capital, giving rise to over-production, fall of the rate of profit (and hence stagnation of economic growth) and absolute impoverishment. The same law, under socialism, guarantees the uninterrupted technical progress and economic development. How on earth can such a convenient law exist?

The law of the priority growth of Department I is, in reality, logically entailed by the law of the falling rate of profit. Let us go back to Table 8.2. If we assume that in Pd_1 100c consists of consumer goods (Department I), 100v consists of consumer goods (Department II) for labourers and 100s in divided equally into additional means of production and consumer goods for capitalists, the total value of Department I is 150 and that of Department II is 150. Then, in Pd_2c is increased to 400 and v, s remain as in Pd_1 in value terms. Thus, the total value of Department I is increased to 450 and that of Department II remains 150. That is to say, the ratio of Department I to Department II rises from 1 to t in Pd_1 to 3 to 1 in Pd_2. From Pd_3 on, if continued by Marx, a process of the same nature should operate, i.e. the productivity rises, the value-amount of constant capital increases while that of both variable capital and surplus value remains constant, making the share of Department I ever larger.

As for the relation between Marx's law of the falling rate of profit and Lenin's reproduction scheme, it was already examined in detail in the foregoing chapter. Here I show the crux of the matter. Lenin's expanding reproduction scheme consisting of two departments is intended to give a numerical illustration of the priority growth of Department I. As shown in Table 8.4, the one-sector model of the law of the falling rate of profit and the two-sector model of the reproduction scheme by Lenin are of just the same nature, with rising c/v more rapidly growing Department I and a falling rate of profit.

Thus, it is an evident contradiction to assert that the law of the falling rate of profit is the demonstration of over-production ($S > D$) and the reproduction scheme by Lenin, an illustration of the falling rate of profit, is the demonstration of balanced ($S = D$) growth. This contradiction is brought about, as illustrated in foregoing Table 8.2, from Marx's error of forgetting price fall and therefore mistaking $S = D$ for $S > D$. (See Sec. III, Ch. 7, present book.)

It might be thought by those who do not understand this inconsistency that the law of the priority growth of Department I, seen as a logically necessary component of the law of the falling rate of profit, inevitably gives rise to $S > D$ leading capitalism to its collapse, and the same law, developed as the expanding reproduction scheme, guarantees $S = D$ and the balanced growth of the socialist economy. In reality, however, phenomena contradictory to the 'law of the priority growth of Department I common to all types of society' are seen both in socialist and capitalist countries.

2 The priority growth of Department II in USSR

In the USSR, as shown in Table 8.5, the priority growth of Department II, consumer goods, had been realised from 1968 through 1970, aiming at an 'affluent society'. In the 9th five year plan, 1971–75, the priority growth of consumer goods was also a target, although it did not materialise. In the 11th five year plan the priority growth of consumer goods was again a policy target and it was realised although in a slower rate. In the 12th five year plan the same policy is pursued.

Regarding the 9th five year plan, secretary-general Brezhnev of the Soviet Communist Party, in the 24th Congress in March 1971, made it clear that:

Table 8.4   Priority growth of Department I = falling rate of profit = Lenin's reproduction scheme

---

1 sector model illustrating the falling rate of profit (the 5th of the 'hypothetical series')

$$400c + 100v + 100s = 600 \quad\dots\dots\dots\dots\dots\dots\dots\dots\dots\dots (1)$$

(1) multiplied by 15 is

$$6000c + 1500v + 1500s = 9000 \quad\dots\dots\dots\dots\dots\dots\dots\dots (2)$$

(2) divided in a ratio of 2 to 1 is:

$$\left.\begin{array}{l} 4000c_1 + 1000v_1 + 1000s_1 = 6000 \\ 2000c_2 + 500v_2 + 500s_2 = 3000 \end{array}\right\} \dots\dots\dots\dots\dots\dots\dots\dots (3)$$

(3) is Marx's 2 sector simple reproduction scheme. If we change the figures of the 2nd sector a little, we obtain:

$$\left.\begin{array}{l} 4000c_1 + 1000v_1 + 1000s_1 = 6000 \\ 1500c_2 + 750v_2 + 750s_2 = 3000 \end{array}\right\} \dots\dots\dots\dots\dots\dots\dots\dots (4)$$

---

(4) is the 1st year figures of the expanding reproduction scheme by Marx and Lenin. From the comparison of the 1st year figures and the 4th year figures of Lenin's reproduction scheme, we obtain:

Ratio: in % except $\frac{c}{v}$	Organic composition $\frac{c}{v}$		ratio: Dept. I & II $\frac{c_2+v_2+s_2}{c_1+v_1+s_1}$		Profit rate $\frac{s}{c+v}$	
	I	II	I	II	I	II
1st year	4	2	100	50.0	20.0	33.3
4th year	4.99	2.12	100	41.4	16.7	32.0

(See Table 7.11)

This measure, of course, does not mean the alteration of our basic line, the priority growth of the department of means of production.[30]

Ten years later, however, when the policy of the priority growth of consumer goods was again adopted, Prime Minister Tikhonov in February 1981 in the 26th party Congress simply declared that:

The principal feature of the 11th five year plan is the more rapid growth of group B compared with group A.

Table 8.5   The priority growth of consumer goods
in USSR[31]

(Increase-ratio, compared with previous year, %)

Year		A	B
1968	Result	8.0	8.3
1969	Result	6.9	7.2
1970	Result	7.9	8.3
1971–5	Plan	7.1–7.9	8.1
	Result	7.8	6.5
1981–5	Plan	4.7–5.0	4.9–5.2
	Result	3.6	3.9
1986–90	Plan	3.9–4.2	4.1–4.6
1986	Result	5.2	4.0
1987	Result	3.8	3.8
1988	Result	3.9	4.5
1989	Plan	2.5	6.0

Note: Figures for 1971–5 and 1981–5 are the yearly
averages during the periods.

And yet he did not go as far as positively to deny 'the law common to
all societies'.

Now under Gorbachev's *perestroika* the priority growth of
Department II became further noteworthy. The planned growth rates
in 1989 are 2.5% for group A and 6% for group B.

[*Note*:   In the Soviet statistics group A and group B represent the means
of production and the means of consumption within the industrial sector.
But very often they also mean heavy industry and light industry, or the
means of production and the means of consumption in the total social
product. These three kinds of categories are used almost synonymously.

I met K. Protonikov, President of the Economic Research Institute,
Academy of Sciences, USSR, on 28 December 1964, just after the national
economic plan for 1965 was made public, in which the target for the
annual growth-rate of group B was set at 7.7%, coming close to that of
group A, 8.2%. I asked him if there was a possibility of the growth-rate of
group B surpassing that of group A some time in the future. He flatly
denied it on the ground that 'the principle of the priority growth of
Department I is a fundamental law of Marxian economics'. It was only

four years later in 1968 that his assertion was betrayed by the real Soviet economic development as is shown in Table 8.5.

Several years later, in 1970 or so, N.A. Tsagolov, economics professor at Moscow University, visited Waseda University. I asked him, 'Don't you think that the faster growth of group B nullifies Marx's law of the priority growth of Department I?' 'No. Group A and group B cover only the industrial sector. Over the total social product the law continues to be effective.'

This was his answer. (It was not persuasive to assert that the priority growth of Department I continued while group B was growing faster.) In Protonikov's case Departments I and II are equivalent to groups A and B. But Tsagolov meant the priority growth of Department I of the total social product.

In the following section 3 we will see a virtually synonymous usage in China of heavy industry and light industry (plus agriculture) with Department I and Department II. Marx himself defined the two departments as follows:

The total product, and therefore the total production, of society may be divided into two major departments: I. Means of Production (*Produktionsmittel*) . . . II. Articles of Consumption (*Konsumtionsmittel*).[32]

The abstract character of this definition gave rise to equivocal interpretations. Sometimes they are treated as representing the total social product, and sometimes they mean heavy and light industries, the demarcation of the three interpretations being very often blurred in the arguments.]

In connection with Professor Tsagalov's answer above a close friend of mine gave me the following comment: 'Tsagalov must have meant (1) productive transportation (freight) grows faster than unproductive (passengers), (2) fodder and technical crops and meat for sausage factories grow faster than direct foodstuffs, and (3) the excesses in (1) and (2) outweigh the deficit in industry.'

I am quite sceptical of this comment. (1) Professor Tsagalov should have a good access to Soviet statistics, if the trend pointed out above were a fact he could have told it me on the spot. (2) In 1970 in the total social product industry occupied 64%, agriculture 16% and productive transportation and communication 4% (*The National Economy of the USSR*, Russian edn, p. 47: % calculated from roubles by T.H.). We can assume from these figures the following: It is hardly thinkable that in the late 1960s the priority growth of Department I in the spheres of agriculture and transportation outweighed the priority growth of Department II in industry. (3) Therefore, I suppose that Professor Tsagolov merely asserted Marx's proposition of the priority growth of Department I in the total social product presumably without any factual ground.

3 The Chinese policy of restraint on heavy industry

We see a similar policy in China too. Table 8.6 is taken from *The Study of Economic Problems in Socialist China*[39] by Xue Muqiao, a famous economist born in 1904 who was ousted during the Cultural Revolution. His book is noted for his bold criticism on the past erroneous economic policies. Quoting the figures in Table 8.6 he argues as follows: In 1957 agriculture, light industry and heavy industry were well balanced, but in the following three years the heavy industry was disproportionately swollen, giving rise to severe distortion to the structure of the economy and contracting production as a whole. Thereafter, through the adjustment period of five years, a normal situation was recovered in 1965. The relative ratio in 1979 was 30% for both agriculture and light industry and 40% for heavy industry. The share of heavy industry is again disproportionately large as a result of hasty modernisation efforts. So he concludes: 'The ratio of heavy industry must be properly checked.'[34]

Table 8.6   The change of relative ratio of agriculture, light industry and heavy industry in China

Year	Agriculture	Light industry	Heavy industry
1957	43.3	30.1	26.6
1960	20.1	26.6	53.3
1965	29.8	35.4	34.8

The underlying theoretical basis of the balance-destroying growth of heavy industry is the law of the priority growth of Department I. Toward the end of 1979 a large scale discussion meeting was held in China on the theme of 'What is the objective of socialist production?' There it was pointed out that the 'mistaken application' of the law of the priority growth of Department I caused 'production for the sake of production' and one lost sight of the fundamental principle of 'production for the sake of consumption'. But 'the majority of the participants of the meeting made no doubt of the rightness of the law itself.'[35] What the discussants should have done in this case was to disclose the fallacious nature of the law *per se* (see Table 8.2) and thereby straightforwardly justify the policy of proper restraint on heavy industry.

4 The priority growth of consumer goods in capitalist countries

Now coming to the capitalist world let us have a look at Table 8.7. In Japan from 1970 through 1981 consumer goods increased by 100% whereas producer goods increased only a little more than 40%. In the US from 1967 through 1983 consumer goods increased 50% and equipment 40%. In West Germany even in the 1950s we find the priority growth of industries roughly coinciding with Department II.

Table 8.7   The priority growth of consumer goods in Japan, US and West Germany

Japan [36] *(Index numbers)*		
Year	Consumer goods	Producer goods
1970	100.0	100.0
1981	200.5	142.5

US [37] *(Index numbers)*		
Year	Consumer goods	Equipment
1967	100.0	100.0
1983	151.7	140.8

West Germany[38] *(Percentages)*		
Year	Consumer goods food processing	Mining, general materials, capital goods
1950	30.0	70.0
1958	37.3	62.7

In other advanced industrial countries, thinking of the nature of recent technological development and the rise in the standard of living, the trend should be similar, the more rapid growth of consumer goods. Now let us compare these facts with the following contention by Zheng-lizhi in his essay:

> The expansion of the capitalist market first of all depends on the expansion of the market for the means of production. The progress of science and technology necessarily gives rise to the rise of the organic composition of capital, bringing about the more rapid increase of means of production than that of means of consumption.[39] . . . Productive consumption is after all connected with individual consumption . . . In the capitalist system the contradiction between production and consumption cannot find a way to its solution . . . Thus it caused the 1973–75 economic crisis, the most severe one since the end of the war.[40]

In the 1970s the department of the means of consumption had been growing more rapidly in Japan, in the United States and presumably also in other advanced capitalist countries. The first oil-shock depression, which occurred under these conditions, is explained away by the imbalanced rapid development of the means of production and the following over-production, relying on the theory described in *Capital* of the rise of organic composition of capital leading to the priority growth of Department I. This is not inductive reasoning starting from facts, but a wrong deductive method based on the assumption of the 'infallible' law of Marx. It is a matter for regret as Zheng's essay contains an excellent positive analysis of the current situation in the major capitalist countries.

American economist Paul M. Sweezey also sets out from the 'infallibility' of *Capital*. On the rapid growth of capitalism in the 1960s he argues:

> The *normal* state of the system in its monopoly stage is one of cyclical ups and downs in a context of continuing stagnation. If during any period of time this is not the *actual* state of the system, this fact requires to be explained by historical forces which operate on the system but are not presupposed as being essential to its existence.[41]

This reminds us of the following statement by Marx in *Capital*:

> The development of the productivity of labour creates out of the falling rate of profit a law which at a certain point comes into antagonistic conflict with this development and must be overcome constantly through crises . . . the capitalist mode of production . . . comes to a standstill at a point fixed by the

production and realisation of profit, and not the satisfaction of requirements.[42]

Sweezy asserts, on the ground of 'infallible' law of the falling rate of profit (and hence, of the growth rate) that the rapid growth of the 1960s is exceptional because it does not match the law and the stagflation in the period of the oil shock is the normal state corresponding with the law. This is also an unwarranted deduction, standing on its head.

5   The still surviving law of *Capital*

Now let me present three examples of contemporary Marxists' interpretation of the law of the falling rate of profit, the origin of the 'law common to all social systems'.

First, Zue Muqiao writes in the preface of his book mentioned above:

> Marx . . . clarified the essence and the law of motion of the capitalist productive relations and reached the conclusion that the collapse of capitalism and the victory of socialism are both inevitable.[43]

Second, Tetsuzo Fuwa, secretary-general of the Japan Communist party, asserts in his article entitled *Capital and the present age*:

> It is evident that this book has become *the most* terrible one for the ruling class in charge of capitalism because it elucidated, through the power of science, the inevitable collapse of capitalist society, which they wish to continue eternally and its replacement by a new society; that this is the law of motion of social development.[44]

This 'law of motion' of social development pointed out by the above two Marxists is, in other words, the law of the falling rate of profit developed in *Capital*. The inadmissible inconsistency involved in this law and hence the invalidity of the law itself should be already clear as demonstrated in the foregoing chapters and in this one.

Third, Wodzimierz Brus, who visited Waseda University on 7 April 1982, once served in Poland as a distinguished scholar and an important economic-policy maker. Since October 1972 he has been in the United Kingdom and is now Professor and fellow of Wolfson College, Oxford. In the Foreword to his book, *Socialist Ownership and Political Systems*, he mentions of his methodological basis as 'materialistic concept of history by Marx', which is no more than a 'working hypothesis' for him.[45]

He gave a lecture at Waseda University under the title: *Social Theory and Political Practice – Marxism and Communism*. The gist of it was, in a word, that Marxist social theory has 'use-value' for the understanding of and hence for offering solutions to the problems faced by the communist system.[46] After his lecture I asked him:

> The fundamental law of historical materialism that production relations must correspond to productive forces is quite an ambiguous one. And its application to capitalist system, the law of the falling rate of profit, contains impermissible self-contradiction. [I explained to him the main points of my argument as in this book.] Is it not after all necessary to carry out a fundamental reappraisal of the whole body of Marxian social theory in order to introduce economic and political reform in the communist countries?

He held his position that the Marxian theoretical system is fundamentally valid. On the law of the falling rate of profit he replied:

> The conclusion of the falling profit rate and hence the falling growth rate comes from Marx's assumption that, in the terminology of contemporary economics, technological progress is always capital coefficient raising. [This interpretation is the same as T.H.'s.] But one qualification is added by Marx. The law is that of *tendency* of the profit rate to fall.

So that this law is not necessarily a statement of the inevitability of the falling profit rate. This was his implication. In conjunction with that I called his attention to the following:

> At the beginning of Chapter 14, 'Counteracting influences' (on the law), Book III, *Capital*, Marx writes that 'counteracting influences . . . cross and annul (*aufheben*)' the law (p. 227) and a few pages later that 'counter-effects . . . do not do away with (*nicht aufheben*) the law, but impair its effect'.[47]

He replied:

> Book III of *Capital* was unfinished manuscripts published by Engels after Marx's death. Scholars and thinkers should be careful not to let their manuscripts be published after death without permission.

Brus's humour does not save him from his ambiguous position. If this law is only that of a tendency which might be realised or might not be realised, then, as a logical corollary, capitalism might collapse or might not collapse. This uncertainty nullifies Marx's prophecy of the inevitable downfall of capitalism. Brus seemed unaware of this crucial point.

On the law of the obligatory correspondence of production relations to the productive forces he stated in his lecture:

> To the productive forces of socialism should correspond the production relations of political freedom, which is lacking in contemporary socialism. This is the contradiction which propels the political system in the direction of correspondence with the productive forces.[48]

He added that this is not a necessary law, but a working hypothesis which he wishes to come true. I agree with him on the necessity of political freedom for the economic reform in Poland. But the dialectics of productive forces and production relations is superfluous in this case. What I could not tell him due to lack of time was this: Marx could not have envisaged the contradiction between productive forces and production relations in socialism. He expected the advent of a *free* socialist society after overthrowing the capitalist society. His image of a socialist society was 'a community of free individuals, carrying on their work with the means of production in common'.[49] Marx's line of thinking was as follows: when all the productive forces within a limit of a social system have been fully developed, 'then begins an era of social revolution . . . the material transformation of the economic conditions of production, which can be determined with the precision of natural science'.[50]

But 'productive forces' is an abstract and inexact concept unsuitable for a quantitative measurement 'with the precision of natural science', as is already explained in Chapter 5 of the present volume (Section II, subsection 2). It is a nonsense, for instance, to make prophecy that when GNP per annum reaches three hundred trillion Yen in Japan, capitalism will be superseded by communism.

I am sympathetic with Professor Brus's emotional and political stance which makes him plead the fundamental rightness of Marxism and its usefulness for the reform of Poland. However, the call for liberty in Poland and other socialist countries is essentially of a nature that demands to break down the wall of 'infallible' Marxism from its theoretical foundations.

III   SOME DISCUSSIONS WITH SOVIET ECONOMISTS

An international symposium sponsored by Japan–USSR Economists' Society was held from 4 to 6 October 1983 in Moscow. The problems taken up were the prospect of Japan–USSR economic co-operation, the influence of rapid progress in high technology on the Japanese economy, the evaluation of contemporary world capitalism, etc.

But what I intend here is to review only some theoretical issues developed in the course of the symposium which are closely related to the theme of this book. Dr V. K. Zaitsev, Institute of World Economy and International Relations, made a report entitled, *The present stage of scientific and technical progress and growing instability of capitalist economy*. I raised two questions related to the basic propositions of Marxian economics.

1 High-technology and the law of the falling rate of profit

Dr Zaitsev admitted that the high-technological investments, in the fields such as 'the information-computing complex', 'microelectronics', etc., now in progress in Japan have a large multiplier effect, contributing to the fast growth of the Japanese economy. And at the same time he asserted that these investments accelerate 'the replacement of physical labour by machines' and lead to 'an increase in the organic composition of capital and a fall in the average rate of profit'.[51]

I pointed out the self-contradiction involved in his statement as follows: Paraphrased in Marxian terminology, he means that a small investment of c in the field of high technology produces large $v + s$. When $c/v + s$ ($= K/Y$, capital coefficient) is small, $s/c + v$, the rate of profit, becomes large, enabling rapid economic growth. And on the other hand, he claims that the same investment raises c/v (and so $c/v + s$ too), thus decreasing $s/c + v$, the rate of profit.

The two opposite conclusions, the rise of the rate of profit and its fall, coming out of the same premise, are evidently incompatible. Considering that high technology in the above-said field is generally acknowledged to be capital-saving, the latter conclusion, and with it the wrong belief in the 'law' itself 'discovered' by Marx, should be discarded.

Dr Zaitsev answered my comment by saying that he knew also of the cases of other Western economists who regard high-technology to be generally capital-saving. But he kept silent on the 'contradiction' I brought up and the law of the falling rate of profit.

2 Re-examining the concept of 'unproductive labour'

On the relation between the material sector and the non-material sector of production, Dr Zaitsev reported that 'scientific and technical progress in the sphere of material production has assumed today such a form that it must rely on the support of the non-material sector – the service industry and information. An ever growing need of replacing material exchange by exchange of information will determine an accelerated growth of the share of the non-material production sphere in the future.'[52]

I agreed with him in his prospect of an increased share of the non-material sector, and added that this prospect itself raises the following theoretical problem.

Before the 1960s the orthodox interpretation among Soviet economists of labour engaged in non-material industries had been that it is unproductive labour which does not create value. But, in the 1960s in advanced capitalist countries the share of the non-material sector came close to that of the material sector and in the 1970s even surpassed it in some of these countries. (See Table 1.9 in the present book.) The increasing trend of the workers in the non-material sector is the same in the Soviet Union. As shown in Figure 8.8, the share of the workers in the 'unproductive sector' increased from 13% in 1940 to 25% in 1984. If we add to them the workers in goods-transportation, commerce, etc. (classified as productive services in Soviet statistics), their share increased from 23% in 1940 to 42% in 1984.

If Marxists cling to the theory that labour of the material sector alone creates value, in the near future the larger part of social labour will be barred from the labour-value theory. Perhaps reflecting this apprehension a series of controversies took place in the late 1960s among Soviet economists, touched off by V. Kovyzhenko's article, *Value of Service – Reality or Fiction?*, 1967,[54] in which he came up with his view that labour in service industries except that in commerce is productive and so creates value. Two years later this new interpretation of value-creating labour was extended to include commercial labour by Y.A. Pevsner in his article, *There is no double calculation of service.*[55] This amounts to a substantial denial of Marx's view of commercial labour, although he does not openly admit it.

As Professor Pevsner happened to be present as one of the discussants of our symposium I particularly stated that I support his view.[56]

On this point Dr Zaitsev answered me that the view of Professor Pevsner is now prevalent in the Soviet Union. A young Soviet economist who was also attending the symposium told me later that Professor Pevsner's view is already prevalent in academic circles, but it is not yet taught in schools.

Table 8.8   The rising share of the workers engaged in unproductive fields in USSR[53]

		1940	1960	1975	1984
1.	Industry, construction, agriculture	77	71	61	58
2.	Transportation, communication, commerce, etc.*	10	13	17	17
	1 + 2	87	84	78	75
3.	Unproductive sector **	13	16	22	25
	2 + 3	23	29	39	42
	Total	100	100	100	100

Note: *   Freight and business communications.
       **   Health, education, welfare, science, culture, housing, public establishments, administration, management, finance, insurance, etc.

Lastly, an important qualification should be added here. I gave support to Professor Pevsner's view only in the sense that his inclusion of commercial labour in value creation is the establishment of consistency within the framework of Marx's labour value theory. This consistency does not give operationality to 'labour hour' calculation, as already explained in Chapter 2 of this book (Section II, subsection 4). (For particulars of this symposium see its official record.[57])

[*Note*:   The controversies introduced above on the nature of labour in service industries, especially in commerce, are of the theoretical dimension. In the practical area of statistics commerce has long been classified as one of the branches of *material production*. (For instance, see Alexandr Petrov, *Textbook for economic statistics*, 1954.[58]) How can this treatment be compatible with Marx's assertion that commercial labour is unproductive and does not create value? Marx divides the process of circulation into two categories: (1) the 'genuine' circulation, the pure act of selling and buying in which new value is not created; (2) the 'processes of production which are only continued in circulation', i.e. storage, transportation, etc. (See Ch. 6, 'The costs of circulation', Book II, *Capital*. Esp. see citation, note 24, Ch. 1 of the present book.)

It is almost impossible to distinguish (1) from (2) in statistical aggregation. Therefore, Soviet statisticians regard all the commercial activities as category (1) for convenience' sake. (And arguing a step further, this distinction itself is an absurdity. Can you suppose that a shop-girl carrying a commodity is creating value, but selling that commodity is not creating value?!)

As for transportation and communication industries, only freight transport and communication for productive purposes are counted as value-creating material production. This clearly differs from Marx's definition, according to which all kinds of transportation and communication are value-creating.[59]

IV EPILOGUE

Now we want to confirm that contemporary Marxists, irrespective of whether they live in communist or capitalist countries, are still in essence holding to the inheritance of Marxian ideology, its dialectics, its historical materialism, and the economics of *Capital*. The probable refutation of this conclusion of mine by believers in Marxism would be that doctrine set by Marx has been continually developed by his successors observing the spirit of Lenin who said:

> We do not regard Marx's theory as something completed and inviolable; on the contrary, we are convinced that it has only laid the foundation stone of the science which socialists must develop in all directions if they wish to keep pace with life.[60]

Here we should not overlook that Lenin also said that 'the Marxist doctrine is omnipotent, because it is true'.[61] Lenin who 'does not regard Marx's theory as something inviolable' does not dare to examine 'the foundation stone' itself and limits socialists' task to inheriting and developing along the guide-lines established by Marx. Note that even so unorthodox a Marxist as Wodzimierz Brus (above) cannot, it seems, shake himself free.

Irrespective of socialism or capitalism, to perform necessary reforms based on objective analysis, one must emerge from the unscientific way of thinking named scientific socialism. It might not be easily expected in the circle of its believers at the moment. But someday even among them the truth will become widely known that scientific socialism does not deserve its name. And then, a solid ground will be prepared for establishing a trustworthy world peace connected with a common tie of free thinking in the literal sense of the word.

> The real advantage which truth has consists in this, that when an opinion is true, it may be extinguished once, twice, or many times, but in the course of ages there will generally be found persons to rediscover it, until some one of its reappearances falls on a time when from favourable circumstances it escapes persecution until it has made such head as to withstand all subsequent attempts to suppress it.

John Stuart Mill, *On Liberty*[62]

Appendix: The Two Factors Which Nullify the Law of the Falling Rate of Profit

I   CAPITAL COEFFICIENT LOWERING TECHNICAL PROGRESS

Let us assume an abstract society where capital technological progress prevails (Table A.1).

Table A.1   The illustration of the rising rate of profit

Pd_1	$400c + 100v + 100s = 600h$	$(300G)$	$p' = 20\%$
Pd_2	$100c + 100v + 100s = 300h$	$(30,000G)$	$p' = 50\%$

This table is the same as Table 4.3, except for one thing: the order of the two equations is reversed. The implication of this change is that capital coefficient is lowered from $400c/100v + 100s = 2$ in Period 1 to $100c/100v + 100s = {}^1/2$ in Period 2. Owing to its effect, the total social product increases from $300G$ in Period 1 to $30,000G$ in Period 2, i.e. by 100 times. And the rate of profit rises from $100s/400c + 100v = 20\%$ in Period 1 to $100s/100c + 100v = 50\%$ in Period 2.

We can assume, of course, less capital-saving technique, e.g., $200c$, $300c$, etc, in Period 2. Then the rate of rise of the profit rate becomes smaller. In the case of neutral technology, $400c$, the rate of profit remains unchanged.

In Period 1, $600h$ are 'embodied' in $300G$, so the value (price) of $1G = 2h$. In Period 2, $30,000G$ 'embody' $300h$, so $1G - 1/100h$. Thus with $100s$ only $50G$ are obtainable in Period 1, but in Period 2, $10,000G$. The increase of surplus value in real terms is 200 times.

'Constant' capital, which should be *constant*, was *reduced* to $^1/4$ in value, and it *boosted surplus value* 200 times, contradicting Marx's definition that constant capital does not produce surplus value.

We can conclude now that if we acknowledge capital coefficient lowering technology, we should also acknowledge that Marxian concept of 'constant' capital is quite obsolete. Marx was living in the age of iron and coal, and we are living in that of high technology. There might have been several hundred times productivity rise between the two.

II THE EFFECT OF THE TURNOVER OF CAPITAL ON THE RATE OF PROFIT

There exists another factor which nullifies the law of the falling rate of profit: the turnover of capital.

The rate of profit in Ch. 13 'The law as such', Book III of *Capital* is the ratio of surplus value, s, to the value of 'total capital',[1] $c + v$. But what sort of a total capital? In this chapter Marx first defines it as 'employed' total capital,[2] and just a few pages later as 'advanced' total capital.[3] And we find in Ch. 9, Book I that Marx writes as follows: 'By constant capital *advanced* . . . We always mean . . . the value of the means of production actually *consumed*'.[4] (emphasis – T.H.). In short, 'advanced' is the same as 'consumed'. However, advanced capital and consumed (turned-over) capital belong to unmistakably different categories according to his own explanations elsewhere.[5] Then again in the latter part of Ch. 13, Book III we read: 'The rate of profit is calculated on the total capital *employed*'[6] (emphasis – T.H.).

Reading through these confusing definitions of capital as the denominator in the profit-rate calculation in all the three books of *Capital*, we know that what Marx should adopt and principally adopts is *advanced* (expended in advance or invested) capital.

However, as far as Ch. 13, Book III is concerned, this perplexity does not come to the fore, because Marx ignores in his 'hypothetical series', $100c + 100v + 100s$, etc., the distinction between fixed capital and circulating (fluid) capital, and accordingly, the difference of turnover periods among various components of total capital. Thus the difference between advanced capital, employed capital and turned-over capital substantially vanishes and the rate of profit counted on these three kinds of capital comes to be one and the same. This might have been the reason why Marx and Engels could remain unaware of the apparent inconsistency lying in their statements.

Marx himself writes, however, in Ch. 8, Book III: 'Different compositions of capitals . . .' that 'we shall have to analyse: (1) the difference in the organic composition of capitals, and (2) the difference in their *period of turnover*'.[7] (emphasis – T.H.). And Ch. 4, Book III, supplemented by Engels, bears the title 'The effect of the turnover on the rate of profit'.

If we take into account the turnover of capital, the law of the falling rate of profit loses its validity, as Table A.2 shows.

Let us assume that the model society of Table A.2 has in Period 1 the total capital of $100c + 100v$ and produces a total social product of $100c + 100v + 100s$, so the rate of profit is 50%. The yearly turnover rate of c and v are thought to be both 1. This means, in a more concrete imagination, all the equipments of this society perishes in one year and the production period of all the goods is also one year, so they are completed at the end of the year.

Then in Period 2, as a result of technical progress, the duration period of the equipments is extended to two years, in other words, the yearly turnover rate of $50fc$ (fixed constant capital) is now $1/2$. And these equipments shorten the production period of all the goods to $1/5$ years. So the yearly turnover rate of cc (circulating constant capital) becomes 5: 10(advanced or invested)$cc \times 5 = 50$(employed or consumed)cc. The same amount of the total social product is made, not at the year end, but successively 5 times through the year.

Table A.2   Shortening of the turnover period raises the rate of profit

---

Pd_1 (Yearly turnover rate: $c = 1$, $v = 1$)

   $100c + 100v + 100s$ $p' = 50\%$

Pd_2 (Yearly turnover rate: $fc > = 1/2$, $cc = 5$, $v = 1$)

   Calculated on employed capital:

      $25fc + 50cc + 100v + 100s$ $p' = 50\%$

   On turned-over (consumed) capital:

      $25fc + 50cc + 100v + 100s$ $p' = 57.1\%$

   On advance capital:

      $50fc + 10cc + 100v + 100s$ $p' = 62.4\%$

Note: *fc*: fixed constant capital.
         cc: circulating constant capital.

As shown in Table A.2 above, the *employed* capital is $50fc$ (amount of equipments in use) and $500cc$ (amount of materials used in a year). So the rate of profit remains the same as in Period 1, 50%. But the *turned-over* capital is smaller, with $25fc$ (amount depreciated of the employed or advanced capital) and $50cc$ (amount of materials consumed in a year), so the rate of profit rises to 57.1%. The *advanced* capital is again smaller, with $50fc$ (amount of equipments invested) and $10cc$ (amount advanced or invested for procuring $50cc$ materials), so the rate of profit further rises to 62.5%.

The illustration above, although quite simple and abstract, shows the essence of a common-sense fact clearly described in *Capital* that 'reduction in the period of turnover . . . increases the rate of profit'.[8]

Thus we know that not only the application of capital-coefficient lowering technique but also the shortening of turnover period nullifies the 'inevitability' of the law of the falling rate of profit.

Moreover, the above figures invalidate the fundamental concept of 'organic composition' (c/v). In Period 1 the organic composition of capital is $100c/100v = 1$. But in Period 2 there appear three kinds of organic composition. That of the employed capital is $50fc + 50cc/100v = 1$, same as that of Period 1. In the case of the turned-over capital it *falls* to $25fc + 50cc/100v = 3/4$. In the advanced capital it *falls* further to $50fc + 10cc/100v = 3/5$.

Therefore, we have to conclude that the law of the rising organic composition reflecting technical progress comes to be unwarranted. It is valid only under two unrealistic assumptions: that all the components of constant capital (and variable capital) have one and the same turnover period and that technical progress always raises capital-coefficients.

One last word. Reduction of turnover period in both production and circulation spheres and the development of capital-coefficient lowering technique seem to be prevalent in this age of high technology and managerial innovation. It goes without saying that these trends encourage the rise of the rate of profit.

Notes

Abbreviations

Capital: Karl Marx, *Capital*, Foreign Languages Publishing House, Moscow. Three volumes of this English edition are identical with three books (Bücher) of the German text.

Kapital: Karl Marx, *Das Kapital*, Dietz Verlag, Berlin, 1953.

Lenin, *C.W.*: V.I. Lenin, *Collected Works*, Foreign Languages Publishing House, Moscow.

Preface

1. See Gorbachev's speech at UN general assembly, 8 Dec. 1988: 'To utter the ultimate truth is the last thing to which we aspire.' This is an implicit denial of the 'infallibility' of Marxism-Leninism.

Chapter 1

1. '. . . when a society has got upon the right track for the discovery (*auf die Spur gekommen is*t) of the natural law' (*Capital*, Book I, p. 10, Preface to the first German edition, Kapital, S.7; 'these laws . . . working with iron necessity (*eherner Notwendigkeit*) towards inevitable results' (*ibid*, pp.8–9, S.6.); 'discovering it (*es zu entdecken*)' (Book III, p.209, S.240).
2. *Capital*, Book III, p. 767.
3. Resembling what Oscar Lange intended in his 'Marxism and Bourgeois Economics', *Zycie szkoly wyzszej*, April and May 1958: Japanese translation in *Keizai Seminar*, Feb. 1959.
4. John Strachey, *Contemporary Capitalism*, Victor Gollancz, London, 1956, pp. 63–4.
5. *Ibid.*, p. 100.
6. *Capital*, Book III, p. 224.
7. 'total price' (*ibid.*, p. 225); '*Gesamtpreis*' (S.258); 'sum of the prices of the commodities' (Book I, p. 120); '*Preisumme der Waren*' (S.125).
8. Book I, p. 46.
9. *Ibid.*, p. 46. For a more detailed citation and explanation, see Ch.2, note 54 in the present volume, and the following.
10. *Ibid.*, p. 10.1
11. Book III, p. 347.
12. Book I, p. 94.

13. *Ibid.*, p. 95.
14. *Ibid.*, p. 98.
15. *Ibid*, p. 319. For a more detailed citation see Ch.2, note 55 in the present book. Here Marx prescribes that 'an average social working-day of . . . 12 hours produces the same new value, six shillings'. In Book I, p. 40, we find a proposition to the same effect in which 'value' also means 'price'. 'The value of a commodity . . . varies . . . inversely as the productiveness of the labour incorporated in it.'
16. *Capital*, Book 1, p. 99.
17. Strachey, *Contemporary Capitalism*, p. 87.
18. Joseph M. Gillman, *The Falling Rate of Profit – Marx's Law and its Significance to Twentieth Century Capitalism*, Dennis Dobson, London, 1956, p. 89.
19. 'To rescue Marxian theory on economic crises from its dilemma – Does the law of the falling tendency of the rate of profit really exist?' *Sekai-keizai-hyoron (World Economic Review)*, June 1956.
20. Karl Marx, *Theories of Surplus Value* (Sections), translated by G.A. Bonner and Emile Burns, Lawrence & Wishart, London, 1951, p. 194.
21. *Capital*, Book II, p. 52.
22. *Ibid.*, pp. 54–5.
23. Алекцандр Петров, ред, *Курс экономической статистика*, 2--ое изд, Тосфиннзиат, москва, 1954г, стр. 2 22; Alexander Petrow, red, *Grundriss der Wirtschaftsstatistik*, übersetzt v. W. Fickensher, Verlag Die Wischaft, Berlin, 1954, S. 149; А. И. Тозулов, *Экономическая статистика*, Госфиннздат, Москва, 1953 г, стр. 172.
24. Book II, p. 149: 'The general law is that all costs of circulation which arise only from changes in the forms of commodities do not add to their value.'
25. Book II, p. 283.
26. Book II, p.149: 'The capital spent to meet those costs (of circulation) . . . must be . . . a deduction from the surplus value.' Book III, p. 288: 'The former (commercial capital) appropriates a portion of this surplus value by having this portion transferred from industrial capital to itself.'
27. Политическая экономия – учебник, 3. изд, москва, 1959, стр. 152.
28. *Political Economy*, a textbook issued by the Institute of Economics of the Academy of Science of the USSR, English translation, Lawrence & Wishart, London, 1957, p. 242.
29. *Capital*, Book III, p. 344.
30. Book II, p. 136.
31. Paul A. Baran, *Political Economy of Growth*, Monthly Review Press, New York, 1957, p. 24.
32. *Capital*, Book II, p. 132.
33. Ronald L. Meek, *Studies in the Labour Theory of Value*, Lawrence & Wishart, London, 1956, p. 7.
34. Я. А. Певзнер, 'Повторного счетд услуг не существует', *Мировая экономика и межднародные отношения*, no. 3, 1969, стр. 92.
35. Nobuo Iimori, *Theory of Productive Labour – Economics of Service Sector (Seisanteki-rodo-no-riron–Service-Bumon no Keizaigaku)*, 1977, p. 173.

Chapter 2

1. Lenin, *C.W.*, vol. 38, p. 319.
2. Translation by T.H. from German text in *Marx Engels Werke*, Dietz Verlag, Berlin, BD.32. S.552.
3. *Capital*, Book III, p. 826.
4. John Locke, *Two Treatises of Civil Government*, Everyman's Library, pp. 136–7.
5. Adam Smith, *The Wealth of Nations*, vol.1, Everyman's Library, pp. 41–2.
6. David Ricardo, *Political Economy and Taxation*, Everyman's Library, p. 13.
7. *Ibid.*, pp. 28–9.
8. John Gray, *The Social System, A Treatise on the Principle of Exchange*, Edinburgh 1831, reprinted 1973 by Augustus M. Kelley Publishers, USA, p. 18.
9. *Ibid.*, p. 63.
10. *Ibid.*, pp. 67–8.
11. John Gray, *Lectures on the Nature and Use of Money*, Edinburgh, 1848, Adam & Charles Black, London: Longman, Brown, Green & Longmans, 1898, p. 169.
12. Gray, *The Social System*, p. 64.
13. *Ibid.*, pp. 99–100.
14. Gray, *Money*, pp. 165–6.
15. Robert Owen, *A New View of Society and other Writings*, Everyman's Library, pp. 250, 262–3.
16. G. D. H. Cole, *Life of Robert Owen*, Macmillan, 1930, pp. 63–4.
17. Marx, *A Contribution to the Critique of Political Economy*, Progress Publisher, Moscow, 1970, pp. 83–4.
18. *Ibid.*, pp. 84–5.
19. *Capital*, Book I, p. 94.
20. My quotations from Gray (notes 9, 10, 11) are among the passages cited by Marx.
21. *Capital*, Book I, pp. 74–5.
22. Owen, note 15, p. 263.
23. *Capital*, Book I, pp. 78–9.
24. Friedrich Engels, *Anti-Dühring* (*Herr Eugen Dühring's Revolution in Science*), Foreign Languages Publishing House, Moscow, 1954, pp. 429–30.
25. Marx, *Marginal Notes to the Programme of the German Workers' Party (Critique of the Gotha Programme), Marx Engels Selected Works*, vol.II, Foreigh Languages Publishing House, Moscow, 1958, pp. 23–4.
26. *Ibid.*, p. 24.
27. *Programme of the Communist Party of the Soviet Union*, adopted by the 22nd Congress of the CPSU, 31 October 1961, Foreign Languages Publishing House, Moscow, 1961, pp. 62, 82.
28. *Политическая экономия -- учебник*, 3. издание, москва, 1959, стр. 652.

29. Lenin, *The State and Revolution, A Handbook of Marxism*, Haskell House Publishers, New York, 1970, vol.II, p. 749.
30. Reuter-dispatch, Moscow, *The Japan Times*, 27 April 1984. This line of argument by Chernenko was followed in the newly revised Programme of the CPSU adopted in the 27th Congress held in Feb.–Mar. 1986. It stipulates that 'socialism and communism are two successive phases of a single demarcation between the two'.
31. *Capital*, Book I, p. 44.
32. Marx, (note 25), p. 24.
33. Marx and Engels, *The German Ideology*, Progress Publishers, Moscow, 1964, p. 47.
34. Minoru Oka, *Keikaku-Keizairon Josetsu* (*An Introduction to the Theory of Economic Planning*), Iwanami-Shoten 1963, pp. 163–4.
35. *Ibid.*, p. 65.
36. See Oka (note 34), pp. 165–7. С. Сотрумилин, К вомросу об учете стоимости лродукции, *Волресы экномики*, no. 16, 1956, стр. 4; Стумилим, *Проблемы социализма и коммунизма в ссср*, москва, 1961, стр. 202–3
37. Charles Bettelheim, *L'Economie Soviétique*, 1950 (Japanese translation by Heihachirō Ōsaki, *Soviet Keizai no Kōzō*, 1954, pp. 368–9.
38. *Capital*, Book I, pp. 37, 105.
39. *Ibid.*, p. 94.
40. *Ibid.*, pp. 172–3.
41. *Ibid.*, p. 316.
42. *Ibid.*, p. 520.
43. *Capital*, Book III, p. 207.
44. See note 39.
45. Michio Morishima, *Marx's Economics – A Dual Theory of Value and Growth*, Cambridge Univ. Press, 1973, pp. 12-1-3.
46. George Stigler, 'Ricardo and the 93% Labor Theory of Value', *American Economic Review*, XLVIII, no. 3 1958, pp. 357–67. (Requoted from Murray Wolfson, *A Reappraisal of Marxian Economics*, Columbia Univ. Press, 1966, p. 199.
47. *Capital*, Book I, p. 38.
48. *Ibid.*, p. 46.(Also cited in Ch. I, note 8, present volume.)
49. *Ibid.*, p. 51.
50. *Ibid.*, p. 38.
51. *Ibid.*
52. *Ibid.*, p. 101. Also cited in Ch.I, 10.
53. *Capital*, Book III. p. 347.(Also cited in Ch. I , note 11, present volume.)
54. Book I, p. 46.
55. *Ibid.*, p. 319.
56. Book III, p. 224.
57. See present book, Ch. 1, Sec. I, 2; and Ch. 2, Sec.I, 2.
58. See note 55.
59. See note 49.
60. *Capital*, Book I, p. 94: 'Money as a measure of value, is the phenomenal form that must of necessity be assumed by that measure of value which is immanent in commodities, labour-time.'

61. See note 55.
62. *Capital*, Book I, p. 94.
63. *Ibid.*, p. 98.
64. *Ibid.*, p. 117.
65. *Ibid.*, p. 54.
66. *Ibid.*
67. *Ibid.*, p. 55.
68. *Ibid.*, p. 49.
69. See note 39.
70. See notes 54, 55, 56 and related explanations.
71. *Capital*, Book I, p. 118.
72. Book III, pp. 207–13.
73. Also see John Strachey's words cited in the present volume, Ch.1, 4.
74. See note 51.
75. *Capital*, Book I, p. 39.
76. *Ibid.*, p. 50.
77. See note 40.
78. See note 40.
79. Paul M. Sweezy, *The Theory of Capitalist Development*, Dennis Dobson, London, 1952, p. 109. Meghnad Desai also writes: 'The problem of values and prices – the transformation problem – has been at the heart of the controversy regarding Marx's Theory' (*Marxian Economics*, Basil Blackwell, Oxford, 1979, p. 5)7.
80. David Laibman, 'Values and Prices of Production: The Political Economy of the Transformation Problem', *Science and Society*, Winter, 1973–4, vol. 37, no. 4, p. 405.
81. Michio Morishima, George Catephores, *Value, Exploitation and Growth*, McGraw Hill, UK, 1978, p. 179.
82. Marx usually assumes: 1 hour = 1/2 shilling. See citations, notes 40, 41, 42 and 43. In Book III, P.52: 1 hour = 1 shilling.
83. See citations notes 59 and 60.
84. *Capital*, Book I, p. 78.
85. Ch. 2, Sec.I.2.(4) present volume: The so-called labour-time calculation.
86. Peter Wiles, 'Karl Marx as a Religious Philosopher', *Festschrift for Tadao Horie's 61st Birthday*, 1974, p. 353.
87. H.D.Dickinson, 'A Comment on Meek's "Note on the Transformation Problem"', *The Economic Journal*, December 1956, pp. 740–1.
88. See Marx's transformation tables in *Capital*, Book III, pp. 153–5.
89. Price of Production is 'cost-price plus average profit', $K(= c + v) + P$. *Capital*, Book III, p. 155.
90. Murray Wolfson, 'The Empirical Content of the Labor Theory of Value: the Transformation Problem Once Again', *Keio Economic Studies*, vol.14, no.2, 1978, p. 70.
91. Sweezy (note 79), p. 117.
92. F. Seton, 'The Transformation Problem', *Review of Economic Studies*, 25, June 1957, pp. 150–1.
93. Paul A. Samuelson, 'Understanding the Marxian Notion of Exploitation: A Summary of the So-Called Transformation Problem Between Marxian Values and Competitive Prices', *Journal of Economic Literature*, June 1971, vol.IX, no.2, p. 400 ff.

94. 'In this case every one of the departments happens to use various materials and machine services in the same proportions that society produces them *in toto*' (p. 415).
95. Michio Morishima, *Marx's Economics: A Dual Theory of Value and Growth*, Cambridge Univ. Press, 1973, p. 13 ff.
96. See *ibid.*, p. 72 ff.
97. David Laibman (note 80), pp. 414–31.
98. Sweezy (note 79), pp. 128–9.
99. Seton (note 92), p. 160.
100. Samuelson (note 93), pp. 400, 421.
101. Laibman (note 80), pp. 433–4.
102. Wiles (note 86), p. 336.
103. Ulrich Krause, *Money and Abstract Labour: On the Analytic Foundations of Political Economy* (*Geld und abstrakte Arbeit: Über die analytischen Grundlagen der Politischen Ökonomie*, 1979, translated by Pete Burgess, NLB and Verso Editions, London, 1982, p. 10.
104. *Ibid.*, p. 79.
105. On 'standard reduction' see *ibid.*, ch. 7.
106. *Capital*, Book III, p. 47.
107. Book I, p. 218.
108. Book III, pp. 47–8.
109. Marx's definition of the 'organic composition of capital' is cited in Ch.5, note 59, present volume.
110. Sweezy (note 79), p. 121.
111. *Capital*, Book III, p. 826.
112. *Ibid.*, p. 161.
113. Book I, pp. 612-1-3:

> 'In this chapter we consider the influence of the growth of capital on the lot of the labouring class. The most important factor in this inquiry is the composition of capital and the changes it undergoes in the course of the process of accumulation . . .
> The many individual capitals invested in a particular branch of production have . . . more or less different compositions. The average of their individual compositions gives us the compositions of the total capital in this branch of production. Lastly, the average of these averages, in all branches of production, gives us the composition of the total social capital of a country, and with this alone are we . . . concerned in the following investigation.

114. *Ibid.*, p. 10. For a more detailed citation, see Ch. 4, note 13, present book.
115. Book III, p. 209. For particulars see Ch 1, note 1, present book.
116. Book I, pp. 8–9. For a more detailed citation see Ch. 5, note 3.
117. Book III, p. 245. 'Unconditional development of the productive forces of society.'
118. *Ibid.*, p. 240. 'the narrow basis on which the conditions of consumption rest.'
119. In Marx's terminology the rise of the 'technical composition of capital'.
120. *Capital*, Book III, pp. 207, 13.
121. Book I, p. 319. For a more detailed citation see note 55.

122. For a more detailed explanation of this apparently number and its
     nature, see p. 94, esp. Ch. 4, citation(note 16) and *(Note)* on two kinds
     of productivity, Ch. 4, p. 98.
123. *Capital*, Book III, p. 207. (For a more detailed citation see Ch. 4, note
     19.)
124. *Ibid.*, p. 231

Chapter 3

1. I say this on purpose because I know that some people believe that the
   whole structure of *Capital*, arrangements of books, parts, chapters,
   section . . . are all strictly dialectical and thus they form for those
   believers a sort of 'sanctuary' leaving no room for criticism or alteration.
2. *Capital*, Book I, p. 174.
3. *Ibid.*, p. 751.
4. *Ibid.*, p. 721.
5. *Ibid.*, p. 723.
6. *Ibid.*, p. 751.
7. *Ibid.*, p. 715.
8. *Capital*, Book III, p. 173.
9. Book I, p 742, p. 750.
10. *Ibid.*, p. 165.
11. See note 5.
12. Footnote, Book I, p. 184.
13. Book III, p. 826. See Ch. 2, note 3 for a more detailed citation with the
    interpretation by T.H.
14. Book I, p. 568.
15. Book III, p. 766.
16. *Ibid.*, p. 799.
17. Book I, p. 511.
18. *Ibid.*, p. 235.
19. *Ibid.*, pp. 146–7.
20. *Ibid.*, p. 150.
21. *Ibid.*, p. 158, 159.
22. *Ibid.*, p. 160.
23. *Ibid.*, p. 161.
24. *Ibid.*, p. 165.
25. *Ibid.*
26. See note 8.
27. See note 20.
28. See note 21, 22, 23, 24.
29. See note 25.
30. Book I, pp. 165–6. For reference: We find in Hegel's *Grundlinien der
    Philosophie des Rechts* the expressions '*Hic Rhodus, his saltus*' and '*Hier
    ist die Rose, hier tanze*'. (In Latin, Hic rhodon, hic salta.)
    (G.W.F. Hegel, *Werke in zwanzig Bänden, theorie Werkausgabe*,
    Suhrkamp Verlag, Bd. 7, S.26.). These might be the origin of Marx's
    '*Hic Rhodus, hic salta!*'

('*Hic Rhodus, hic saltus*' is from a fable by Aesop: A man boasting that he was the jumping champion in Rhodes was told by an accuser 'Well, jump then.' He said 'I only jump in Rhodes.' His accuser replied 'Here is Rhodes, jump here.')

31. Book I, p. 167.
32. *Ibid.*, p. 194.
33. *Ibid.*, pp. 194–5.
34. *Ibid.*, p. 164.
35. *Ibid.*, p. 569.
36. *Ibid.*, p. 579.
37. *Ibid.*, p. 585.
38. See note 32.
39. Book I, p. 713.
40. *Ibid.*, p. 714.
41. *Ibid.*, pp. 732–3.
42. See note 6.
43. Book I, p. 751.
44. *Ibid.*, p. 760.
45. See note 35.
46. See note 14.
47. Book I, p. 569.
48. *Ibid.*
49. See note 39.
50. Book I, p. 715.
51. *Ibid.*, p. 742.
52. *Ibid.*, p. 750.
53. See note 8.
54. Book I, p. 713.
55. *Ibid.*, p. 309.
56. *Ibid.*, p. 322, 326
57. *Kapital*, Bd. I, S.341.
58. *Le Capital*, Paris, 1872 (reprinted by Kyokuto-shoten, 1967. p. 141.
59. See P.J.Proudhon, *Qu'est-ce que la propriété?* ed. Rivière, p. 215 and elsewhere.
60. See note 50.
61. Uno: founder of the so-called 'Uno school' interpretation of *Capital*. Ōtsuka: famous for his unique explanation of the genesis of industrial capitalism.
62. Kōzō Uno, Chosakush (Uno, *Collected Works*), Iwanami-Shoten, vol. III, p. 207 ff.
63. Uno, *Collected Works*, vol. IV, p. 309 ff.
64. Uno criticised Smith and Ricardo with regard to their explanations of exchange of equivalents 'in the early and rude state of society', and called them 'very awkward'. But, if we interpret their assumption of primitive society (or rather their theoretical model) as the one where factors of production are limited only to homogeneous human labour, it serves as an ideal framework for fundamental explanation of labour-value theory.
65. See note 8.
66. Uno, *Collected Works*, vol. VI, p. 175.

67. Uno, vol. III, p. 226.
68. Hisao Ôtsuka, *Kindaiōshūkeizaishi-Josetsu* (*An Introduction to the Economic History of Modern Europe*), Kōbundō, Tokyo, 7th edn, 1957, p. 7.
69. Ôtsuka, *Kindaishihonshugi-no-Keifu* (*The Genealogy of Modern Capitalism*), Kōbundō, Tokyo, 5th edn, 1957, p. 10.
70. *Capital*, Book I, p. 750.
71. *Ibid.*, p. 308.
72. See note 40.
73. Common sense tells us that 'constant' capital also yields profit (surplus value), i.e. 'constant' capital does not remain constant. For a more detailed explanation on this point, see Appendix, I, present volume, and T.H. *Marx Keizaigaku Nyumon* (*An Introduction to Marxian Economics*), Nihohyronsha, 1962, ch. 9, esp. Sec .5.

Chapter 4

1. *Capital*, Book I, p. 19, Afterword to the second German edition.
2. *Ibid.*, p. 20.
3. Georg Wilhelm Friedrich Hegel, *The Philosophy of Right*, Great Books of the World, vol. 46, 1952, p. 77.
4. Marx, *Economic and Philosophic Manuscripts of 1844*, Foreign Languages Publishing House, Moscow, p. 29.
5. Marx and Engels, *Manifesto of the Communist Party*, Foreign Languages Publishing House, Moscow, 1957, pp. 69–70.
6. *Capital*, Book I, p. 645.
7. *Ibid.*, p. 763.
8. Rosenkranz, *Hegels Leben*, 1844, SS.85–6. At that time he read *Untersuchung der Grundsätze von der Staatswissenschaft*, 1769–72 (German translation of Sir Denham Steuart's *An Inquiry into the Principles of Political Economy*, 1767). Later when he was in Jena he read Adam Smith's *The Wealth of Nations*.
9. *The Times*, 14 Feb. 1843. (Requoted from *Capital*, Book I, p. 651
10. A passage of Professor E. J. Hobsbawm's lecture at Waseda University, 2 October 1973, entitled 'The formation of the working class in England'. The following sentence was: 'As the mass of the marginal and apparently unemployable population became absorbed, the growth of the class consciousness went hand in hand with a lowering of the social temperature: capitalism was going to last, and the class antagonism which was accepted no longer implied the hope of its imminent overthrow.'.
11. W. W. Rostow, *The World Economy – History and Prospect*, Macmillan, 1978, p. 157. Sources: 1840-50, R .S. Tucker, *Real Wages of Artisans in London*; 1850-80, G. H. Wood, 'Real wages at full work' (in Walter T. Layton and Geoffrey Crowther, *An Introduction to the Study of Prices*, Macmillan, 1938, p. 273).
12. On Marx's phraseology of 'discover', 'discovery', etc. in German, see Ch. 1, note 1, present volume.
13. *Capital*, Book I, p. 10.

14. *Ibid.*, p. 622.
15. *Ibid.*, p. 635.
16. *Ibid.*, p. 623.
17. *Capital*, Book III, p. 253.
18. Book I, p. 319.
19. Book III, p. 207.
20. *Ibid.*, p. 240.
21. *Ibid.*, pp. 214–15.
22. Book I, p. 643.
23. *Ibid.*, p. 644.
24. John Lewis, *Marxism and the Open Mind*, Routledge & Kegan Paul, London, 1957, p. 152.
25. Marx, *Economic and Philosophic Manuscripts of 1844*, Foreign Languages Publishing House, Moscow, p. 102.
26. John Strachey, *The Great Awakening – Or: From Imperialism to Freedom*, Encounter, Pamphlet no. 5, p. 6.

Chapter 5

1. Lenin, *C.W.*, vol. 19, p. 23.
2. *Capital*, Book I, p. 10.(Also see Ch. 1, note 1, present volume.)
3. *Ibid.*, pp. 8–9.
4. Book III, p. 800.
5. Marx and Engels, *Selected Works*, Foreign Languages Publishing House, Moscow, 1958, vol.II, p. 405.
6. '*List der Vernunft*', G.W.F. Hegel, *Vorlesungen über die Philosophie der Geschichte*, Theorie Werkausgabe, Suhrkamp Verlag, Bd.12, S.49. For explanation see Ch. 6, note 45, present volume.
7. Gunnar Myrdal, *Beyond the Welfare State*, Gerald Duckworth, London, 1961, p. 3.
8. Lenin, *C.W.*, vol. 38, p. 319.
9. *Ibid.*,vol. 1, p. 142.
10. Edward Hallett Carr, *What is History?*, Macmillan, London, 1962, p. 52.
11. Marx and Engels, *Selected Works*, vol. II, pp. 89–90.
17. Marx, Preface to *A Contribution to the Critique of Political Economy*, Progress Publishers, Moscow, 1970, pp. 20-1.
18. I.V. Stalin, *Economic Problems of Socialism in USSR*, Bolshevik, no. 18, 1952, p. 4. (Translation from Russian text by T.H.)
19. Lenin, *C.W.*, vol. I, pp. 140-1.
20. Marx and Engels, *The German Ideology*, The Progress Publishers, Moscow, 1964, p. 81.
21. *Capital*, Book I, p. 180.
22. Engels, *Dialectics of Nature*, Foreign Languages Publishing House, Moscow, 1954, p. 83.
23. *Ibid.*
24. As to a strict causal explanation of an event, see an illustration by Karl Popper of a thread broken in *The Logic of Scientific Discovery*, Hutchinson, London, 1959, p. 59 ff.

25. *Basic Knowledge of Political Economy (Zhengzhi-jinjixue jichuzhishi)*, published during the Great Cultural Revolution in 1974 from Shanghai Renmin Chubanshe, is composed of two volumes, *Socialism* and *Capitalism*. The USSR is classified into the latter and is characterised as 'Revisionist Imperialism', 'Socialist Imperialism', built on the economic basis of 'State monopoly capitalism'.

26. Marx, *The Poverty of Philosophy*, Foreign Languages Publishing House, Moscow, p. 122.

27. Lenin, *C.W.*, vol. 1, p. 142. This is the passage just preceding the sentence quoted in note 9.

28. *Capital*, Book I, p. 19. (Also see citation, notes 14 and 15).

29. *Ibid.*, p. 763.

30. Engels, *Anti-Dühring (Herr Eugen Dühring's Revolution in Science)*, Foreign Languages Publishing House, Moscow, 1954, pp. 179–80.

31. *Ibid.*, pp. 185–6.

32. Marx, *Economic and Philosophic Manuscripts of 1844*, p. 114.

33. Marx and Engels, *The German Ideology*, p. 49.

34. Joan Robinson, *Marx and Keynes* (originally in Italian in *Critica Economica*, November, 1948, English edition in Japan p. 6)1. For more detailed explanation related to this, see next Sec.III, 3, 'Negation of the negation – The rise of the capital coefficient', and Ch. 8, Sec. I, 2, 'The rapid economic growth of postwar capitalism and Marx, Keynes, Harrod'.

35. *Capital*, Book I, p. 35.

36. *Ibid.*, p. 36.

37. *Ibid.*, pp. 72–3.

38. See *ibid.*, Ch.1, Sec.4 'The Fetishism of Commodities and the Secret thereof'.

39. *Ibid.*, p. 86, 'contrast (*Gegensatz* = opposition) . . . between use-value and value'. Also see Ch. 4, note 3, quotation and T.H.'s note.

40. In Hegelian and Marxian terminology contradiction and opposition are used interchangeably; for an exact explanation on this point see Ch. 6, Sec. II in the present volume. As for examples in *Capital*, see Ch. 6, Sec. II, 4.

41. See Lenin's remark, Ch. 6, note 40.

42. Д. Розеньерт, коммрнтии к первому тому *Капитала*, Карла Маркса, Государственное издателиство полити-уеской литературы, москва, 1931. Translation from Japanese version, 1933, p. 98.

43. *Ibid.*, pp. 102–3. On yes–yes vs. yes–no, also see Engels' remark cited in Ch. 6, note 6, present volume.

44. *Capital*, Book I, p. 36. 'The utility of a thing makes it a use-value. But this utility is not a thing of air. Being limited by the physical properties of the commodity, it has no existence apart from that commodity.'

45. *Ibid.*, p. 46, 'All labour...in its character of identical abstract human labour...creates and forms the value of commodities.'

46. Of T.H.'s criticism on the 'dialectical contradiction' of use-value and value, also see Ch. 6, Sec. II, 4.

47. *Capital*, Book I, p. 37.

48. Eugen von Böhm-Bawerk, *Karl Marx and the Close of His System*, Augustus M. Kelley, New York, 1966, p. 69.
49. Murray Wolfson, *A Reappraisal of Marxian Economics*, Columbia Univ. Press, New York, 1966, pp. 42–3.
50. *Capital*, Book I, p. 38. 'the value-creating substance, the labour'. Also see Ch. 2, notes 47 and 50, in the present book.
51. *Capital*, Book I, p. 583.
52. *Ibid.*, pp. 165–6. For a more detailed citation and T.H.'s explanation see Ch. 3, note 30.
53. *Capital*, Book I, pp. 194–5. For a more detailed citation see Ch. 3, note 33.
54. *Capital*, Book III, p. 173. For a more detailed citation see Ch. 3,note 8.
55. Edward Hallet Carr, *Karl Marx – A Study in Fanaticism*, 1934, p. 26.
56. *Capital*, Book III, p. 20. For a more detailed citation see Ch. 4, note 19.
57. *Ibid.*, p. 240. For a more detailed citation see Ch. 4, note 20.
58. Book I, p. 319: For a more detailed citation see Ch. 2, note 121, and Ch. 4, note 18.
59. Book I, p. 612.
60. Paul M. Sweezy, *The Theory of Capitalist Development*, Dennis Dobson, London, 1952, p. 102: 'If both the organic composition of capital and the rate of surplus value are assumed variable, as we think they should be, then the direction in which the rate of profit will fall if the percentage increase in the rate of surplus value is less than the percentage decrease in the proportion of variable to total capital.'
61. According to Steindl's survey, the ratio of business capital to net national product had been between 2.5% and 3.2% in the period from 1869–78 (average) to 1929–38. J. Steindl, *Maturity and Stagnation in American Capitalism*, Oxford, Basil Blackwell, 1952, p. 170.
62. Marx and Engels, *The German Ideology*, p. 38.
63. *Capital*, Book I, p. 20.
64. Engels, *Anti-Dühring*, p. 185.
65. Myrdal, *Beyond the Welfare State*, p. 165.
66. Quoted by Carr in *What is History?*, p. 43.

Chapter 6

1. Zeno's arguments are explained in detail in the *Physics* of Aristotle.
2. *The Logic of Hegel*, translated from *The Encyclopaedia of the Philosophical Sciences* by William Wallace, 2nd ed, Oxford, 1892, pp. 213-1-4, Sec. 115. On Hegel's reference to the absurdity of the Law of Identity also see Hegel's *Science of Logic* translated by Johnston and Struthers, George Allen & Unwin, London, vol. I, Preface to the 2nd edn, p. 47. 'The 1st part: the Science of Logic', of *The Encyclopaedia of the Philosophical Sciences* (*'Erster Teil: Die Wissenschaft der Logik' der Enzyklopädie der philosophischen Wissenschaften*, 1817. is commonly called 'Small Logic' (*Die Kleine Logik*) and Science of Logic (Wissenschaft der Logik, 1812. is called 'Large logic' (*Die grosse Logik*).
3. *Logic of Hegel*, p. 223, complementary note (2) to sec. 119.

4. *Science of Logic*, vol. II, p. 67.
5. *Capital*, Book I, Afterword to the 2nd edn, p. 20.
6. Engels, *Anti-Dühring*, pp. 34–5.
7. *Ibid.*, p. 167.
8. *Ibid.*, Preface to the three editions, p. 14.
9. Mitsushige Sawada, *Shutaisei no Gainen to Tetsugaku-riron* (*The Concept of Subjectivity and Philosophical Theory*), *Gendai jin no Shisoo* (*The Thoughts of Contemporaries*), vol. XX, p. 365.
10. *Capital*, Book I, p. 104.
11. With respect to the elliptical motion of celestial bodies, Hegel gives a more sophisticated dialectical interpretation in his 'Large Logic' (*Science of Logic*) vol. I, p. 399.
12. *Science of Logic*, vol. II, p. 68. In this English version the word for '*Gegensatz*' is 'contradiction'. This is not correct. So I put 'Opposition' in its place. See Hegel, *Wissenschaft der Logik II, Werke* 6, Theorie Werkausgabe, Suhrkamp Verlag, 1969, S. 77.
13. *The Logic of Hegel*, p. 222, Complementary note 1. to Sec. 119.
14. *Science of Logic*, vol. II, p. 52.
15. *Ibid.*, p. 68.
16. In the terminology of ordinary logic, above and below are contrary concepts and father and son are relative concepts. They do not as such have any implication of real antagonism or struggle.
17. *Science of Logic*, vol. II, p. 52.
18. Kazuto Matsumura, *Hegel no Ronrigaku* (*Logic of Hegel*), Iwanami Shoten, 1959, p. 282.
19. Hans Reichenbach, *The Rise of Scientific Philosophy*, University of California Press. 1954, pp. 8–9.
20. 'Middle' would be better for the German word '*Mitte*' in this case than 'mean'. the latter has too many meanings and so might obscure the 'dialectics' of 'Extreme' (extreme) at the same time being '*Mitte*'. And the word '*Mitte*' leads one to the concept '*Vermittlung*' (mediation), which is the function Hegel expects of the Diet between the monarch and the people. Also see citations from Marx on Hegel in notes 50, 51 and the related explanation by T.H.
21. *Hegel's Philosophy of Right*, translated by S. S. Dyde, London, George Bell and Sons, 1896, p. 312. In this English version '*Stände*' is translated as 'classes'. I put the word 'Diet' in its place as '*die Stände*' was the Diet where the classes were represented. See Hegel, *Grundlinien der Philosophie des Rechts*, Werke 7, S. 472.
22. See note 3.
23. *Science of Logic*, vol. II, p. 67.
24. Lenin, C.W, vol. 38, *Philosophical Notebooks*, Foreign Language Publishing House, Moscow, 1961, p. 141.
25. 'Rationalistic' (not 'rational') is the adjective for 'rationalism', a philosophical method which regards reason as a source of synthetic knowledge. See Reichenbach, *Rise of Scientific Philosophy*, pp. 31–2.
26. My English translation from a Japanese version of Mao Tse-Tung's *Essay on Contradiction* (*Selected Works of Mao Tse-Tung*, vol. III, p. 17.

27. *Hegel's Phenomenology of Mind*, translated by J. B. Baillie, vol. I, London, Swan Sonnenschein, 1910, p. 70.
28. *Capital*, Book I, p. 20. Afterword to the 2nd German ed.
29. *Ibid.*, p. 35.
30. *Ibid.*, p. 61.
31. *Ibid.*, p. 48. In this English version the wodk for '*entgegegesetzte*' is 'antagonistic', but I put 'opposite' in its place. See *Das Kapital*, Bd. I, S. 53.
32. *Ibid.*, pp. 103–4. In this English version the word for '*Widersprüche*' is 'inconsistencies', I put 'contradictions' in its place. See *Das Kapital*, Bd. I, S. 109.
33. *Ibid.*, pp. 86–7. In this English version the word for '*schlummernde*' is 'latent', that for '*Gegensatz*' is 'contrast' and for '*Bedürfnis*' is 'necessity'. I put 'sleeping', 'opposition' and 'want' respectively in their places.
34. *Capital*, Book I, pp. 76–7.
35. *Ibid.*, p. 94: 'Throughout this work, I assume, for the sake of simplicity, gold as the money-commodity.'
36. See Engels, *Dialectics of Nature*, pp. 27 and 83.
37. See Lenin, 'On the Question of Dialectics', *C.W.*, vol. 38, p. 359 ff.
38. *Ibid.*, p. 361.
39. *Science of Logic*, vol. II, p. 266 ff.
40. Lenin, *ibid.*, pp. 360–1.
41. *Capital*, Book I, pp. 113–14. *Kapital*, Bd. I, S. 118.
42. *Ibid.*, p. 138, *ebd.*, S. 144.
43. Marx, *Theory of Surplus-Value*. vol. II, Progress Publishers, Moscow, 1968, p. 513. *Theorien über den Mehrwert*, Teil 2, Dietz Verlag, Berlin, 1959, S. 509.
44. *Science of Logic*, vol. I, p. 60. *Wissenschaft der Logik*, I, Werke 5, S. 44. This passage reminds us of the beginning sentences of 'The gospel according to John', New Testament: 'In the beginning was the Word, and the Word was with God, and the Word was God ... all things were made through him.' 'Word' is in Greek '*logos*' and Hegel himself quoted the first sentence of the gospel in Greek in his *Philosophy of History* (Hegel, *Vorlesungen der Philosophie der Geschichte*, Werke 12, 1970, S.401. Thus we know the definite affinity between Christianity and Hegel's logic.
45. Hegel, Werke 12, S. 49. '*Das is die List der Vernunft zu nennen, dass sie die Leidenschaften für sich wirken lässt, durch was sie sich in Existenz setzt, einbüsst und Schaden leidet.*' Translated into ordinary language: 'Reason' (philosophical counterpart of God) lets 'Passions' (individuals with passion and power like Caesar, Napoleon, etc.) work for the realisation of his grand design, in the course of which he is damaged and hurt. This is to be called the *Cunning of Reason*.
46. *Science of Logic*, vol. II, *The Absolute Idea*, p. 466 ff.
47. *Hegel's Philosophy of Right*, pp. 348–9, Hegel, *Grundlinien der Philosophie des Rechts*, Werke 7, S.511.
48. *Capital*, Book I, Preface to the 2nd German edn, p. 20.

49. *Ibid.*
50. Marx, *Kritik des Hegelschen Staatsrechts, Karl Marx-Friedrich Engels Werke*, Bd. 1, Dietz Verlag, Berlin, 1957, S. 292. Also see my citation from Hegel's Philosophy of Right on 'the Diet' (note 21), and Shakespeare, *A Midsummer-Night's Dream*, 5. 1. 217 ff (Cambridge Univ. Press edn, 1949, p. 67).
51. Marx, *ibid.*, S. 290.
52. *Capital*, Book I, p. 763.
53. *Ibid.*, pp. 8–., For a more detailed citation see Ch. 3, note 3, present volume. The passage directly following this is Ch. 5, note 29.
54. See note 20.
55. *Capital*, Book I, p. 20.
56. Lenin, *C.W.*, vol. 38, p. 360.
57. Karl Popper, *The Poverty of Historicism*, London, Routledge & Kegan Paul, 2nd edn, 1960. p. 64ff.
58. 'Economics is the science which studies human behaviour as a relationship between ends and scarce means which have alternative uses' (Lionel Robbins, *An Essay on the Nature and Significance of Economic Science*, London, Macmillan, 2nd edn, 1952, p. 16).
59. The notion very often used by Gunnar Myrdal in his methodological arguments. See, for instance, Myrdal, *An International Economy – Problems and Prospects*, 2nd printing in Tokyo, 1964, p. x, p. 336.
60. *Ibid.*, p. 336.
61. 'The great man of the age is the one who can put into words the will of his age, tell his age what its will is, and accomplish it. What he does is the heart and essence of his age; he actualises his age' (Hegel, *Philosophy of Right*, English transl, 1942, p. 295). (Quoted by E.H. Carr, *What is History?*, Macmillan, 1962, p. 48.)
62. Werner Sombart, *The Quintessence of Capitalism*, English translation, 1915, p. 354. (Requoted from Carr, *What is History?*, p. 54.)

Chapter 7

1. Joan Robinson, *An Essay on Marxian Economics*, Macmillan, London, 2nd edn, 1966, p. ix.
2. *Capital*, Book III, p. 207. For a more detailed citation see Ch. 4, note 19, present book.
3. *Ibid.*,
4. *Capital*, Book I, p. 319. For a more detailed citation see Ch. 2, note 55.
5. *Ibid.*, p. 315.
6. *Ibid.*, p. 315.
7. *Ibid.*, p. 316.
8. *Ibid.*, pp. 316, 318.
9. *Ibid.*, p. 316–7.
10. *Ibid.*, p. 318.
11. *Ibid.*, pp. 318–9.
12. *Ibid.*, p. 319.
13. *Ibid.*, p. 321.

14. See T. Horie, *Marx-Keizaigaku Nyumon* (An Introduction to Marxian Economics), Nihonhyoronsha, 1962, pp. 118–24. T. Horie *'Shihonron' to Shihonshugino Unmei* (*Capital and the Fate of Capitalism*), Gakubunsha, 1981, pp. 85–93.
15. *Capital*, Book I, pp. 612–13.
16. *Ibid.*, p. 623.
17. *Ibid.*, p. 319.
18. *Capital*, Book III, p. 207.
19. *Capital*, Book II, p. 510.
20. *Ibid.*, pp. 505, 513.
21. *Ibid.*, p. 513.
22. *Ibid.*, pp. 513–9.
23. Lenin, *C.W.*, vol. 1, p. 85. (Note: 'both develop on parallel lines' but except in the transition process from Y_1 to Y_2 in which Department 1 grows faster than Department 2 owing to Marx's mistaken selection of concrete figures.)
24. *Ibid.*
25. *Ibid.*, pp. 86–7.
26. *Capital*, Book III, p. 239.
27. *Ibid.*, p. 240.
28. Lenin, Reply to Mr. Nezhedanov, 1899, *C.W.* vol. 4, pp. 162–3.
29. 'Капитал' К. Маркса и проблемы Современного Капитализма лод редакцией Н. А. Цаголова и В. А. Кирова, издательство Московского университета, 1968, стр. 3.
30. Lenin, *C.W.*, vol. 22, p. 200: On the inevitable tendency to monopoly. *Ibid*, p. 216: On the capitalist banking system having the 'form' of universal bookkeeping and distribution of means of production on a social scale.
31. *Capital*, Book III, p. 245.
32. *Capital*, Book I, p. 581, note 1.
33. Lenin, *C.W.* vol. 22, p. 241.
34. *Ibid.*, p. 244.
35. *Capital*, Book III, p. 239.
36. *Ibid.*, p. 233.
37. *Ibid.*, pp. 250-1.
38. *Ibid.*, p. 232.
39. Lenin, *C.W.*, vol. 22, p. 260.
40. *Capital*, Book II, p. 470.
41. Lenin, *The Development of Capitalism in Russia*, *C.W.*, vol. 3, pp. 46–7.
42. Lenin, Reply to Mr. Nezdanov, *C.W.*, vol. 4, p. 162.
43. *Ibid.*, p. 161. The source of Lenin's idea here is supposed to be the following statement by Marx: 'The fact that the production of the commodities is the general form of capitalist production . . . engenders certain conditions of normal exchange peculiar to this mode of production and therefore of the normal course of reproduction . . . conditions which change into so many conditions of abnormal movement, into so many crises, since a balance is itself an accident owing to the spontaneous nature of this production.' (*Capital*, Book II, p. 495).

44. Lenin, *C.W.*, vol. 3, p. 590.
45. *Ibid.*, p. 590.
46. *Ibid.*, p. 66.
47. Lenin, *C.W.*, vol. 22, p. 257.
48. *Partners in Development – Report of the Commission on International Development*, Praeger Publishers, New York, 1969 (the so-called 'Pearson Report'), p. 8.

Chapter 8

1. The alleged revision by the Japanese Education Ministry of high school history text books – a typical example: crossing out of the work 'aggression' and replacing it with the word 'advance' in connection with the Japanese war of invasion in China.
2. Lenin, *C.W.*, vol. 22, p. 300.
3. 1820–1913: Jürgen Kuczynski, *Studien zur Geschichte der Weltwirtschaft*, S.54, 1913 = 100, manufacturing and mining. 1913–51: W. S. Woytynski, *World Economy* (Japanese edition), p. 916, 191 100, manufacturing and mining, world excluding USSR. 1952–89: UN statistics, 1963, 1970, etc. = 100, all converted into 1913 = 100, manufacturing, mining, electricity, gas and water; 1952–82, world excluding USSR, China, East-European countries, North Korea, North or Vietnam, Outer Mongolia; 1983–89, including USSR and East European countries except Albania. (But the growth-rates of these countries are not much different from those of the capitalist countries, so the tabulated figures would be useful as showing rough trend.)

1820	2	1879	25	1912	95	1957	311
		1880	27	*1913*	*100*	1958	308
1840	5	1881	28			1959	332
		1882	30	1921	84	1960	351
1850	9	1883	32	1922	101	1961	363
1851	9	1884	31	1923	109	1962	391
1852	10	1885	30	1924	113	1963	410
1853	10	1886	32	1925	122	1964	437
1854	10	1887	35	1926	125	1965	473
1855	10	1888	36	1927	133	1966	510
1856	11	1889	39	1928	139	1967	522
1857	11	1890	41	1929	148	1968	563
1858	12	1891	42	1930	131	1969	605
1859	13	1892	42	1931	121	1970	625
1860	13	1893	41	1932	91	1971	645
1861	13	1894	42	1933	103	1972	691
1862	12	1895	46	1934	112	1973	754
1863	12	1896	47	1935	125	1974	760
1864	13	1897	50	1936	140	1975	716

1865	15	1898	54	1937	149	1976	778
1866	16	1899	58	1938	136	1977	816
1867	16	1900	59			1978	852
1868	18	1901	61	1946	157	1979	895
1869	18	1902	66	1947	175	1980	903
1870	20	1903	67	1948	190	1981	895
1871	23	1904	67	1949	191	1982	895
1872	23	1905	74	1950	216	1983	898
1873	23	1906	78	1951	240	1984	953
1874	23	1907	80	1952	249	1985	982
1875	23	1908	74	1953	265	1986	1012
1876	23	1909	81	1954	265	1987	1054
1877	24	1910	86	1955	292		
1878	24	1911	88	1956	302		

4. J. M. Keynes, *The General Theory of Employment, Interest and Money*, Macmillan, London, 1936, p. 220.
5. J. Stalin, *Economic Problems of Socialism in the USSR*, Foreign Languages Publishing House, Moscow, 1952: 'The disintegration of the single, all-embracing world market must be regarded as the most important economic sequel of the Second World War and of its economic consequences. It has had the effect of further deepening the general crisis of world capitalism.' (p. 34).

   'It is evident that, after the world market has split, and the sphere of exploitation of the world's resources by the major capitalist countries (U.S.A, Britain, France) has begun to contract, the cyclical character of the development of capitalism – expansion and contraction – must continue to operate. However, expansion of production in these countries will proceed on a narrower basis, since the volume of production in these countries will diminish' (p. 63).
6. *Capital*, Book III, p. 209, For detailed citations see Ch. 1,note 1.
7. In Chapter 25, 'The general law of accumulation', *Capital*, Book I, technical composition of capital is described as the ratio of the quantity of the means of production employed to the mass of labour time expended for their employment and value (organic) composition; its equivalent in value-terms as the ratio of constant capital, $\frac{c}{v}$. Here we find an error by Marx. The labour time expended is unmistakably necessary labour plus surplus labour, $v + s$, so that the value-terms equivalent of technical composition must be $\frac{c}{v+s}$. For more detailed explanation, see citation (note 59) of Ch. 5 and the following interpretation by T.H. in the present book.
8. *Capital*, Book III, p. 225. Explanation by Marx follows: 'If the increase in the productiveness of labour acts uniformly and simultaneously on all the elements of the commodity . . . so that . . . the mutual relation of the different elements [*c, v, s* – T.H.] of the price of the commodity remains the same.' This amounts to: if $\frac{c}{v+s}$ remains the same.
9. See Ch. 5, note 61, present volume.

10. $GC = s$: R. F. Harrod, *Towards a Dynamic Economics*, Macmillan, 1954, p. 77.

11. $\frac{c}{v}$ – or rather $\frac{c}{v+s}$ mistaken as $\frac{s}{v}$ by Marx. When $\frac{s}{v}$ is given, $\frac{c}{v}$ changes in exactly the same ratio with $\frac{c}{v+s}$. (For more detailed explanation on this point, see Table 5.1 and the following exposition.)

12. *Capital*, Book III, p. 207. For a more detailed citation see Ch. 4, note 19, in the present volume.

13. Book I, p. 631:'The labouring population...produces, along with the accumulation of capital produced by it, the means by which itself is made relatively superfluous, is turned into a surplus-population; and it does this to an increasing extent.' Also see citation Ch. 4, note 23, present volume.

14. Lenin, *C.W.*, vol. 22, p. 241. The following passage is; 'for both uneven development and a semi-starvation level of existence of the masses are fundamental and inevitable conditions and constitute premises of this mode of production. As long as capitalism remains what it is, surplus capital will be utilised not for the purpose of raising the standard of living of the masses in a given country, for this would mean a decline in profits for the capitalists.'

15. Percentages are calculated by T.H. from the real income figures presented by Fritz Sternberg in his *Capitalism and Socialism on Trial*, The John Day Company, New York, 1950, p. 26.

16. *Ibid.*, p. 198.

17. *Capital*, Book I, p. 180. for a more detailed citation see Ch. 5, note 21.

18. Book III, p. 227.

19. *Ibid.*, p. 233.

20. *Ibid.*, p. 254.

21. Friedrich Engels, *Vorwort zur deutschen Auflage de 'Lage der arbeitenden Klasse'*, Marx-Engels Werke, Bd. 22, S.326.

22. *Marx-Engels, Selected Works*, vol. I, Foreign Languages Publishing House, Moscow, 1958, p. 45.

23. Lenin, *Impoverishment in capitalist society, C.W.*, vol. 18, p. 435.

24. Lenin, *Review of Karl Kautsky's Book, C.W.*, vol. 4, p. 201.

25. B. R. Mitchell, *International Historical Statistics, 1750–1975*, Macmillan Press, Japanese edition, pp. 31, 301, 302.

26. Its abridged version in English is *Hegelian Fallacy in Marxian Economics, Waseda Economic Papers*, no. 12. The German translation of it is carried in the Festschrift for my seventieth birthday.

27. А.Х. СССР, Институт экономики; полтическая экономия – Учеьник; 4. изд. Москва, 1962, стр. 199. *Political Economy*, a Textbook issued by the Economic Institute of the Academy of the Sciences of the USSR. Also English translation of 2nd edn, London, 1957, p. 256.

28. *Ibid.*, стр. 635, p. 721.

29. Курс политческой экономии, том II, социализм, подредакцией Н.А. Цаголова; 3. изд Москва, 1974, стр. 209.

30. *Ibid.*, p. 212.

31. Figures are taken from, or calculated on the basis of official USSR publications. In the *Soviet Dictionary and Handbook of Social-Economic Statistics*, 1944, A and B are defined as follows:

Means of Production and objects of consumption

The whole global social product is divided into means of production and objects of consumption. This analysis of the product of each branch of the national economy is determined by the actual use of the product and in general depends on its material utility (*Material 'noi-potrebitel' – skoi prirody*). To the means of production belong such commodities and articles as enter into the sphere of productive consumption. Thus semi-fabricates, for example, yarn and sugar, destined to be worked up into other objects of consumption, should be counted among the means of production. To the objects of consumption belong commodities and products that serve the ends of the unproductive consumption of the population and of unproductive establishments.

The means of production are commonly designated with the letter A, the objects of consumption with the letter B.

The separation of gross industrial production into 'A' and 'B' is achieved in the practice of economic statistics by various means. Since the establishment of the actual utilisation of production is often difficult in the absence of the necessary data, the separation of production into 'A' and 'B' is done approximately on the basis of the predominant category into which one or another product falls. For example, all refined sugar belongs to 'B' irrespective of the fact that a part of it went into the production of confectionery. Or kerosene, for example, belongs entirely to 'A' even though part of it was used by the population for lighting and cooking. (Requoted from P. J. D. Wiles, *The Political Economy of Communism*, Basil Blackwell, Oxford, 1964, p. 272.)

But since the late 1950s separation has been done according to the end-use of products in principle, and incorporation of one product as a whole into one category has become exceptional. For example, coal, which had been classified as 'A', is now divided into 'A' and 'B' according to its end-use. (From Toshio Wada, *Soviet Keikakukeizai no Kozo to Kino, The Structure and Function of the Soviet Planned Economy*, 1976, p. 116.

The statistically calculated ratio between group 'A' and group 'B' reflects the division of products into the means of production and the objects of consumption only in one branch of national economy – industry. Partition of industry into light and heavy characterises the relation between the two departments more inaccurately. Some part of heavy industry produces objects of consumption and some part of light industry produces means of production. (*Курс политической экономии*, том II, социализм, Москва, 1974, стр.210).

32. *Capital*, Book II, p. 395.
33. Xue Muqiao, *Zhongguo-shehuizhuyi-jingji-wenti-yanjiu*, Shanghai, 1982, p. 160. 1st edn, 1979.
34. *Ibid.*, p. 162.
35. From *Jingji-yanjiu*, 1980, no. 12, article by Liu-Xun.
36. *Toyo-keizai-nenkan* (*Yearbook of economic statistics*), Tokyo-keizai-sha, 1982, p. 260. Figures are converted from 1975 = 100 into 1970 = 100.

37. *Economic Report of the President*, 1985, p. 281. Equipment includes defence and space equipment.
38. In P. J. D. Wiles, *The Political Economy of Communism*, Basil Blackwell, Oxford, 1964.)
39. From Japanese translation of 'The economic development of major capitalist countries since the war', *Sekai-keizai-hyoron* (World economic review), July 1980, p. 41. (Chinese text, *Fudan-xuebao*, 1978, 1st and 2nd period.)
40. *Ibid.*, August 1980, p. 76.
41. Harry Magdoff and Paul M. Sweezy, *The End of Prosperity: The American Economy in the 1970s*, Monthly Review Press, 1977, p. 56.
42. *Capital*, Book III, p. 253. Also see citation (note 20).
43. Datum (note 33), pp. 3–4.
44. *Zen-ei (Vanguard)*, no. 474, Jan. 1982, pp. 36–7. Fuwa is now the chairman of the presidium (June 1989).
45. Japanese translation, p. 9. The original book in English: Routledge & Kegan Paul, London, 1975.
46. Based on the résumé by Brus of his lecture.
47. Also see notes 18. and 19.
48. See datum of note 45. for details.
49. *Capital*, Book I, p. 78.
50. Marx, *A Contribution to the Critique of Political Economy*, p. 21. For a more detailed citation see Ch. 5, note 17, present volume.
51. Dr V. K. Zaitsev's report paper, *Present Stage of Scientific and Technical Progress and Greater Instability of Capitalist Economy (on the Example of Japan)*, pp. 3–4.
52. *Ibid.*, p. 7.
53. Народное жозяйство, СССР, 1984г, стр. 407.
54. В. Ковыженко, *Стоимосты усиуг или фикция?* «Мировая экопомика и международные отношения» no. 8 – 1967.
55. See Ch.1, note 34, present volume.
56. I have known Professor Pevsner since 1957. When I visited him in Moscow in 1966 and argued that labour in service industries including commerce should be counted as value creating, he replied, already at that time, that he was in agreement with me.
57. An official record of the 15th Soviet-Japanese Symposium of economists is issued by the Institute of World Economy and International Relations, USSR Academy of Sciences: Материалы XV Советско-Японского Симпозиума Ученыж-экономистов, Сокращенная Стенограмма, Москва, 4/X-6/X 1983г.
58. See Ch.1, note 23, present volume.
59. *Capital*, Book II, p. 52. 'There are certain independent branches of industry in which the product of the productive process is not a new material product . . . Among these only the communications industry, whether engaged in transportation proper, of goods and passengers, or in the mere transmission of communications, letters, telegrams, etc, is economically important . . . What the transportation industry sells is change of location. The useful effect is inseparably connected with the process of transportation, i.e. the productive process of the transport

industry. Men and goods travel together with the means of transportation, and this travelling . . . constitutes the process of production . . . The exchange-value of this useful effect is determined . . . by the value of the elements of production (labour-power and means of production) consumed in it plus the surplus value created by the surplus labour of the labourers employed in transportation.'

60. Lenin, *Our Programme, C.W.*, vol. IV, pp. 211–12.
61. Lenin, *Three Origins and Three Component Parts of Marxism, C.W.*, vol. XIX, p. 23. Also see Ch. 5, note 1, present volume.
62. J.S. Mill, *On Liberty*, Everyman's Library, no. 482, 1968, p. 90.

Appendix

1. *Capital*, Book III, p. 208. '*Gesamtkapital*', *Kapital*, Bd. 3, S. 238.
2. *Ibid.*, p. 209. '*angewandt*', *Ebenda*, S.240. In the English edition the word for '*angewandt*' is 'invested'. But I changed it to 'employed', because 'invest' is also the word for '*auslegen*' (*ibid.*, p. 211, *Ebenda*, S.243) and 'anlegen' (Book II, p. 169. Bd. 2, S.163) which are used as synonyms of '*vorschiessen*' (advance).
3. Book III, p. 211. '*vorgeschossen*', Bd. 3, S.243.
4. Book I, p. 213. '*vorgeschossen*' . . . '*verzehrt*', S.221.
5. For instance, see Book II, Ch.9, 'The aggregate turnover of advanced capital. Cycles of turnover', esp. p. 184. Bd.2, Kap.9, '*Der Gesamtumschlag des vorgeschossnen Kapitals. Umschlagszyklen*', bes. S.179.
6. Book III, p. 222, original translation 'invested'. Bd. 3, S.255, '*angewandt*'. This is the part supplemented by F. Engels.
7. *Ibid.*, p. 142, *Ebenda*, S.168.
8. *Ibid.*, p. 70. *Ebenda*, S.9.0

Index

absolute impoverishment, 64, 65, 172, 180; discussion on, 83–4
agricultural collectivisation, horrors of, xviii
Anti-Dühring, Engels
    direct labour-time calculation begins with common possession of means of
        production, 33
    Dühring criticises Marx's demonstration of the advent of communism relying
        on the law of the negation of negation, 111
    Engels defends Marx's application of the law of the negation of negation,
        112
    proving the advent of communism, 121
    metaphysician excludes positive and negative absolutely from one another,
        127
    motion itself is a contradiction, 127; *see also* Engels

Baran, Paul A., potential economic surplus, 18
Beijing Weekly, 10 Dec. 1985, in *Capital* we cannot find ready-made answers,
    187
Berlin, Isaiah, 139
Bernstein, Eduard, 139
Böhm-Bawerk, Eugen von, most vulnerable point in Marxian system, 116, 139
Bortkiewicz–Sweezy solution of transformation problem, 62
Boulding, Kenneth, 139
Boyle, Robert, law on the volume of gases, 107, 109
Brezhnev, Leonid I., priority growth of department I, 189–91
Brus, Wlodzimierz, materialist concept as a working hypothesis, 197–8, 202
Buckle, Henry Thomas, principle of universal regularity, 107
Burke, Edmund, laws of commerce, 107

capital, advanced, consumed, turned-over, employed, 206
Capital, Marx
    backbone of the economics of, 91
    closed system, 167
    controversies on, xxi
    cornerstone of the ideological edifice of Marxism, 106
    dialectical method applied in, 107, 108
    full of primitive errors, 23
    fundamental character of, xx
    fundamental defects of, xviii, xx
    infallibility of, xviii
    main theme of, 91
    Newtonian rigidity of, 1
    systematic defects in, 23
    ultimate aim of, 92

236 *Index*

Capital elevated the materialist concept of history to the level of proven truth, 123

Capital is a model application of dialectical logic, 23, 106

capitalism's need for foreign market is not to be explained from the impossibility of realisation on the home market, 170

Capital made the materialist concept of history a proven proposition, 106

even with fully proportional realisation, we cannot imagine capitalism without contradiction between production and consumption, 165

exchange of commodities reveals all the contradictions of modern society, 136

Marxist doctrine is omnipotent, 105, 202

Marx's theory not completed and inviolable, 202

Marx was first to put sociology on a scientific basis, 109

reduction of production relations to the level of productive forces is the basis for understanding development of society, 19

second conception (dialectics) gives key to transformation to the opposite, 140

Lewis, John, Marxism is the highest development of humanism, 102

Locke, John, products are effects of labour, 25

logic of contradiction, 126, 127, 129

logos, 139; *see also* Ch. 6, end-note 44

Malthus, Thomas R., law of population, 107

Manifesto of the Communist Party, Marx and Engels; modern labourer sinks deeper below the condition of existence, 183; pauperism develops more rapidly than wealth . . . bourgeoisie produces its grave diggers, 89, 90; *see also Communist Manifesto*

Maoism, 181, 187

Mao Zedong, xviii; without contradiction the world does not exist, 132

marginal utility, 135

Marx, Karl, *see Capital, Capital* Book I, *Capital* Book II, *Capital* Book III, *Communist Manifesto, Contribution to the Critique of Political Economy, Critique of the Gotha Programme, Critique of the Hegelian State-Philosophy, Economic and Philosophical Manuscripts of 1844, German Ideology, Manifesto of the Communist Party*, Marx's *letter to Kugelmann, Poverty of Philosophy, Theory of Surplus Value, Wage Labour and Capital*

Marx, Karl, on, Arnold Toynbee evaluates, 103; crisis is establishment of unity, 137; falling rate of economic growth, 175; feudal lord with hand-mill, industrial capitalist with steam-mill, 110; history does nothing, man does everything, 124; producer receives according to labour he expended, 33;